D0793595

Civic Agendas
and
Religious Passion

Habent sua fata libelli

Volume XXXV
of
Sixteenth Century Essays & Studies

Charles G. Nauert, Jr. and Raymond A. Mentzer

General Editors

Composed at Truman State University, Kirksville, Missouri 63501 USA. Cover art and title page by Teresa Wheeler, Truman State University designer.Manufactured by Edwards Brothers, Ann Arbor, Michigan. Text is set in Minion 11/13.

Civic Agendas AND Religious Passion

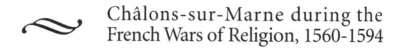

Châlons-sur-Marne during the
French Wars of Religion, 1560-1594

Mark W. Konnert

Sixteenth Century Essays & Studies
Volume XXXV

*This book has been brought to publication
with the generous support of
Truman State University, Kirksville, Missouri*

Library of Congress Cataloging-in-Publication Data

Konnert, Mark W.
    Civic agendas and religious passion : Châlons-sur-Marne during the
French wars of religion, 1560–1594 / Mark W. Konnert.
        p.   cm. —(Sixteenth century essays and studies ; v. 35)
    Includes bibliographical references and index.
    ISBN 0-940474-37-9 (alk. paper)
    1. Châlons-sur-Marne (France)—History. 2. France—History—Wars of
the Huguenots, 1562–1598—Influence. 3. Municipal government—
France—Châlons-sur-Marne. 4. Cities and towns, Medieval—France—
Social conditions. I. Title. II Series.
    DC801.C34K66   1997
    944'.32—dc2096-27645
    CIP

Contents

Figures   vi

Preface   vii

Acknowledgments   x

Civic Agendas and Religious Passion

Introduction   3

Part 1   ~   The Structures of Power

Chapter 1	The Province and the City	25
Chapter 2	Portrait of a City Council	40
Chapter 3	The Community Defended: Structure and Challenge	51
Chapter 4	Fiscal Impact of the Wars	72

Part 2   ~   Châlons during the Wars of Religion

Chapter 5	The Community Challenged, 1560–1576	91
Chapter 6	The Community Subdued, 1576–1588	122
Chapter 7	The Community Liberated, 1588–1594	145
Chapter 8	Châlons, Ideal of the Bonne Ville	162

Bibliography   172

Index   179

Figures

Figure 1.1	Champagne	27
Figure 1.2	Location and Spread of Châlons	29
Figure 1.3	Châlons in the Sixteenth Century	39
Figure 2.1	Frequency of and attendance at Council Meetings, 1560–1593	48
Figure 3.1	Fortifications of Châlons in the Sixteenth Century	53
Figure 3.2	Fortifications Expenditures, selected years	54
Figure 4.1	City Council Revenues	74

Preface

N December 30, 1588, the inhabitants of the predominantly Catholic city of Châlons-sur-Marne swore an oath "to guard and ... maintain this city of Châlons under the obedience and authority of the king ... and to employ to this end their lives, bodies and goods...."[1] What makes this event noteworthy is its context: A week earlier, on December 23, King Henry III (the same king to whom the inhabitants were now swearing their oath) ordered the murder of his two chief rivals, who were leaders of the Catholic League: the duc de Guise and his brother, the cardinal de Guise. Since 1584, the League, led by the Guises, had attempted to exclude from the succession to the throne the heir apparent, the Protestant Henry of Navarre. In addition, the Leaguers attempted to force their policy of extirpation of heretics upon a king who was reluctant to adopt such a program. The king had tried to balance the religious and political factions, but to no avail; these events led him into the desperate measures of political murder in an attempt to cripple the League by eliminating its leaders.

Far from crippling the League, however, the king's actions only galvanized militant Catholics. Condemned as a tyrant by the Sorbonne and vilified in the streets of Paris, Henry—it was claimed—had, by his criminal acts, forfeited his right to rule. All over France, towns and nobles previously hesitant to join the Catholic League now flocked to its banner.

Yet Châlons still resisted the pressure to join the League, as it had on numerous occasions. Indeed, in the week between the murder of the Guises and the swearing of the oath by its inhabitants, the Châlons city council had acted to prevent the city from falling into Leaguer hands. On December 24, the day after the assassinations, the city council, acting on directions from the king, expelled the baron de Rosne, Châlons' Leaguer governor, and turned the city over to Joachim de Dinteville, the royalist *lieutenant-général* of Champagne. Several months later, in February 1589,

---

[1]"De garder et maintenir ceste ville de Chaalons soubz l'obéissance et auctorité du Roy ... et ad ce employer leurs vies, corps, et biens"; Archives départementales Marne, E suppt. 4789, fol. 41.

the council refused to allow Cosme Clausse, the bishop of Châlons and an ardent Leaguer, to enter the city. Two days after the assassination of Henry III in August 1589, at a moment of supreme crisis and danger, the city council unanimously declared its loyalty to the Protestant Henry of Navarre as the rightful King of France, one of the very few Catholic towns to do so. In the early 1590s, Châlons was virtually alone as an isolated royalist outpost in Champagne.

Châlons' actions were even more remarkable by virtue of its situation in heavily Leaguer and Guisard Champagne, so close to the Guises' power base in Lorraine and Burgundy. Both Reims and Troyes were League cities, Guise had been the military governor of the province, and Châlons itself had been given to the duc de Guise as security by the Treaty of Nemours in 1585, since which time he had imposed a virtual military occupation on the town.

Why the city councillors of Châlons-sur-Marne should have embarked on such an impolitic and seemingly dangerous course is in one sense the central focus of the pages that follow. Briefly, through an exploration of the minutes, or *livres des conclusions*, of the city council, we will see that the councillors were motivated by a common commitment to a civic agenda, an agenda which they pursued to the best of their ability in the midst of religious civil war and impending national disintegration. This, however, is not the initial focus of this study. Initially, the aim was to examine the inner workings of a French town of the early modern period, a subject about which very little detail is known. It seemed that a period of crisis and turmoil such as the Wars of Religion of the sixteenth century might reveal the city's administrative structures and processes as those in charge of the city's safety and welfare scrambled to improvise solutions to the problems they faced.

Châlons-sur-Marne seemed an ideal town for this original project. Of medium size and importance, it suffered from none of the anomalies produced by either great size and significance or by obscurity and isolation. In addition, the minutes of the city council from the sixteenth century are preserved virtually complete, providing a detailed view of the council's workings. But Châlons proved to be an intriguing case, with the councillors pursuing a course so contrary to what seemed prudent or logical.

So what began as a study of urban government in a time of conflict and crisis soon became much more. It became apparent that the actions of 1588 and 1589 were consistent with the attitudes and policies pursued by the council over the previous three decades of civil religious war. The city council of this ordinary and not very important town pursued policies which could (and nearly did) bring the town to utter ruin. Questions arose about what led them to this course and why they rejected what seems to have been the obvious and safe course of action.

In answering these questions we are dealing with issues—not mutually exclusive—of both structure and policy. The structure of power within and outside of Châlons provided the councillors with a range of policy options from which they had to select. Why were the city councillors of Châlons able to pursue the course they did? Perhaps more significantly, why did they choose these particular policies from the range of the possible ones? It is in answering this latter question that this study transcends the purely local, for in its answer we discover hitherto little noticed aspects of urban and communal life in early modern France: a devotion to ideals of urban solidarity and integrity along with commitment to a civic agenda, both of which were pursued in the midst of and despite religious division within the city and within France at large.

Acknowledgments

LTHOUGH IT IS A PLATITUDE, this book could indeed never have been written without the assistance of many people. This project was begun as a Ph.D. dissertation at the University of Southern California, under the supervision of Lloyd Moote. I am eternally grateful for the assistance and friendship supplied to both myself and my wife by Lloyd and his wife, Dorothy. I could not have wished for a better supervisor or a better friend. Thanks are also due to the John Randolph and Dora Haynes foundation, whose generous fellowship made possible the initial research trip to France. I would also like to thank Frederic J. Baumgartner, who read an earlier version of this work, and whose suggestions and encouragement were enormously helpful.

My parents, Bill and Ileen Konnert, have never faltered in their encouragement and support, both emotional and financial, throughout the years. My debt to them can never be repaid. Although this book was begun before our children were born, Heidi and Samuel have been a constant source of joy and inspiration. Finally, to my wife, Candy, I owe the greatest debt of all. For ten years, she has encouraged, supported, and inspired me. It is to her that this book is lovingly dedicated.

Civic Agendas
and
Religious Passion

A gate of the Louvre, after St. Bartholomew's Day

Introduction

NTIL QUITE RECENTLY, the history of French towns in the early modern period has been relatively ignored.[1] The *annalistes* concentrated, on the one hand, on the *longue durée* of the agricultural world: the cycle of crops, depression, and recovery. On the other hand, they concentrated on the great movements of international commerce. In both cases, attention was drawn away from the history of towns except insofar as they are international ports, such as Marseille, Bordeaux, Nantes, or Saint-Malo. Anglo-Saxon history of this same period has by and large been the history of social elites such as the nobility and the burgeoning "fourth estate" of royal venal officeholders. Again, towns are relatively ignored, except as the birthplaces or residences of these elites.

At first sight, the literature on the Wars of Religion seems to redress this imbalance. It is true that older histories of the wars tend to treat towns merely as military objectives, prizes to be conquered or defended by this or that noble commander. More recently, there have been a number of studies of towns in this period. Most of these studies, however, are rather circumscribed in their scope. Some deal with the social composition of the Protestant community, with the elements of collective action, or with the composition and motivation of the Catholic League. Others deal with the period of the wars, but are fundamentally concerned with other questions. Still others seem to fit the bill, but examine only the fascinating cases— cities in which dramatic and violent events took place, where passions were so enraged that the cities stand out from others.

Treatments of towns and municipal institutions in general works about the institutions of early modern France tend to be slight and general. For example, Roland Mousnier's magisterial work, *The Institutions of France under the Absolute Monarchy, 1598–1789*, a tome of nearly eight hundred pages, devotes only forty-three pages to towns and their

---

[1] On the relative lack of works of urban history during the Wars of Religion, see also Wolfgang Kaiser, *Marseille au temps de troubles: Morphologie sociale et luttes de factions, 1559–1596*, trans. Florence Chaix (Paris: L'Ecole des Hautes Etudes en Sciences Sociales, 1992), 7–12.

3

institutions. By way of contrast, Mousnier devotes almost eighty pages to the seigneurie and over a hundred pages to the nobility. In addition, his treatment of towns is largely schematic, dividing French towns into three types: seigneurial, villes de bourgeoisie, and communal, with Paris as the exemplar of the first type, Bordeaux of the second, and Beauvais of the last.[2]

Among older works of this type, we see the same tendency. Gaston Zeller, in his *Les institutions de la France au XVIe siècle*, gives towns a somewhat more thorough treatment than does Mousnier, and is seemingly more aware of the wide variety of municipal institutions. Nevertheless, his observations are generalized in the extreme (as they probably must be) and then so heavily qualified with local and regional variations that they are almost meaningless. And again, as with Mousnier, Zeller's attention is drawn quite naturally to the largest and most important cities, which, while many times larger than most towns, are still a small number among the many French towns.[3]

Roger Doucet's work of the same title treats towns in the same way: a brief description of the major types of civic constitutions, followed by a cursory description of officers, finances, and military affairs. As with Zeller, Doucet's observations are generalized and largely confined to a few examples.[4]

By far the most comprehensive and useful general work on French towns in this period is Albert Babeau's *La ville sous l'ancien régime* with its detailed descriptions of civic institutions, offices, finances, and defense. This work, like those of Zeller and Doucet, suffers from a static point of view. Babeau's attempt to describe civic institutions over the course of two centuries results in a good deal of telescoping and generalization. Also, as the title suggests, he is concerned primarily with towns in France under the absolute monarchy of the seventeenth and eighteenth centuries. Thus, his descriptions are more relevant to that period than to the sixteenth century or, specifically, the Wars of Religion. Indeed, one of Babeau's

---

[2]Roland Mousnier, *The Institutions of France under the Absolute Monarchy*, trans. B. Pierce, 2 vols. (Chicago: The University of Chicago Press, 1979); 1:563–605; on the *seigneurie*, see 1:477–550; on the nobility, 1:112–213.

[3]Gaston Zeller, *Les institutions de la France au XVIe siècle* (Paris: Presses Universitaires, 1948), 37–56.

[4]Roger Doucet, *Les institutions de la France au XVIe siècle*, 2 vols. (Paris: Picard, 1948), 1:360–95.

major themes is the confrontation of local privilege and the centralizing state.[5]

Taken in aggregate, these works suffer several shortcomings. The descriptions and catalogues of institutions are necessarily interested in generalization. The authors seek categories into which a particular town can be fit. As a result, they do little justice to the wide and bewildering variety of municipal institutions to be found in early modern France. In addition, although paying lip service to historical process and change, they tend to be rather static. More precisely, change is part of their treatment, but only in the big picture. Thus, they may see, as does Zeller, a weakening of municipal autonomy, but the specifics and mechanics of this weakening are ignored.[6]

Histories of individual towns tend to be defective in the opposite direction. By and large, these works (and there are many fine ones) treat a particular town in isolation. Thus, we may know a great deal about Toulouse or Bordeaux, but next to nothing about the regional or national significance of the developments in those towns. In addition, the specialization of historical research being what it is, the authors of these works are experts in one period, which is usually seen as the period of greatest and most lasting significance in the city's history. For other periods, they tend to rely, as they must, on older (often nineteenth-century) histories, many of which run to the provincial and antiquarian.

There have, of course, been many fine studies of individual towns. One's attention is drawn in particular to the "Histoire des Villes" series of the Univers de la France et des pays francophones, published by Privat under the general direction of Philippe Wolff. These are collaborative efforts and deal with the entire history of the city in question. In theory, having an expert write on each period should cover all areas equally; in reality, this is not so. For example, in the volume on Reims, edited by Pierre Desportes, the Reformation and the Wars of Religion are covered in three-and-a-half pages. By contrast, the events of the Revolution take up twenty pages.[7]

---

[5] Albert Babeau, *La ville sous l'ancien régime,* 2 vols. (Paris, 1884), 1:1–2.

[6] Zeller, *Les institutions de la France,* 38, 42–44.

[7] Pierre Desportes, ed., *Histoire de Reims* (Toulouse: Privat, 1983), 175–78 on the Reformation and the Wars of Religion, and 257–79 on the Revolution. Other cities covered in this series include Bordeaux, Lyon, Marseille, Rouen, and Toulouse, to name only a few.

Recently, there has been something of a renaissance in the study of towns as opposed to a particular town. One must mention in this respect especially the *Histoire de la France urbaine*, published under the direction of Georges Duby. The third volume, *La ville classique de la Renaissance aux Révolutions*, takes in the period of the Wars of Religion, at least chronologically. Yet as the broad sweep of the title indicates, the authors are more concerned with continuity than with change. What makes this collaborative work so significant is its broad scope and inclusiveness; it is nothing less than a total history of urban France, intended to complement the enormous body of historical research on French rural history.[8]

Like most works of histoire totale, *Histoire de la France urbaine* tells us at once too much and too little. It tells too much in the sense that it presents a vast and perplexing panorama of urban history in which it is all too easy to lose sight of the realities of urban life. It tells too little in that one looks in vain for a continuous narrative of the development of a single town.

Of more immediate interest is the volume edited by Philip Benedict, *Cities and Social Change in Early Modern France*. As implied by the title, the main focus of the book is the ancien régime, rather than the sixteenth century, and it is more concerned with the changing role of cities in French society than with any one city in particular.[9] Moreover, as Benedict points out, both the source material and the secondary literature are much more abundant for the eighteenth century than the sixteenth.[10] The essays themselves deal with a wide variety of topics, from Robert Descimon's social geography of Paris in the sixteenth century to Claire Dolan's microanalysis of social relations in Aix-en-Provence. With the exception of Robert Schneider's essay "Crown and Capitoulat: Municipal Government in Toulouse, 1500–1789," none of these contributions take as their focus

---

[8]*Histoire de la France urbaine*, 3 vols. (Paris: Seuil, 1980), 1:9. Or, as Wolfgang Kaiser, *Marseille*, 8, observes, "pour l'*Histoire de la France urbaine* … le XVIe siècle ne constitue qu'un prologue à 'la ville classique.'"

[9]Philip Benedict, ed., *Cities and Social Change in Early Modern France* (London: Unwin Hyman, 1989). In the lengthy introduction, Benedict draws attention to the ways in which French cities played a different role in national life in the eighteenth century than in the sixteenth. Although the population of cities grew only slightly faster than the general population (7), the cities' "place in the country's economic and social life was very different" (8).

[10]Benedict, ed., *Cities and Social Change*, 8.

issues of urban governance.[11] Furthermore, as Benedict himself points out in his introduction, "few aspects of the Ancien Régime are as poorly understood as the dynamics of local politics."[12]

Of more immediate relevance is Bernard Chevalier's excellent *Les bonnes villes de France du XIVe au XVIe siècles*. Chevalier argues that French towns of the fourteenth through sixteenth centuries (the *bonnes villes*) were qualitatively different from both medieval towns and those of the absolute monarchy in their internal organization, civic mentality, and relations with the royal government.

The bonne ville is differentiated from the medieval city first of all by its origins and functions. Following Jacques Le Goff in *Histoire de la France Urbaine*, Chevalier characterizes the medieval city as "above all an economic centre of artisanal production and mercantile exchange; it is as much an extraordinary grouping of churches, abbeys, convents and oratories gathered around steeples and cemeteries, as it is a city distinct from many others. The medieval city is rarely unified, but on the contrary, is most often split up among rival seigneurial jurisdictions, even when the communal association was able to insert itself into this game of opposing powers."[13] The bonne ville, on the other hand, is characterized by its autonomy and self-sufficiency. Born out of the crises and catastrophes of the Hundred Years' War, it took to itself the independent powers of defense, taxation, sanitation, and justice, which had previously been the province of its feudal seigneurs.

The reestablishment of royal authority in the later fifteenth century did nothing to detract from the autonomy and power of the bonnes villes. On the contrary, kings, most especially Louis XI, chose to rule through them. Though Estates General were rare, at the meetings of provincial estates or assemblies of one kind or another, it was not some mythic "third estate" which deliberated with the clergy and nobility; they served to

---

[11]Benedict, ed., *Cities and Social Change;* the other essays in the book are Frederick Irvine, "From Renaissance City to Ancien Régime Capital: Montpellier, c.1500–c.1600"; James Farr, "Consumers, Commerce, and the Craftsmen of Dijon: The Changing Social and Economic Structure of a Provincial Capital, 1450–1750"; and René Favier, "Economic Change, Demographic Growth and the Fate of Dauphiné's Small Towns, 1698–1790."

[12]Benedict, ed., *Cities and Social Change*, 22.

[13]Bernard Chevalier, *Les bonnes villes de France du XIVe au XVIe siècles* (Paris: Aubier Montaigne, 1982), 12.

represent the bonnes villes. Indeed, "representatives" is probably misleading, for "they owe their 'election' to no regulation of public power; they are truly 'ambassadors' (the word is used) and do not form a group."[14] The royal government and the bonnes villes coexisted in an *entente cordiale*, with the government acting more as an administrative tribunal than as a ministry of the interior attempting to suppress civic liberties and privileges.[15]

This "state of bonnes villes" could not last, however, opposed as it was to the state's own internal logic of development.[16] The idea of the bonne ville perished before the growing power of the state, the "treason of the bourgeois" in exchanging their civic and communal roles for royal offices, and the upheaval of the Wars of Religion.

The real significance of Chevalier's work is that it provides a historical and theoretical framework against which the experience of particular towns can be tested. It furnishes a degree of sophistication and an analytical tool to deal with towns in early modern France. In distinguishing among the medieval city, the bonne ville, and the city under the thumb of the absolute monarchy, he provides us with a construct which does greater justice to the complexity and vitality of urban history than one of an incessantly rising bourgeoisie or of isolated communities jealously guarding their ancient liberties. In particular, with respect to the Wars of Religion, his thesis helps to explain the importance attached to the possession of towns by both sides and the success of civic elites in managing the crises of the period. After all, they had had long experience in managing their own affairs.[17]

When we turn to urban studies dealing with the sixteenth century, we find a number which deal with specific aspects of civic life. For example, Barbara Diefendorf has written a study of Parisian city councillors, dealing with their wealth, families, and marriage patterns. She stops short of the Wars of Religion, however, "to avoid the confusion of social and political issues that occurred as the quarrels between Politiques and Ultra-Catholics polarized Parisian society in the later decades of the century."[18]

---

[14]Chevalier, *Les bonnes villes*, 45.   [15]Chevalier, *Les bonnes villes*, 104.
[16]Chevalier, *Les bonnes villes*, 93.   [17]Chevalier, *Les bonnes villes*, 109.
[18]Barbara Diefendorf, *Paris City Councillors in the Sixteenth Century: The Politics of Patrimony* (Princeton: Princeton University Press, 1983), xviii.

In her latest book she deals with Paris through the St. Bartholomew's Day Massacre in 1572, but the focus is on the uniqueness of Paris in its size and importance as well as its religious culture and the sequence of events leading to the massacre.[19] Philip Hoffman's work on Lyon deals primarily with the Counter-Reformation. As a result, the events of the Wars of Religion play a largely tangential role, and examination of civic institutions and politics is largely limited to church-city relations.[20] Similarly, James Farr has dealt with events in Dijon, but his main concern lies in demonstrating the transformation of Dijonnais artisans into a middle class by the middle of the seventeenth century.[21] Natalie Davis, in a number of her essays, has dealt with various aspects of the Reformation and the Wars of Religion, but her main interests lie elsewhere than in civic politics and institutions: the "rites of violence," social inversion, "City Women and Religious Change," and "Poor Relief, Humanism, and Heresy."[22] One might also mention here Emmanuel Le Roy Ladurie's *Carnival in Romans*, which although examining the events of the Wars of Religion is more concerned with the themes of carnival and patterns of collective violence than with the city of Romans itself.[23]

One of the few full-scale treatments of the impact of the Wars of Religion on municipal institutions concerns the three Breton towns of Rennes, Nantes, and Saint-Malo.[24] In his *Essai sur le régime municipal en Bretagne pendant les guerres de religion*, Charles Laronze stresses the opportunity presented to these towns to recover the "ancient liberties" by "the liberal breeze of the Reformation and the political necessities of the era which furnished the occasion and the means of conquering and organizing municipal liberties."[25] These towns "governed themselves through their

---

[19]Barbara Diefendorf, *Beneath the Cross: Catholics and Huguenots in Sixteenth-Century Paris* (New York: Oxford University Press, 1991), 6–7, 48.

[20]Philip Hoffman, *Church and Community in the Diocese of Lyon* (New Haven: Yale University Press, 1984).

[21]James Farr, "The Rise of a Middle Class: Artisans in Dijon, 1550–1650" (Ph.D. diss., Northwestern University, 1983); idem, *Hands of Honor: Artisans and Their World in Early Modern France* (Ithaca: Cornell University Press, 1988).

[22]Natalie Zemon Davis, *Society and Culture in Early Modern France* (Stanford: Stanford University Press, 1975).

[23]Emmanuel Le Roy Ladurie, *Carnival in Romans* (New York: G. Braziller, 1979).

[24]Charles Laronze, *Essai sur le régime municipal en Bretagne pendant les guerres de religion* (Paris, 1890).

[25]Laronze, *Essai sur le régime municipal*, 5.

mayors, procureurs, and échevins, administered their finances, provided for their security, met all the needs of public assistance and of instruction, and claimed and defended their political rights.... We will not only indicate the workings of this municipal administration, we will see it function despite the opposition of officers of all kinds and amidst the dangers of civil war and we will see it disappear, regretfully, after heroic efforts, tamed or overcome by the powerful hand of the Béarnais."[26] Laronze's choice of the three towns of Rennes, Nantes, and Saint-Malo is in some ways inevitable, since these are the three major Breton towns. In another way, however, this choice is significant, for it is his purpose to show that the same short-lived urban independence operated regardless of the town's political and religious affiliation. Nantes was a Leaguer town and a seat of one of the League's provincial councils, Rennes remained loyal to the king, while Saint-Malo remained steadfastly neutral and independent.[27] This point is especially significant because it illustrates that the same processes were operative regardless of the town's position in national politics. Clearly, then, whether or not a town remained loyal to the crown or took up arms against it is a function of the town's experiences and internal politics. The same impulses could produce dramatically opposed results.

The study of the social composition of the French Protestant movement has led willy-nilly to urban studies, since its strength in cities is one of its most striking characteristics. Ever since Henri Hauser's pioneering work, historians have looked at urban Protestant movements with an eye to their social and occupational composition: Were Protestants primarily artisanal or bourgeois? What groups or trades are especially well represented or conspicuously absent?[28]

---

[26]Laronze, *Essai sur le régime municipal*, 5–6.

[27]Laronze, *Essai sur le régime municipal*, 6.

[28]See Henri Hauser, *Etudes sur la Réforme Française* (Paris, 1909). For works on the sociology of the French Reformation, see David L. Rosenberg, "Social Experience and Religious Choice: A Case Study; The Protestant Weavers and Woolcombers of Amiens in the Sixteenth Century" (Ph.D. diss., Yale University, 1978); James Farr, "Popular Religious Solidarity in Sixteenth-Century Dijon," *French Historical Studies* 14 (1985): 192–214; Janine Garrisson-Estèbe, *Protestants du Midi, 1559–1598* (Toulouse, 1980); David Nicholls, "The Social History of the French Reformation: Ideology, Confession, and Culture," *Social History* 9 (1984): 25–44; idem, "Social Change and Early Protestantism in France: Normandy,1520–1562," *European Studies Review* 10 (1980): 279–308; Joan Davies, "Persecution and Protestantism: Toulouse, 1562–1575," *Historical Journal* 22 (1979): 31–53; Maryélise S. Lamet, "French Protestants in a Position of Strength: The Early Years of the Reformation in Caen, 1558–1568," *Sixteenth Century Journal* 9 (1978): 35–56; Raymond A. Mentzer, "Heresy Suspects in Languedoc prior

Henry Heller in *The Conquest of Poverty* emphasizes the economic and social problems of mid–sixteenth-century France that gave rise, in his view, to Calvinism as a national movement. Following Hauser in his view of the artisans as the social base of the French Reformation, Heller underlines the division between artisanal religious protest, based on political and economic factors, and the religious heterodoxy of civic elites.[29] Using towns throughout France as examples, he illustrates the various stages and processes by which popular and elite Calvinism came to be reconciled in the 1550s. These processes are primarily economic: "Spurred by the increasingly dark economic and fiscal prospects notables and merchants were prepared to make common cause with plebeians."[30] Heller's purpose in writing the book is to show how "we are forced to the conclusion that the wars of religion were an abortive form of what Marxists after Engels refer to as an early bourgeois revolution.... Calvinism was an abortive bourgeois movement because it was economically and politically immature. Economically it was based on a mode of production which was only partially distinguished from feudalism and which accordingly could not establish an independent basis for itself. This economic weakness expressed itself politically in the subordination of the Calvinist movement in France to the ambitions of a party among the aristocracy. Such a compromise was of course made necessary by the weakness of French capitalism."[31] It is evident that this is where Heller was headed all along. His examples, or case studies, are carefully chosen to lead us to this conclusion. By picking

---

to 1560: Observations on Their Social and Occupational Status," *Bibliothèque d'Humanisme et Renaissance* 39(1977): 561–68; Ann Guggenheim, "The Calvinist Notables of Nîmes during the Era of the Religious Wars," *Sixteenth Century Journal* 3 (1972): 80–96; Philip Benedict, *Rouen during the Wars of Religion* (Cambridge: Cambridge University Press, 1981), 71–94; Emmanuel Le Roy Ladurie, *The Peasants of Languedoc*, trans. J. Day (Urbana: University of Illinois Press, 1974), 149–64; Natalie Z. Davis, "Strikes and Salvation at Lyon," and "City Women and Religious Change," in Davis, *Society and Culture*. For a summary of much of this literature, and one which argues that the socioeconomic approach has reached a dead end, see Denis Crouzet, *Les guerriers de Dieu*, 2 vols. (Seyssel: Champ Vallon, 1990), 1:61–75.

[29]Henry Heller, *The Conquest of Poverty: The Calvinist Revolt in Sixteenth-Century France*, Stud-

[30]Heller, *Conquest of Poverty*, 204.

[31]Heller, *Conquest of Poverty*, 258. Henry Heller, *Iron and Blood: Civil Wars in Sixteenth-Century France* (Montreal: McGill-Queen's University Press, 1991), does not examine the urban experience during the Wars of Religion, but rather extends his theme of class warfare in religious guise to the sixteenth century as a whole, thereby attempting to refute the long-established division of the sixteenth century in France into a stable and prosperous first half and a second half riven by religious and civil war.

and choosing he is able to construct an "ideal type" of Calvinist evolution, which did not take place in any one city, but certainly should have.

Heller's book does not enhance our understanding of how Protestantism affected urban life in the Wars of Religion. Indeed, for him, the wars are irrelevant; the early bourgeois revolution was doomed to failure simply because it was early. There is no interest on Heller's part in studying the inevitable. How towns reacted to the disruptions of the wars is simply not important compared with the elucidation of inevitable historic process.

One of the most appealing areas for this kind of social history has not been on the Protestant side at all, but rather the study of the Catholic League and the Paris Sixteen. Henri Drouot's thesis treating the urban Leaguers as a frustrated group of socially mobile lawyers has come in for substantial revision, but the League itself has remained a topic of great interest to historians of the period. In recent years in particular, debate on the League and the Sixteen has centered around the work of Elie Barnavi and Robert Descimon.[32] Both agree with Drouot and an earlier article by J. H. M. Salmon in denying that the urban Leaguers were the rabble portrayed by politique propaganda.[33] Both see the Leaguers as coming from the middle ranks of Parisian officialdom. Here, however, their agreement ends. For Barnavi, the Sixteen are real revolutionaries and form a party in the modern sense. That their revolution failed does not make it any less revolutionary. For Descimon, on the other hand, the Parisian Leaguers are essentially backward-looking, motivated by medieval ideals of communal solidarity against an intrusive and centralizing state. As Barbara Diefendorf points out, "one test of Descimon's theory might be to apply it to the activities of the League in other cities. Can we find evidence that the provincial Leagues also embodied notions of communal virtue and civic

[32]Elie Barnavi, *Le Parti de Dieu, Etude sociale et politique des chefs de la Ligue parisienne, 1585–1594*, Publications de la Sorbonne, N.S. Recherches, 34 (Brussels: Editions Nauwelaerts, 1980); idem, "Réponse à Robert Descimon," *Annales: Économies, Sociétés, Civilisations* 37 (1982):112–21; Robert Descimon, *Qui étaient les Seize? Mythes et réalités de la Ligue parisienne (1585–1594)* (Paris: Fédération des sociétés historiques et archéologiques de Paris et de l'Ile de France, 1983); idem, "La Ligue à Paris (1585–1594): Une révision," *Annales: Économies, Sociétés, Civilisations* 37 (1982): 72–111; idem, "La Ligue: Des divergences fondamentales," *Annales: Économies, Sociétés, Civilisations* 37 (1982): 122–28.

[33]Henri Drouot, *Mayenne et la Bourgogne*, 2 vols. (Paris: Picard, 1937); J.H.M. Salmon, "The Paris Sixteen, 1584–94: The Social Analysis of a Revolutionary Movement," *Journal of Modern History* 44 (1972): 540–76.

liberties?"[34] Studies of the League in provincial cities, however, often tend to treat civic institutions and mentalities as a given, and in general reveal no pattern among Leaguer towns corresponding with either Barnavi's or Descimon's theories.[35]

One must admit the possibility that Descimon's views in particular might also work in the opposite direction. Could not devotion to ideals of civic virtue and communal solidarity have led a community to oppose the League as an ideology? It is true that Descimon finds a number of congruencies between the ideology of the Parisian Sixteen and these "medieval" ideals: "A particularly dense socialization could have contributed to forming in the Sixteen a system of representations of solidarity very receptive to the themes of integral Catholicism (such as the collective expiation of sins and of the heretic stain) or of charismatic propaganda (the duc de Guise as redeemer of the French monarchy)."[36] Nevertheless, it does seem possible that these ideals lay behind resistance to the League as well, provided, of course, that the League was perceived as foreign and somehow inimical to communal solidarity and civic virtue.

Urban studies of the Wars of Religion tend to suffer from another shortcoming. Quite understandably, they concentrate on the exciting or noteworthy cases. Paris, of course, is extremely important in its own right as the chief city of the kingdom. But it has also drawn the lion's share of

[34]Barbara Diefendorf, "Recent Literature on the Religious Conflicts in Sixteenth-Century France," *Religious Studies Review* 10 (1984): 364.

[35]For local and regional studies of the League, see Peter Ascoli, "French Provincial Cities and the Catholic League," *Occasional Papers of the American Society for Reformation Research* 1 (1977); Elie Barnavi, "Centralisme ou fédéralisme? Les relations entre Paris et les villes à l'époque de la Ligue (1585–1594)," *Revue Historique* 259 (1978): 335–44; René Crozet, "Le protestantisme et la Ligue à Vitry-le-François et en Perthois," *Revue Historique* 156 (1927): 1–40; Henri Drouot, "Les conseils provinciaux de la Sainte-Union (1589–1595): Notes et questions," *Annales du Midi* 45 (1953): 415–33; Marc Fardet, "Nantes au temps de la Ligue: La lutte contre les protestants au sud de la Loire sous le gouvernement du duc de Mercoeur," *Revue du Bas-Poitou* (1969), a.80, no. 1, 36–51; no. 2, 117–28; Mark Greengrass, "The *Sainte Union* in the Provinces: The Case of Toulouse," *Sixteenth Century Journal* 14 (1983): 469–96; Louis Guibert, *La Ligue à Limoges* (Limoges, 1884); Robert Harding, "Revolution and Reform in the Holy League: Angers, Rennes, and Nantes," *Journal of Modern History* 53 (1981): 379–416; François Hauchecorne, "Orléans au temps de la Ligue," *Bulletin trimestriel de la Société archéologique et historique de l'Orléannais* n.s. 5, no. 39 (1970): 267–78; idem, "Orléans ligueur en 1591," *Actes du 93e Congrès de la société des savantes*, Tours, 1968 / *Bulletin philologique et historique du comité des travaux historiques et scientifiques* 2 (1971): 845–59; Ernest Prarond, *La Ligue à Abbeville, 1578–94*, 3 vols. (Paris, 1868–73); Georges Viard, "Propagande politique et campagnes d'opinion à Langres au temps de la Ligue," *Cahiers Haut-Marnais* 138 (1979), 121–33.

[36]Descimon, *Qui étaient les Seize?* 281.

attention, one suspects, because of the exciting nature of the conflicts there. Events in Paris, especially after 1588, have a highly dramatic quality which, when combined with the city's importance and wealth of documentation, serve as an almost irresistible magnet for historians.

The same might also be said of other recent works on urban history in the Wars of Religion, and in particular, Philip Benedict's study of Rouen, which has been called "a model of the local study that transcends its geographic focus."[37] Nevertheless, Rouen, as the second or third largest city in France, the seat of a Parlement, and a thriving center of industry and international trade, can hardly be taken as typical. Benedict himself addresses this question, and while allowing that "Rouen's fate in these years was not typical of most French communities; in few other towns did the First Civil War produce so disastrous a denouement as the siege and sacking of Rouen, and in few, if any cities were the subsequent scenes of unrest so numerous. But if not typical, the pattern of violence could be considered archetypal.... Few towns of any importance escaped at least a minor *émeute* or imbroglio. Communities throughout France were bitterly divided over the religious issues."[38]

What is significant here is the equation of "a minor *émeute* or imbroglio" with "bitter division." While Benedict is no doubt correct for Rouen, surely other cities must be examined in the same depth and over the same length of time. What is important is not one riot, but the totality of civic experience over a period of some thirty-five years. For Châlons-sur-Marne, the significance of minor disturbances has been greatly exaggerated, on the one hand by Protestant historians to show the long-suffering martyrdom of the true faith, and on the other by Catholics to show the city's devotion to its traditional religion. Clearly, one must look at the total experience of the community, rather than at one or two *émotions*, over the course of three-and-a-half decades.

Similarly, Wolfgang Kaiser, in his recent work on Marseille during the Wars of Religion, elucidates the religious, political, and social basis of factional struggles during the period of the wars.[39] Though a model of urban history, Marseille can hardly be taken as a "typical" French city. A cosmo-

[37]Diefendorf, "Recent Literature," 362.
[38]Benedict, *Rouen*, 240.
[39]Kaiser, *Marseille*.

politan and wealthy port, recently added to the kingdom, Marseille possessed its own strong sense of identity and privileges, which affected its history during the last half of the sixteenth century.

~

THERE EXISTS, THEREFORE, A SIGNIFICANT GAP in the historical literature on French towns in the early modern period in general and the Wars of Religion in particular. First of all, general institutional works, with the exception of Babeau, treat towns in a static and almost superficial manner. In addition, these works, including Babeau's, are usually intended to demonstrate the growth of absolute monarchy and the attendant withering of communal autonomy and institutions. Chevalier's work in some sense provides a corrective to this view, but even he shares the assumption that the Wars of Religion sounded the death knell of the bonne ville. Works specifically on urban history during the Wars of Religion tend to have their focus elsewhere than on the town itself. What is important is not so much the town as the arena it provides for religious division and its resulting conflict. Yet how inevitable was this conflict? Did the mentality of the bonne ville really perish so easily? How important was religious division to people who were actually responsible for the town's welfare? As suggested above, could not the same devotion to such so-called medieval ideals of civic virtue and communal solidarity advanced by Descimon as the ideology of the Sixteen have functioned in a somewhat different manner? Could not the mentality of the bonne ville, in certain circumstances, have led city fathers to disavow the League as an alien ideology and a threat to their communal solidarity? Studies of towns in the Wars of Religion have also tended to focus both on the largest and most important cities, such as Paris, Rouen, Marseille—and on the cities which saw the most dramatic and violent conflicts.

Châlons-sur-Marne, a smaller and less nationally important town, provides a different perspective on the urban experience during the Wars of Religion. How did those responsible for the security of such a town deal with the problems and pressures that confronted them? How concerned were they with internal religious division, and how did this affect what they actually did, rather than what they said? How did they balance the demands of powerful external agents upon their loyalty and material resources? How severely did they feel the weakness and drift of the royal government and what did they do in the face of contradictory and often nonexistent direction from the center? Thrown back upon their own resources and ingenuity, how did they confront the military, fiscal, and economic threats posed by an extended period of civil and religious war? This study is an attempt to view the Wars of Religion from the inside out, so to speak, from the perspective of those responsible for the order and security of their town, to evaluate the degree to which the ideals of civic virtue and solidarity provided for continuity, and to determine the direction in which those ideals led the town leaders.

This brings me to the question of representativeness. I do not contend that Châlons is representative of anything except Châlons. This is a study of one particular town, and not a different one. The question of representativeness, of whether or not Châlons' experience was similar to that of other towns, can only be pursued by similar research in other towns. On the other hand, it is surely no less representative of the urban experience in the Wars of Religion than Paris, Rouen, or Marseille. What is suggested is that here at least is an alternative experience, one which needs to be kept in mind as other towns' experiences are further researched.

Moreover, by virtue of its geographic position and administrative functions, Châlons was in and of itself a relatively important city in the sixteenth century, and one which has not been intensively studied. As shown in chapter 1, the city's strategic geographic location made it an important military entrepôt. This is especially important for the Wars of Religion, since whoever controlled the open plains of Champagne was in a position to bring in reinforcements from Germany, and to deny the same to adversaries. Location, therefore, explains the importance attached by the duc de Guise to controlling the city in the 1580s, and also the city's many encounters with German *reiters* on their way to or from the major theaters of war. Châlons was also important in an administrative sense. It was the seat not only of a *grenier à sel,* or royal salt warehouse, and a *siège particulier* of the *bailliage* of Vermandois, but also of both fiscal jurisdictions in sixteenth-century France, the *élection* and the *généralité.*

This work also contributes to a recent trend in the historiography of early modern France, that is, the importance placed on the local community and on the elites who governed it. Clearly, France could not be governed effectively from a single center without extensive support and cooperation at the local level. W. H. Beik has pointed out the importance of the cooperation of at least parts of the provincial elite of Languedoc in the construction of royal absolutism.[40] Daniel Hickey has pushed the examination of this process further back in time, concentrating on Dauphiné, "the first major French province into which the new absolutist institutions were pushed."[41] Similarly, in his examination of the early modern fiscal system, James Collins points out the crucial role of local elites: "France was a collection of local economies and local political societies dominated by local elites. Absolutism was strictly limited in practice; the king could do little without the cooperation of local notables. One of the most important means of obtaining such cooperation was the tax system."[42]

If such elites were able to frustrate, delay, and defeat the ambitious plans of powerful kings and ministers in the seventeenth century, surely it is at least equally important to understand their roles during a period of royal weakness such as the Wars of Religion, when we could logically expect them to have a much greater effect on national affairs.

The treatment that follows is divided into two major parts. Part 1 is primarily analytical in nature and provides the structure and context for the events of the Wars of Religion in Châlons. Chapter 1 deals with the history of Châlons-sur-Marne prior to the Wars of Religion. It demonstrates the circumstances and developments which forged the city, its institutions, and the mentality of its inhabitants. In particular, attention is drawn to the paradoxical fact that while the city of Châlons-sur-Marne had no juridical or legal existence, in fact there *was* a city, and this city was governed by a council which, like the city itself, had no legal basis or constitution. The

[40]William H. Beik, *Absolutism and Society in Seventeenth-Century France: State Power and Provincial Aristocracy in Languedoc* (Cambridge: Cambridge University Press, 1985).

[41]Daniel Hickey, *The Coming of French Absolutism: The Struggle for Tax Reform in the Province of Dauphiné, 1540–1640* (Toronto: University of Toronto Press, 1986), 3. Hickey, ibid., 190, argues that the crown was able to introduce absolutist fiscal institutions into Dauphiné because of breakdown in the provincial consensus in Dauphinois society, "that local and provincial conflicts … were far more important than national priorities in explaining the eventual reduction of provincial 'liberties.'"

[42]James B. Collins, *The Fiscal Limits of Absolutism: Direct Taxation in Early Seventeenth-Century France* (Berkeley: University of California Press, 1988), 3–4; according to Collins, ibid., 106–7, 219–22, the introduction of intendants in the 1630s was made necessary by the inability or unwillingness of local elites to collect what was seen as excessive taxation.

consequences of this paradoxical situation are taken up in chapter 2. Unencumbered by rigid constitutions and regulations, the city councillors were able to adopt and adapt as they saw fit. Moreover, it seems that because of this flexibility and freedom, there was very little anti-oligarchical sentiment in Châlons of the type that caused so much grief elsewhere. In chapter 3, the defensive structures and procedures of the city are examined. The city council of Châlons-sur-Marne was able to pursue an independent course throughout much of the period only because there were already in place well-established norms of civic defense. Furthermore, unlike the situation in Paris, as described by Barbara Diefendorf, these structures predated the wars and had an unambiguous raison d'être: the well-being of the city and its inhabitants, and the defense of their civic autonomy and the institutions which expressed it.[43] Chapter 4 deals with the fiscal aspects of civic administration. The annual accounts or *comptes* of the city receivers are examined, as are the extraordinary demands placed upon the city's resources by the vicissitudes of the wars. In particular, can the council's actions be explained by financial issues? Did they have any effect on the council's decisions to reject the League and remain loyal first to Henry III and then to Henry IV?

Part 2 is predominantly narrative in nature, and unapologetically so. History takes place in a temporal continuum. Of course the analysis of structure is important. Equally important is the impact of events on those structures. This can best (and perhaps only) be evaluated in chronological sequence. Moreover, one of the major theses of this work is the continuity of conciliar actions and attitudes throughout the period of the Wars of Religion. This continuity can only be appreciated and explained through narrative. Earlier actions of the council necessarily influenced later actions. Again, only the narrative method can make this clear.

Chapter 5 is divided into two parts. The first begins with the outbreak of the Wars of Religion and their impact on Châlons, the establishment of a Huguenot community in the city, and the emergence of basic patterns which persist throughout the wars. The second carries the sequences of events from 1567 through 1576, demonstrating the persistence of the

---

[43]Diefendorf, *Beneath the Cross*, 160–68; idem, "The Background to the League: Civic Values in Paris at the Beginning of the Wars of Religion," address delivered to the Society for French Historical Studies, Québec, 1986; the author is grateful to Professor Diefendorf for providing a copy of this paper.

attitudes elucidated in the first part. Chapter 6, taking in the years from 1576 to 1588, examines the efforts of the duc de Guise to impose his control on Châlons and transform it into his military headquarters in Champagne, in large part through attempting to force the city council to join the Catholic Leagues of 1576 and 1584. In 1585, the Treaty of Nemours ceded Châlons to Guise as a security town, but even then the councillors continued to resist the agenda of the Guise and Catholic League as far as they were able. Chapter 7 opens with the assassinations of the duc and cardinal de Guise at Blois, and the immediate expulsion of Châlons' Leaguer governor, the baron de Rosne. It takes us through the murder of Henry III, and Châlons' immediate allegiance to the Huguenot Henry IV to the end of the Wars of Religion in Champagne with the submission of Reims to Henry IV in 1594. It was during this period that Châlons was an isolated royalist outpost in heavily Leaguer Champagne.

THIS IS A STUDY OF A CITY COUNCIL and its efforts to navigate safely the treacherous waters of religious division and civil war. Therefore, I have used the sources most appropriate to this end: the *livres des conclusions* or minutes of the city council meetings, letters to and from the city council, various administrative documents, such as those concerning military affairs, and city budgets. The livres des conclusions are a contemporary and continuing account of the actions of the city council. There is absolutely no evidence of retroactive editing. The pages themselves are crisscrossed with addenda and errata, and there are crossed-out lines, sentences, and even pages. With the exception of a period extending from 1569 to 1574, they are complete.

This is not a study of the Huguenot community of Châlons (which is largely precluded by the state of the sources[44]). Although the council's attitudes towards and actions regarding the Huguenots constitute an important theme, the focus is always squarely on the council rather than on the Huguenots.

[44]The earliest Protestant parish records in Châlons date from 1585 for baptisms and from 1592 for marriages (AD Marne 2E, 119/42); nor does there appear to have been a functioning consistory before the establishment of a Protestant church in the suburb of Compertrix following the Edict of Nantes.

Nor is this a study of the socioeconomic composition of the city council. Little attempt has been made here to describe the background or family connections of the Châlonnais notability. Certainly it would be helpful to know this information; however, the state of the sources does not permit it. Moreover, that is not the book I intended to write, for by now a fairly clear picture has emerged of the social, occupational, and economic characteristics of urban elites in early modern France.[45]

My method is admittedly "unscientific," if "scientific" is taken to mean quantitative. Apart from chapter 4 on the fiscal impact of the wars, there are few numbers in this work. To the greatest extent possible, I have attempted to understand the interests and concerns of the city council through its actions as revealed in the livres des conclusions. This involved immersing myself in these voluminous records for a period of several years, trying to make sense of the variety of business and problems which confronted the councillors as well as the ways in which they handled the city's affairs. This method, like any other, has its strengths and weaknesses.

On the one hand, the livres des conclusions are minutes, not records of debates. We are therefore almost ignorant of the internal dynamics of the council. Only on rare occasions are there records of votes or dissent among the councillors. Nor have I been able to supplement these records with journals or memoirs, or with contemporary accounts of the kind so ably exploited by Claire Dolan for Aix-en-Provence;[46] for Châlons-sur-Marne such accounts simply do not exist. On the other hand, we have the record of what the council actually did rather than what individual councillors said. It is indeed quite conceivable that were one to ask the councillors about the burning issues of the day, one might receive answers at

[45]See, e.g., Chevalier, *Les bonnes villes*, esp. 65–83; Duby, *Histoire de la France urbaine*, 3:157–63; Mousnier, *Institutions*, 1:563–98; Diefendorf, *Paris City Councillors*; Farr, *Hands of Honor*; Benedict, *Rouen*, esp. 31–37; idem, *Cities*, esp. 21–24; Kaiser, *Marseille*, 141–157; George Huppert, *Les Bourgeois Gentilhommes: An Essay on the Definition of Elites in Renaissance France* (Chicago: University of Chicago Press, 1977); Heller, *Conquest*, esp. 42–47, 144–45, 181–82; Robert A. Schneider, *Public Life in Toulouse, 1463–1789: From Municipal Republic to Cosmopolitan City* (Ithaca: Cornell University Press, 1989), esp. 16–29, and idem, "Crown and Capitoulat: Municipal Government in Toulouse, 1500–1789," in Benedict, *Cities*; Sharon Kettering, *Judicial Politics and Urban Revolt: The Parlement of Aix, 1629–1659* (Princeton: Princeton University Press, 1978), esp. 41–48; Beik, *Absolutism*, esp. 66–72.

[46]See, "Crown and Capitoulat," in Benedict, *Cities*. See also Claire Dolan, "Image du protestant et le conseil municipal d'Aix au XVIe s.," *Renaissance and Reformation/Renaissance et Réforme* 4 (1980): 152–64; idem, *Entre tours et clochers: Gens d'église à Aix-en-Provence au XVIe siècle* (Sherbrooke, Québec, and Aix-en-Provence: Presses de l'Université de Sherbrooke and Edisud, 1981).

variance with what the council as a whole actually did. We have, therefore, a truer picture of the councillors' concerns than we would if we relied simply on their words. It is fundamental to the approach adopted here that actions really do speak louder than words. What has emerged is a picture which might be surprising to the councillors themselves. Once their initial reaction had passed, however, I am confident it would be replaced by an unexpected and perhaps grudging recognition.

The Coligny brothers; after drawing by J. Visscher

Part 1

The Structures

of Power

Chapter 1

The Province and the City

T HE CITY OF CHÂLONS-SUR-MARNE lies almost exactly in the middle of the province of Champagne. Perhaps more than many other cities, the physical setting of Châlons-sur-Marne has played an important role in its history. Geographically, Champagne consists of three concentric arcs with their open sides facing west, each sloping gently from east to west. Châlons lies in the center of the middle arc, surrounded on all sides by the open plains which give the region its name.[1] The soil of this plain is extremely chalky, hence the appellation *Champagne crayeuse*, or less neutrally, *Champagne pouilleuse* (barren Champagne). This latter term became popular in the eighteenth century, when it appeared in the *Encyclopedia,* and was echoed by other observers: One sees "neither trees nor bushes," "the only shade comes from the ears of a donkey," "a deplorable sterility," and, from Michelet, "a sad sea of stubble amid an immense sea of plaster."[2] Yet, one ought not to be misled by all this. These writers, for the most part, were describing the area at a low point in its agrarian history, after the crises and wars of the seventeenth century took an immense toll, and before the invention of the sparkling wine revitalized it. The chalky soil was light and easy to work, and thus attracted settlers earlier than neighboring areas with their forests and heavy clays. In addition, even where the soil could not be cultivated, it was well suited for pasturing sheep. So if Champagne crayeuse was not a rich agricultural region like the Beauce, neither had it been, before the eighteenth century, the near desert described by the *Encyclopedia* and Michelet.[3]

---

[1]A. N. Galpern, *The Religions of the People in Sixteenth-Century Champagne,* Harvard Historical Studies, 92 (Cambridge, Mass: Harvard University Press, 1976), 8.

[2]Roger Brunet, *Atlas et géographie de Champagne, Pays de Meuse, et Basse Bourgogne* (Paris: Flammarion, 1981), 161.

[3]Galpern, *Religions of the People,* 8.

On the west, the chalky plains submerge beneath the cuesta of the Falaise de l'Ile de France, pierced at Epernay by the river Marne. Beyond the cuesta lies the plateau of Brie (the westernmost of the three arcs), the eastern part of which (Brie Champenoise) belonged to the counts of Champagne and is tied to the rest of the province by both history and economics.[4]

To the east of chalky Champagne we find another cuesta, beyond which lies humid Champagne, the easternmost of the three arcs. From the Ardennes in the north, it sweeps in a broad arc following the Argonne forest, the Perthois, and in the extreme south the Barrois and the Pays d'Othe. The distinction between chalky Champagne and humid Champagne lies not in the amount of rainfall, but in the soil, for the clay soils of the latter repel moisture as much as the chalk of the former absorbs it, resulting in a landscape of forest and swamp.[5]

But it is chalky Champagne that concerns us here (fig. 1.1). Châlons, like all other towns of the region, lies in the bottom of a river valley. Rainfall drains quickly through the chalky soil where it finds its way to the several rivers that drain Champagne toward the west: the Marne, the Aisne with its tributaries, the Suippe, the Vesle, and the Aube, flowing into the Seine below Troyes. Thus, Champagne, without impenetrable mountains or unfordable rivers, and with its wide open plains, is a natural crossroads. It is little wonder that in the Middle Ages the fairs of Champagne were the commercial clearing house of western Europe. The region offered easy passage from north to south—from the workshops and looms of the Low Countries to the ports and banks of Italy—and from east to west—from Germany into France. As with all such areas, this geographic situation has been a curse as well as a blessing, for trade routes become invasion routes very quickly. "Champagne's vocation," says A. N. Galpern, "ever since men have settled there, has been to link more important places to one another."[6]

Indeed, it is this vocation that gave Châlons its beginning as a way station on the Roman road from Milan to Boulogne. Excavations have revealed human settlement on the site as early as the reign of Augustus (ca. A.D. 9).[7] What, if anything, existed on the site before the Roman

---

[4]Galpern, *Religions of the People,* 10.   [5]Galpern, *Religions of the People,* 10–11.
[6]Galpern, *Religions of the People,* 7.   [7]Galpern, *Religions of the People,* 7.

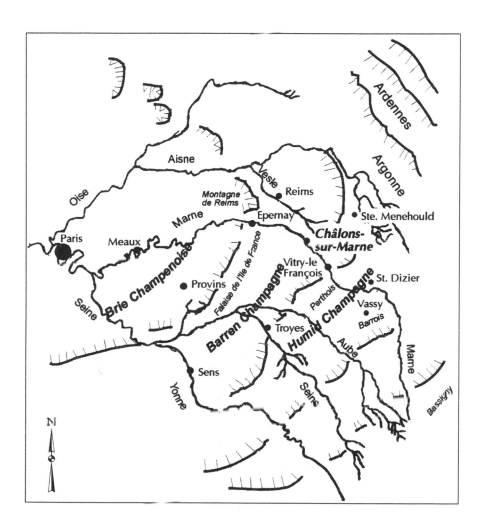

Fig. 1.1. Champagne

settlement, known as Catalaunum or Catuvellanum, is unknown. The name itself derives from the Celtic tribe of the Catalauni or Catuvellani, but there is no evidence that they occupied the site. There is, however, at Cheppes, just north of Châlons, an earthen fortification of the type common in Gaul. In addition, the tribe gave its name to other locations: Châlons-le-Vergeur and Châlons-sur-Vesle near Reims, and to several Vieux Châlons. The Catalauni seem to have been a weak and obscure tribe, caught between their more powerful neighbors, the Remi (hence Reims) and the Lignones (hence Langres).[8] In any case, the Gallic origins of Châlons are negligible.

The Roman settlers found a fortuitous location (fig. 1.2). The Marne at this point separates into several branches, one of which was large enough to merit its own name, the Nau. In addition, two small rivers flow into the Marne on the right bank: the Rognon (since disappeared) and the Mau. Thus the site was easily defensible and the small settlement found itself in a place of some strategic importance. As a result, it grew quite quickly in the first century and by the end of the third century it became the chief city of a Roman *civitas*, whose boundaries would later define the diocese of Châlons, stretching from north of Châlons to Joinville in the south, and from Montmort in the west to Ste. Menehould in the east.[9]

The key event in Châlons' Roman period was the arrival of its first bishop, St. Memmie, at some time around A.D. 325. Although little is known of St. Memmie himself, the creation of a diocese was of key importance, for it allowed Châlons to survive as a city during the twilight of the empire and the rule of the Merovingians, a time when other Roman settlements disappeared entirely. A foreshadowing of times to come occurred in 407, when Vandals crossing the frozen Rhine burned Reims, killing its bishop, St. Nicaise, and kidnapped St. Alpin, bishop of Châlons. In 451, it was the Huns who invaded Gaul and who were defeated near Châlons by the Roman general Aetius.[10]

---

[8]Georges Clause and Jean-Pierre Ravaux, *Histoire de Châlons-sur-Marne* (Le Coteau-Roanne: Horvath, 1983), 17.

[9]Clause and Ravaux, *Histoire*, 18.

[10]Clause and Ravaux, *Histoire*, 22–23; Edouard de Barthélemy, *Histoire de la ville de Châlons-sur-Marne et de ses institutions, des origines à 1848*, 1st ed. (Châlons-sur-Marne, 1854), 133–36. Barthélemy errs when stating that the earlier invaders were the Huns under Attila.

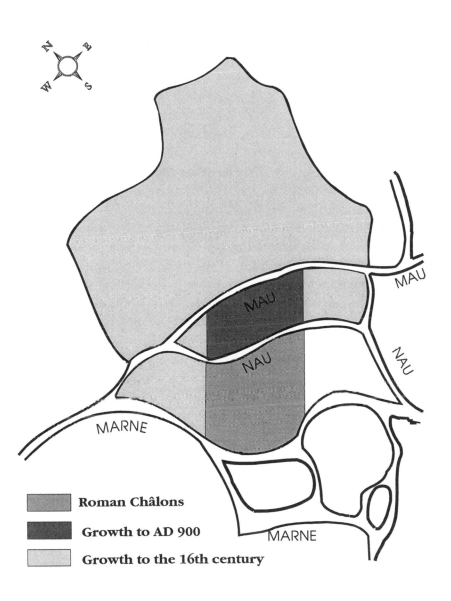

Fig. 1.2. Location and spread of Châlons

The next four hundred years' history of Châlons is obscure, although several of its bishops are mentioned in connection with Merovingian politics.[11] More importantly, Châlons survived and even grew, as witnessed by the establishment of several religious foundations outside the city walls: the Abbey of St. Memmie, about fifteen hundred meters to the southeast of the city; the Church of St. Pierre, the nucleus of what would become in the seventh century the Benedictine Abbey of St. Pierre-aux-Monts;[12] and the Abbey of St. Sulpice, founded before the mid-ninth century, and transformed into a parish church in the eleventh century.

It is significant that these establishments each attracted small settlements and thus demonstrate that Châlons survived intact and even grew during the centuries between the fall of Rome and the revival of the eleventh century. In fact, Châlons shows considerable signs of revival under the Carolingians. By the middle of the ninth century, the market had become a permanent institution, surrounded by a merchants' quarter to the east of the city, between the Nau and the easternmost branch of the Marne.[13] In 864, Bishop Erchenré prevailed upon Charles the Bald to grant him the right to strike his own coins.[14] The ninth century also saw the bishops of Châlons set on the road to domination of the city and to national prominence. In 845, Charles the Bald recognized Bishop Loup as Count of Châlons as well.[15] This revival was short-lived. In 888, Châlons was sacked by the Vikings. In the tenth century, the bishops of Châlons became involved in the dynastic struggles over the crown and the city was sacked in 931 and again in 963.[16]

Despite these setbacks, Châlons continued as before. The continuing viability of the city is evidenced by the construction of a new wall,

---

[11]Clause and Ravaux, *Histoire,* 28–30; Barthélemy, *Histoire,*1st ed., 136–42.

[12]Clause and Ravaux, *Histoire,* 27; other authorities state that St. Pierre was the original cathedral and was supplanted by the newly built St. Etienne in the seventh century; see Edouard de Barthélemy, *Histoire de la ville de Châlons-sur-Marne et de ses institutions, des origines à 1848,* 2d ed. (Châlons-sur-Marne, 1883), 49; Louis Barbat, *Histoire de la ville de Châlons-sur-Marne et de ses monuments depuis son origine jusqu'en 1855* (Chalons, 1865), 17–18.

[13]Clause and Ravaux, *Histoire,* 28–30; Louis Grignon, *Topographie historique de la ville de Châlons-sur-Marne* (Châlons, 1889), 177.

[14]Clause and Ravaux, *Histoire,* 30; Barthélemy, *Histoire,* 1st ed., 116, 145.

[15]Barthélemy, *Histoire,* 1st ed., 145; Barbat, *Histoire,* 194, states that it was Clovis who granted this title, while Clause and Ravaux refer to lay counts whose names are unknown and who were superseded by the bishops in the ninth century.

[16]Clause and Ravaux, *Histoire,* 33; Barthélemy, *Histoire,* 1st ed., 149–51.

probably sometime in the tenth century. The old Roman city was very small, confined between a branch of the Marne and the Nau, comprising no more than seven hectares. Nothing remains of the Roman wall, and in all likelihood it was a simple earthen barrier topped by a palisade. The new wall was double the length and enclosed nearly triple the area, including the market and the merchants' quarter between the Nau and the eastern branch of the Marne. This wall excluded St. Memmie, St. Pierre, and St. Sulpice.[17]

The two centuries from around 1000 to 1200 saw the power of the bishops of Châlons at its height. The growth of episcopal power is tied inextricably to the struggle between the crown and the counts of Champagne. In the course of this struggle, the bishop/counts of Châlons found themselves in an enviable political position, with both sides bidding for their favor.[18]

The eleventh and twelfth centuries were also the period of Châlons' greatest expansion. The foundation of religious establishments provides a rough guide to the growth of the city. By the middle of the thirteenth century, Châlons had grown from the original five parishes of the Cathedral—St. Alpin, St. Sulpice, St. Jean, and Notre-Dame-en-Vaux—to the thirteen it was to maintain until the eighteenth century.[19] In addition, in 1062, Roger II established the Augustinian Abbey of Toussaints de l'Ile on one of the islands lying outside the city walls.[20] Such ecclesiastical expansion was of course made necessary by the physical growth of the city,

---

[17]Clause and Ravaux, *Histoire*, 20, 35.

[18]For example, Bishop Roger I (1011–42) obtained from Eudes II of Champagne a promise not to build fortified places within eight leagues of Châlons. Their respective successors, Roger II (1042–66) and Eudes III (ca. 1048–66), maintained friendly relations, and Eudes ceded to the bishop all his rights over the abbey of St. Memmie and within the city of Châlons. At the same time, the bishop/counts stayed on good terms with the crown, and a number of them played an important part in royal politics. In 1049, Roger I was chosen to go to Kiev to negotiate the marriage of the Grand Duke's daughter to the dauphin. In the 1120s, the bishops supported the king in his wars with the emperor; see Clause and Ravaux, *Histoire*, 43, 47, 51; Barthélemy, *Histoire*, 1st ed., 155, 158.

[19]Bishop Roger I added to the original five parishes of Châlons the two new parishes of St. Jean and St. Alpin in the merchants' quarter, and in 1027 began the Collegiate Church of the Trinity, which from 1095 on served as the parish church for the cathedral quarter. Other parishes founded in this period include: St. Germain, established mid-eleventh century; St. Croix, established 1133; Notre-Dame-en-Vaux, established 1107, in 1246 divided into five parishes, two of which continued at Notre Dame (the three new churches constructed were St. Antoine, Ste. Marguerite, and St. Loup); St. Nicaise created in 1251 out of a division of St. Jean; see Clause and Ravaux, *Histoire*, 37–38, 72; Edouard de Barthélemy, *Histoire*, 2d ed. (Châlons-sur-Marne, 1883), 44–49.

[20]Clause and Ravaux, *Histoire*, 39; Barthélemy, *Histoire*, 2d ed., 49–50.

which by this time had considerably outgrown its walls. In addition to the previous extramural agglomerations of St. Memmie, St. Pierre, and St. Sulpice, were now added Neufbourg to the south of the city, and Neuville de Vigne-l'Evêque to the north.

With such growth, a new wall was again necessary, and was constructed beginning in 1180. This wall subsisted with modifications until the eighteenth century, and was almost three times as long and enclosed almost five times the area of the previous wall. It still excluded most of Neufbourg, part of Neuville de Vigne-l'Evêque, and all of St. Memmie, which from this time on began its own existence independent of Châlons. It also excluded the faubourgs of St. Sulpice and Pont-Ruppé, the inclusion of which would have removed the principal course of the Marne from the city's defenses.[21]

At the same time that Châlons was experiencing its greatest growth and the bishop/counts were exercising supreme authority within the city, these latter were planting the seeds which were to result in the attenuation of their authority. Part of this process involved a feudal habit of mind: As the city grew, the bishops embarked on a process of subinfeudation. In the early eleventh century Roger I granted to the Abbey of St. Pierre feudal rights over part of the city, including the merchants' quarter with its parishes of St. Jean and St. Alpin.[22] Likewise, his successor Roger II, in the mid-eleventh century, granted to the newly erected Abbey of Toussaints seigneurial jurisdiction over the island on which it was situated, and the neighboring parish of St. Sulpice.[23] Neither of these jurisdictions was a serious rival to the bishops' authority. (In the sixteenth century, the bishop was also abbot of St. Pierre and thus ruled both jurisdictions.) More serious competition was to arise from two other quarters: the chapter, and the citizens.

The chapter began its independent existence near the end of the eleventh century when the bishop granted it seigneurial rights over the faubourg of Le Rognon and over Notre-Dame-en-Vaux.[24] The two powers coexisted rather fitfully, as one might imagine, until, by the end of the

---

[21]Clause and Ravaux, *Histoire*, 67–70.
[22]Clause and Ravaux, *Histoire*, 37–38; Barbat, *Histoire*, 18; Barthélemy, *Histoire*, 2d ed., 49.
[23]Clause and Ravaux, *Histoire*, 39; Barthélemy, *Histoire*, 2d ed., 49–50.
[24]Clause and Ravaux, *Histoire*, 39–40.

thirteenth century, the canons of Châlons had succeeded in establishing their independence of the bishop.[25] In its struggle with the bishop, the chapter had several factors working in its favor. By the thirteenth century, the chapter, as was common throughout France, had appropriated to itself the right to elect the bishop. This practice was confirmed by St. Louis in 1265 and again by Charles V in 1357. As a result the chapter was in a position to extort concessions. This right became all the more important when episcopal elections were hotly contested. Between 1100 and 1300, twenty bishops were elected. In the twelfth century, four of eleven elections proved contentious; in the thirteenth, it was seven of nine.[26]

In addition, by the fourteenth century the bishops had lost royal support for their policies. In previous times, the crown had used the bishops of Châlons as a counterweight to the powerful counts of Champagne. In 1285, the county of Champagne escheated to the crown through the marriage of the last count's daughter to Philip the Fair. From then on, the king had no reason to support the independence of the bishop/counts of Châlons, and royal government pressed in more and more on the county of Châlons.

A more serious rival to the bishops' authority than the chapter, which was interested not so much in governing the town as in its own independence, came from the efforts of the lay inhabitants to gain a voice in the government of the city. Despite recurrent attempts, the inhabitants were never able to form a commune, or sworn association of citizens.[27] Nevertheless, by the fifteenth century, they had achieved the substance without the form: de jure Châlons remained subject to its four seigneurs; de facto, the city was self-governing.

---

[25]On the various episodes in this struggle, see: Clause and Ravaux, *Histoire*, 88–91; Barbat, *Histoire*, 229–31; Barthélemy, *Histoire*, 2d ed., 39–41.

[26]Barthélemy, *Histoire*, 2d ed., 35; Barbat, *Histoire*, 195; Clause and Ravaux, *Histoire*, 87.

[27]Edouard de Barthélemy is alone among historians of Châlons in maintaining that Châlons did establish a commune. His argument is based primarily on the reference of contemporary sources to the "bourgeois of Châlons" or the "*cité* of Châlons." This evidence is totally unconvincing. If there was a commune, one might ask why it left no documents behind, what its relationship was to the city council in the fifteenth century, and why the inhabitants continued to agitate for what they were already supposed to have. In short, there are many more problems in maintaining the existence of a commune than in denying it; see Barthélemy, *Histoire*, 2d ed., 6–9.

The first attempt in Châlons at forming a commune occurred in the twelfth century, and met with total defeat despite a royal policy favoring urban communes.[28] In 1210, the bishop authorized a body of Châlonnais to meet for the limited purpose of raising money to complete the new wall. The inhabitants sought to twist this body to serve their own communal purposes. They attempted to tax the chapter, which prevailed upon the bishop to suppress it. This suppression was confirmed by the king, who then also loaned the bishop two thousand livres to complete the wall.[29]

The next clash came over the election of the *échevins*. Châlonnais échevins are not to be confused with officials of the same name in other cities. They were not city councillors. They were judicial officials, and were originally responsible for justice in only the bishop's jurisdiction, or *ban de l'evêque*. The échevins had originally been appointed by the bishop alone. During their struggles with the bishop, the inhabitants began to claim a right to elect them. The standoff continued until 1288, when there were only two instead of the normal seven. The matter was arbitrated by the chapter and the abbot of Toussaints. A compromise was reached by which the échevins were allowed to co-opt their replacements. The candidates would then take an oath to the bishop and be installed by him. We are still far removed from civic self-government, for the échevins remained essentially judges, and not legislators or executives.[30]

Despite these setbacks, the citizens continued to agitate and in 1226, during an episcopal vacancy, they held an assembly on their own authority. (It could not have been otherwise, since there was no bishop to authorize such an assembly.) The disorders became so great that the king sent a representative to reestablish order, and in 1255 and again in 1260, forbade

---

[28]Clause and Ravaux, *Histoire,* 108–9. Bishop Guy II de Montagu maintained that "il soit connu de tous que le comté de Châlons et la seigneurie de la ville et autres droits royaux de l'église de Châlons, ont été concédés et accordés dès les temps plus anciens par les rois des Francs, en toute liberté et perpetuité, sans pouvoir jamais être aliénés, à ladite église et à son évêque; d'où il suit qu'il n'est permis, ni au roi de France, ni à nous, de faire une commune ou d'en laisser faire une aux citoyens dans la ville de Châlons; Barbat, *Histoire,* 288.

[29]Clause and Ravaux, *Histoire,* 71, 110–11.

[30]Clause and Ravaux, *Histoire,* 112–13, 122; Barbat, *Histoire,* 161–63; Barthélemy, *Histoire,* 2d ed., 11–13.

the inhabitants to assemble without the permission of the bishop.[31]

Yet another attempt to gain some measure of self-government focused on the wool industry. Châlons had been the site of a small-scale wool industry throughout the Middle Ages. Beginning in the twelfth century, the town benefited from the technological revolution in weaving and from the general economic and demographic revival of the High Middle Ages. In typical medieval fashion, members of the wool trade organized themselves into a corporation, recognized by the bishop in 1248 and by the Parlement of Paris in 1250. This corporation began to claim more and more power for itself, thereby becoming the focus of the inhabitants' communal aspirations.

The bishops were able to defeat the inhabitants' aspirations by playing on the division between the *drapiers* (merchants) and the *tisserands* (weavers), sponsoring a separate corporation of tisserands. The drapiers were also defeated by their own poorly conceived strategy, by increased competition from newer and more advanced woolen industries in England, Italy, and the Low Countries, and by the economic and demographic catastrophes of the fourteenth century.[32]

The extent to which the inhabitants of Châlons had developed a civic identity is evident in the events of 1306 and 1307.[33] In 1306, Philip the Fair decreed a monetary reform, suppressing debased coinage and replacing it with new coins having twice the precious metal content. The Châlonnais then refused to pay the bishop his revenues with the new coins, which would have doubled his income. The citizens attacked the bishop's officers and the bishop appealed to the king to reestablish order. The royal representatives accepted the citizens' demands under threat of

[31]Barbat, *Histoire*, 288–89; Barthélemy, *Histoire*, 2d ed., 217–19. This prohibition was echoed by the bishop: "Je, Pierre de Hans, évêque et comte de Châlons, pair de France, tiens, connais et avoue tenir en plein fief, foi, et hommage, les choses qui en suivent: 1. Le palais épiscopal avec ses appartenances et les jardins tenant à la rivière de Marne. *Item*: la seigneurie temporelle, haute, moyenne et basse justice dans toute la ville, cité et territoire, fauxbourgs, et rivières dudit Châlons, excepté en certains lieux de ville ès quels les abbés et couvent de Saint-Pierre-aux-Monts, les abbés et couvent de Toussaints et les doyen et chapitre dudit Châlons ont fiefs par concession et don de nos prédécesseurs évêques. *Item*: j'ai le droit qu'il n'est permis aux habitants dudit Châlons de ne faire aucunes assemblées, tailles ou cueillettes en ladite ville, sans ma permission ou celle de mon bailli en mon absence"; Barbat, *Histoire*, 289.

[32]On the woolen industry in Châlons, see Clause and Ravaux, *Histoire*, 74–83, 111–13; Barthélemy, *Histoire*, 2d ed., 148–52; Barbat, *Histoire*, 242–47.

[33]Clause and Ravaux, *Histoire*, 95–96.

being thrown in the river. Between March 3 and 6, 1307, the citizens ruled the city, putting guards on the wall and stretching chains across the streets to impede any efforts at suppression. Eventually, this revolt petered out, and the king imposed a fine of twelve thousand livres on the city: ten thousand livres for himself and one thousand livres for each of his representatives. The bishop received nothing, despite his appeals.

Thus, by the beginning of the fourteenth century, the bishop/counts of Châlons had repulsed all civic attempts at communal organization. It is true that the bishop no longer exercised complete sovereignty over the city. By 1300, Châlons had been divided among four jurisdictions or *bans*. The bishop's jurisdiction or ban de l'évêque covered roughly half the city. The ban de St. Pierre consisted of the southeastern part of the city, about one quarter of the total area. The ban du chapitre covered about 10 percent of the city and was divided into three parts: the cloister and area immediately surrounding the cathedral, the ban des clercs or ban du Rognon in the northeastern corner of the city, and the area surrounding the church of Notre-Dame-en-Vaux. The ban de Toussaints or ban de l'Ile took up about 20 percent of the city, but most of its territory lay outside the walls, and it was the least populated ban. Thus, in a juridical sense, it is technically improper to speak of the city of Châlons-sur-Marne. What we have is an agglomeration of four seigneuries, each with its own powers of justice and government, and each independent of the others. Two other developments would eventually result in the extinction of all but the ceremonial position and power of the bishop and the corresponding institutionalization of the inhabitants' communal mentality. These were the steady encroachment of royal jurisdiction into the county of Châlons and the pressures of foreign invasion and civil war.

When Champagne was definitively brought into the royal domain in the late thirteenth century, the king lost all incentive to maintain the bishop of Châlons as a counterweight to the counts of Champagne. The kings of France had always had a material interest in the county and diocese of Châlons, since during episcopal vacancies, the bishop's revenue went to the king. During the twelfth and thirteenth centuries, royal incursions into the bishops' jurisdiction became more and more direct. Châlons came more and more under the jurisdiction of the *bailli* of Vermandois in Laon, and more and more cases were appealed to the Parlement of Paris.

In the fourteenth century, Châlons became the seat of the fiscal jurisdiction known as the *élection*, and of a royal salt warehouse or *grenier à sel*.

The second development, a series of events that resulted in the extinction of all but the ceremonial power of the bishop, was the Hundred Years' War. During the course of the fighting, Châlons found itself threatened numerous times, first by the English and then alternately by the Burgundians and Armagnacs. There were two basic results of these threats and disorders. First, the inhabitants of Châlons found themselves having to assume responsibility for their own defense. The four seigneurs were not able to coordinate effectively, and this responsibility fell to the citizens, who had already developed a sense of civic solidarity.[34] In doing so, they were not afraid to ask for royal help; in 1348 the first royal captain of Châlons was appointed.[35] The other major development was that during the course of the war Châlons developed the institutions to express their civic consciousness. At some point during the fourteenth century, the citizens of Châlons began to tax themselves for the maintenance of their fortifications. In 1370, the king approved this practice and in 1373 gave the city two thousand livres to aid in their endeavours.[36]

The financial organization of the city was firmly established in 1375, when an assembly of inhabitants confided the affairs of the city to a *receveur* and four *élus* (subsequently known as *gouverneurs* and reduced in number to two).[37] In 1383, the king granted various rights of *octroi* to Châlons, which were to form the base of civic finances throughout the sixteenth century.[38]

The other major institutional development, and the one which really made Châlons self-governing, was the creation of a city council in 1417. In the civil war between the Burgundians and Armagnacs, Châlons was a Burgundian town. Duke John the Fearless of Burgundy, imitating an earlier policy of the French monarchy, sought to solidify his support by upholding civic autonomy. To this end, he established in 1417 a commission of eight inhabitants of Châlons to purge the city of Armagnacs and

---

[34]Bernard Chevalier, *Les bonnes villes de France du XIVe au XVIe siècle* (Paris: Aubier Montaigne, 1982), 50.

[35]Barthélemy, *Histoire*, 2d ed., 79–80; Clause and Ravaux, *Histoire*, 116; Barbat, *Histoire*, 312.

[36]Barthélemy, *Histoire*, 2d ed., 97–98.

[37]Clause and Ravaux, *Histoire*, 117–18; Barthélemy, *Histoire*, 2d ed., 98–102.

[38]Barthélemy, *Histoire*, 2d ed., 102–4.

manage its affairs. The commission quickly asserted its power over all aspects of Châlonnais life, assuming responsibility for defense, finances, public health, and urban planning. Right from its inception, the council kept detailed notes of its proceedings and conclusions. In 1418, the council took the unprecedented step of having an assembly of inhabitants renew its powers and those of civic officials. When Châlons opened its gates to King Charles VII in 1429, he confirmed all its privileges, including those granted by the rival Burgundians.[39]

Thus, by the beginning of the sixteenth century, Châlons-sur-Marne had developed as a self-governing community in all aspects save juridically. Technically, the city was still divided among its four feudal seigneurs (fig. 1.3); in fact, it was the city council which governed Châlons, and the city took its place as one of the bonnes villes of France. The city levied its own taxes, maintained its own fortifications and artillery, and oversaw matters of public health and urban planning.[40] The power of the bishop had been reduced to a pro forma precedence in the annual civic assembly on St. Martin's Day (November 11) and in the city council, on the rare occasions when he chose to attend, and to certain feudal and fiscal privileges within the city. As for the other seigneurs, the bishop was also abbot of St. Pierre. The abbot of Toussaints played a minor role in civic government in the sixteenth century, with most of his ban lying outside the city walls following a diversion of the Marne in the fourteenth century.[41] It was with the chapter that the council clashed most often. This was because the chapter maintained that it was exempt from the council's authority, especially in fiscal and military matters, not because it claimed a powerful voice in the city's government.

[39]On the creation of the council see Barthélemy, *Histoire*, 2d ed., 13–14, 235–36; Clause and Ravaux, *Histoire*, 119–23; Barbat, *Histoire*, 292–93.

[40]See Sylvette Guilbert, "A Châlons-sur-Marne au XVe siècle: un conseil municipal face aux épidémies," *Annales: Economies, Sociétés, Civilizations* 23 no. 6 (1968): 1283; idem, "Les fortifications de Châlons-sur-Marne à la fin du Moyen Age," *Actes du 95e congrès des sociétés savantes*, Reims, 1970. Section d'archéologie et d'histoire de l'art (Paris, 1974), 195–203.

[41]Following an English attack in 1359, the Marne was diverted and a new section of wall built along its bank, in order to eliminate a potentially vulnerable salient. This modification left two-thirds of the ban de Toussaints outside the walls; Clause and Ravaux, *Histoire*, 102.

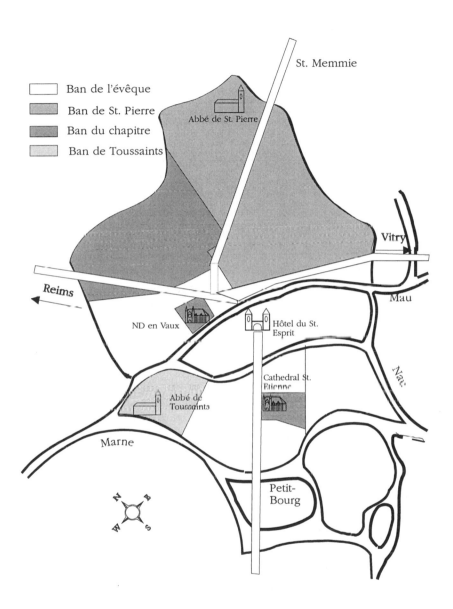

Fig. 1.3. Châlons in the sixteenth century

Chapter 2

Portrait of a City Council

![T]HE CITY COUNCIL OF CHÂLONS-SUR-MARNE, although it could point to no constitution or charter of foundation, was the governing body of the city. The city of Châlons and its council are a vivid witness that in the ancien régime what counted was not the official version of the way things worked, but how the myriad overlapping and at times contradictory institutions functioned on a day-to-day basis. In the case of Châlons, we see a city which technically does not exist governed by a council which has no official power. Yet clearly the city did exist, and just as clearly the council, as the only permanent institution with jurisdiction over the whole city, was ultimately responsible for its government.

The council normally met in the Hôtel du Saint Esprit. It is indicative of the way institutions evolved in this period that as the wars wore on, the term *hôtel de ville* was used at first interchangeably with Hôtel du Saint Esprit, and eventually superseded it altogether. On rare occasions, the council met in other places—such as the Chapelle des Sybilles in St. Etienne Cathedral, the *hôtel épiscopal*, or the Dominican convent—usually for reasons of avoiding the plague.

We know very little of how the councillors were chosen. Each of the four seigneurs was represented. The bishop had the right of precedence, but in fact rarely attended, and was usually represented by his *bailli* or bailiff. The abbot of Toussaints also sat on the council, and although he attended more regularly than the bishop, he still was present at a small percentage of the meetings. The chapter had two representatives, usually the dean and archdeacon; most meetings of the council had at least one chapter representative present. In the later sixteenth century, the bishop was also abbot of St. Pierre; therefore, both seigneuries were represented by the same person.

In addition to the representatives of the seigneurs, several royal officials were ex officio city councillors. Foremost among them was the lieutenant of the *bailli* of Vermandois. In 1551, Châlons had been granted its own branch or *siège particulier* of the *bailliage* of Vermandois based in Laon.

In 1584, the council formally instituted the practice of including the *gens du roi* in the city council. These were the king's legal representatives in the courts and tribunals in the city, and were known as the *avocat du roi* (royal barrister) and *procureur du roi* (royal solicitor).[1] The royal captain of Châlons sat on the council also. The position of captain had been instituted in the fourteenth century for the city's chief military officer. He was appointed by the king and paid by the council. As we shall see in chapter 3, he usually attended council meetings only when his military expertise was required or when the council was dealing with the security of the city.

In addition to these royal officers, there were several other ex officio councillors, among whom were the *échevins*. Châlonnais échevins were not the equivalent of échevins in other cities, where they were essentially aldermen or city councillors. In Châlons, the échevins were the judicial officers of the *ban de l'évêque*. By the sixteenth century, the *échevinage* was cooptive and largely hereditary. Although all échevins were city councillors, not all councillors were échevins.[2]

There were a number of other ex officio city councillors: the two governors, elected for two-year terms at the annual general assembly on St. Martin's Day, November 11, who were essentially the city's chief executive officers, responsible for implementing the council's decisions. The *procureur*, or the city's chief legal officer, was also elected at the St. Martin's assembly and was a city councillor, as were the *receveur* (the city's fiscal officer), the *lieutenant de ville* (the "chief of police"), and the *lieutenant du capitaine*. The council's *greffier*, or clerk, who kept the council's records,

---

[1] AD Marne E suppt. 4788, fol. 70.

[2] On *échevins* in general, see Roger Doucet, *Les institutions de la France au XVIe siècle*, 2 vols. (Paris: Picard, 1948), 38–39; on Châlonnais *échevins*, see Edouard de Barthélemy, *Histoire de la ville de Châlons-sur-Marne et de ses institutions, des origines à 1848*, 1st ed. (Châlons-sur-Marne, 1854), 11–13; Louis Barbat, *Histoire de la ville de Châlons-sur-Marne et de ses monuments depuis son origine jusqu'en 1855* (Chalons, 1865), 260–64; Louis Barbat, *Histoire de la ville de Châlons-sur-Marne et de ses monuments depuis son origine jusqu' en 1855* (Chalons, 1865), 1:144–45; Georges Clause and Jean-Pierre Ravaux, *Histoire de Châlons-sur-Marne* (Le Coteau-Roanne: Horvath, 1983), 112.

was an internal appointment, selected by the councillors from among their own number.[3]

Finally, besides these ex officio members of the council, there were those who were simply councillors. Because the council had no formal constitution, there was no set number of these "councillors-at-large" and thus no prescribed size for the council. The largest number recorded at any regular council meeting was thirty-two, but council business was usually dominated by an informal inner core of members, between ten and twenty in number. We remain ignorant of how these "councillors-at-large" were selected; no elections to the council are mentioned. It seems likely, therefore, that council membership was determined by invitation or co-optation.

This is not a prosopographical study of the city councillors; nevertheless, some impressionistic observations may be made regarding their familial connections and social and occupational status. Of the one hundred fifty councillors recorded over the thirty-five years of this study, one sees the same surnames over and over. There were seven Gorliers, five each of the Cuissotte and Chastillon families, four each of the Aubelin, Braulx, and Godet families, three each of the Hennequins, Beschefers, François, Ytams, de Bars, Daousts, and Cléments. Altogether, sixty-five of the one hundred fifty councillors shared a total of twenty-one surnames.

Although the councillors, with the single exception of the captain, were commoners, they were hardly ordinary citizens. A list compiled in 1587 for the use of the royal captain of those possessing fiefs or parts of fiefs in the countryside around Châlons reveals that sixteen present or former councillors possessed such fiefs.[4]

The council also included a number of royal officers besides those who were ex officio councillors. Châlons was the site of the two major regional fiscal jurisdictions in early modern France: the *élection*, and the superior jurisdiction known as the *généralité*. Nicolas Hennequin was a *receveur des aides* in the élection. G. Godet was a *receveur du taillon*. Pierre du Mouli-

[3]On municipal officers, see Doucet, *Les institutions de la France*, 1:377–80; Albert Babeau, *La ville sous l'ancien régime*. 2 vols. (Paris, 1884), 1:206–7. For Châlons, see Clause and Ravaux, *Histoire*, 122–23.

[4]AD Marne E suppt. 4789, fols. 20–21. See also Anne-Marie Couvret, "Les Châlonnais du XVIe siècle, propriétaires ruraux," *Mémoires de la Société d'agriculture, commerce, sciences et arts du département de la Marne* 78 (1963): 61–81.

net and Jean Dommengin were both *élus* in the élection. Pierre Braulx was a *trésorier de France*, as was T. Cauchon. Guillaume de Champagne was a *receveur-général* in the *généralité* of Châlons.

From its formation in the early fifteenth century, the council quickly assumed overall control of all aspects of civic life. The council held ultimate responsibility for matters of urban planning, public health, commerce, education, poor relief, and defense.

The annual assembly of the city's inhabitants (one assumes of adult male inhabitants) took place in the bishop's palace on St. Martin's Day, November 11. At this assembly, the major officers of the city were elected. The governors were elected for terms of two years, usually staggered, so that one governor always had a year's experience in the office. The procureur, receveur, lieutenant, and lieutenant du capitaine were elected for indefinite terms.

The St. Martin's Assembly was held with the permission of the four seigneurs. Several days before November 11, the council obtained this pro forma permission; it was never refused, and eventually it was dispensed with altogether. The bishop normally presided over the assembly. After 1589, however, when the bishop had been expelled from Châlons because of his affinity for the Catholic League, the assembly was held by leave of the council alone, and was presided over by the dean of the chapter.

Occasionally the council convened extraordinary assemblies to deal with urgent matters. In 1577, when pressed by the duc de Guise and his brother the cardinal de Guise to swear the articles of the Catholic League, the council instructed the captain of each militia unit, or *cinquantenier,* to appoint two or three men to consider the matter in a special assembly.[5] In several instances the council also invited the "principal inhabitants" of the city to deliberate with the regular councillors.[6] The council on several occasions convened extraordinary general assemblies to consider matters of the greatest importance. Thus in January 1589, following the murder of the Guises at Blois, about four hundred inhabitants swore unanimously "to maintain and conserve themselves in the union previously sworn to His Majesty ... to live and die ... under His Majesty's authority, to keep and render the obedience and fidelity they owe to him, to expose their

[5]AD Marne E suppt. 4787, fols. 127-28.
[6]See, e.g., AD Marne E suppt. 4789, fol. 30.

goods and lives in his service and the conservation of this city in his obedience."[7]

Although the city council held ultimate responsibility for Châlons, the four seigneurs also had a limited voice in governing the city. Of the four, the most powerful was the bishop, who was also abbot of St. Pierre. Over the course of the Wars of Religion, the see of Châlons was held by three bishops: Jérôme de Bourgeois or Burgensis (1556–1572); Nicolas Clausse (1572–1574); and his brother, Cosme Clausse (1574–1624). Of these three, only Bourgeois and Cosme Clausse figure in this study; Nicolas Clausse was bishop for only two years, and the council minutes for these years are not extant.

Bishop Bourgeois took little interest in civic affairs. From 1559 to 1569 (when the council records cease for four years), he attended not one meeting of the council. Indeed, he seems to have wished to withdraw completely from the government of the city. By the sixteenth century, episcopal rights in Châlons had been reduced to ceremonial functions, such as presiding over the annual general assembly and to certain feudal dues and levies, such as the *droit de minage* (a fee paid on the weighing of grain for sale) and control over fishing rights in the river Marne. These rights led to a series of conflicts and lawsuits with the council and the inhabitants.[8] Eventually, Bourgeois decided that it would be simpler to sell his rights to the city; the lawsuits would end, and he would still receive some revenue from this source. Thus, in 1565, the council agreed to pay the bishop 800 livres annually in return for these rights.[9]

Cosme Clausse, in contrast, took a much keener interest in city government. Between April 1575 and February 1589, he attended forty council meetings, or 9.5 percent of the total—not a great deal, certainly, but more than his predecessor and enough to cause resentment among the councillors. Moreover, Clausse was a partisan of the Catholic League and

[7]AD Marne E suppt. 4789, fol. 49: "De se maintenir et conserver en l'unyon cy devant jurée à sa Majesté … vivre et mourir … soubz l'auctorité de sadite Majesté, garder et rendre la fidélité et obéissance qu'ilz luy doibvent, exposer leurs biens et vies pour son service et conservation de ladite ville en son obéissance." See also AD Marne E suppt. 4789, fol. 34, where a general assembly concluded "à la pluralité des voix" to negotiate Châlons' entry into the Catholic League with the city council of Paris.

[8]See, e.g., the council's conclusions regarding the lawsuits, in AD Marne E suppt. 4785, fols. 157–58, 161–62.

[9]AD Marne E suppt. 4785, fols. 191–92. For the complete text of the transaction and list of the rights sold, see Barbat, *Histoire*, 199–206.9.

an ally of the duc de Guise; he was therefore perceived as having an agenda of his own in contrast to that of the city council. In addition, Clausse apparently attempted to restore the rights his predecessor had sold to the city, or at least to renegotiate the purchase price.[10]

The abbot of Toussaints also had the right to sit on the city council by virtue of his seigneurie or *ban* in Châlons. Over the period of the Wars of Religion, there were two abbots: Antoine Tousson (abbot until 1575) and Louis de Clèves (from 1575 on). The abbots of Toussaints generally participated more in civic government than did the bishop. From 1560 to 1569, Abbot Tousson attended eighty-seven council meetings, roughly one third of the total. Louis de Clèves attended somewhat fewer meetings: thirty-one between 1575 and 1588, or about 8 percent of the total.

Generally speaking, the abbot of Toussaints attended council meetings only when his abbey or his ban was directly affected by the business taken up at the session. For example, the buildings of the abbey outside the walls (Toussaints dehors) were often used to house plague victims, and the abbot repeatedly requested payment for the use of his facilities.[11]

Of the four seigneurs of Châlons, it was the cathedral chapter which participated most in city government. This was only natural; bishops and abbots came and went, but the chapter as a corporation was in Châlons to stay. The chapter had two seats on the council and was usually represented by the dean and/or the archdeacon. Although the chapter was intimately involved in the council, it had no ambitions of increasing its role in civic government. It was concerned, for the most part, with protecting its own interests, which it felt were challenged on three fronts: the financing of the municipal college of St. Lazaire, duty in the watch or *guet*, and subjection to taxation.

In 1560, after long negotiations with the chapter, the city took over the Hôpital St. Lazaire and transformed it into a municipal college. This was part of a larger movement in Renaissance France in which every city of moderate size attempted to found a college. The royal ordinance of Orléans in 1561 had decreed that each cathedral chapter turn over the revenue of its first vacant prebend for the use of municipal colleges. This was a continual point of contention in Châlons between the city council and

---

[10]AD Marne E suppt. 4787, fols. 197–98; 4788, fols. 23–24.
[11]See, e.g., AD Marne E suppt. 4785, fols. 194–96; 4786, fols. 3, 15; 4787, fols. 101–2.

the chapter. Negotiations over this issue began with the foundation of the college. In 1565, the governors and procureur of the city ordered the chapter to turn over the revenue from the prebend held by the late C. Godet. In 1566, the council asked the king to force the chapter to hand over the prebend. In 1567, the chapter offered an annual payment of two hundred livres in lieu of transferring the prebend. The council refused this offer and wrote to the king asking him to order the bailli of Vermandois to release the prebend to the college, and—should the chapter still refuse—to seize its temporal goods. In 1579, the council once again asked the chapter to remit the revenue to the city and in 1582 asked the king to order the chapter to suppress the prebend.[12]

The clergy of the chapter also claimed exemption from watch duty. In 1586, the council called upon the chapter to do its duty; should they refuse, the council concluded, the duc de Guise would be asked to force them. And in 1588, the council asked the chapter "to do their duty for the conservation of this city, considering the imminent danger."[13]

The chapter also claimed exemption from various of the levies imposed upon the lay inhabitants of Châlons. In 1562, the council asked the provincial governor, the duc de Nevers, to force the chapter to contribute to the supplies needed for an army of German mercenaries, or *reiters*, camped nearby. In September 1589, the commander of the royal army in Champagne, the maréchal d'Aumont, imposed a tax of twelve thousand livres on Châlons to pay for the city's garrison. The clergy were assessed at three thousand. The chapter balked, and by October still had not paid.[14]

The council met according to no regular schedule, but it met when there was business to conduct. As one might expect, the council met more often in times of war and crisis than in more placid times. In 1560 and 1561, the two years immediately preceding the outbreak of the wars, the council met on average once every three weeks. From 1589 to 1594, how-

---

[12]On municipal colleges in general see George Huppert, *Public Schools in Renaissance France* (Urbana: University of Illinois Press, 1984); see also Gaston Zeller, *Les institutions de la France au XVIe siècle* (Paris: Presses Universitaires, 1948), 274–76; Bernard Chevalier, *Les bonnes villes de France du XIVe au XVIe siècle* (Paris: Aubier Montaigne, 1982), 229–33. For the college of St. Lazaire, see Barbat, *Histoire*, 55–60. See also Chevalier, *Les bonnes villes de France*, 232; AD Marne E suppt. 4785, fols. 55–56, 198; 4786, fols. 18, 26; 4787, fols. 197–98; 4788, fol. 28.

[13]AD Marne E. suppt. 4787, fols. 40, 122, 218; 4788, fol. 118; 4789, fol. 37: "Seroit priez messieurs du chappitre de faire leur debvoir à la conservation de lad. ville attendu le péril éminent."

[14]AD Marne E suppt. 4785, fol. 72; 4789, fols. 114, 116.

ever, when Châlons was an isolated royalist outpost in heavily Leaguer Champagne, it met on average twice weekly.

There is good reason to believe that the Wars of Religion revivified a city council on the point of becoming moribund. In the two years preceding the wars, 1560 and 1561, the council met a total of thirty times (16 times in 1560 and 14 in 1561), or just about once every three weeks. From 1562 through 1588, the council met on average a little more than biweekly (.57 times per week). The yearly total fluctuates between a low of 15 meetings in 1582 and a high of 55 in 1568 for a yearly average of 30. From 1589 through 1593, the council met 420 times for an annual average of 105, or two meetings every week (see fig. 2.1).

A more complicated pattern emerges if we look at the average attendance at the council meetings. During the two years before the outbreak of the wars, an average of 17.4 councillors (in 1560) and 18.8 councillors (in 1561) attended meetings. With the increasing number of meetings during the wars, attendance dropped off throughout the rest of the 1560s, from 17.3 in 1565 to 14.0 in 1568. The councillors recognized this problem and took steps to counteract it. In 1564, the council set the quorum for its meetings at 15, and declared that any councillor who missed more than three meetings without a legitimate excuse would forfeit his post, "because often meetings are called and nobody comes."[15] These measures apparently had little effect, for attendance continued to decline: 17.3 in 1565; 14.5 in 1566; 16.6 in 1567; and 14.0 in 1568. There were numerous occasions when lack of a quorum forced the cancellation of a council session.[16] From 1574 to 1588, when the duc de Guise was establishing his control over Châlons, attendance declined to an annual average of 13.61, reaching its nadir in 1583, when an average of only 11.3 councillors attended each meeting.

Attendance levels seem to have been affected by two variables: the relative frequency of meetings (the more often meetings are held, the more difficult it is for every councillor to attend each one) and the degree to which the councillors felt that the important issues were theirs to decide

---

[15]AD Marne E suppt. 4785, fol. 170: "pource que souvent on invite le conseil de la ville et personne sera sy trouvé."
[16]AD Marne E suppt. 4786, fols. 93, 141.

Year	No. meetings	Avg. attendance
1560	16	17.4
1561	14	18.8
1562	30	17.3
1563	33	*
1564	31	*
1565	24	17.3
1566	19	14.5
1567	21	16.6
1568	55	14.0
1569 through 1574	*	*
1575	41	13.2
1576	43	14.0
1577	24	12.3
1578	30	13.0
1579	27	13.0
1580	42	13.6
1581	19	14.3
1582	26	11.9
1583	15	11.3
1584	24	13.9
1585	29	15.9
1586	30	13.9
1587	33	15.3
1588	35	16.0
1589	98	18.8
1590	77	16.8
1591	76	17.8
1592	81	*
1593	88	*

*No data available

Fig. 2.1. Frequency of and average attendance at council meetings, 1560–1593

(with Guise firmly in control, there was very likely a sense of apathy, that the city's destiny was outside the council's control).

Council attendance increased again after 1588, as did the frequency of meetings, when the city declared its independence from Guise and the League. From 1589 through 1593 attendance again reached its prewar level. This by itself is misleading, for the council met many more times in these years: ninety-eight times in 1589 alone. Therefore, the same number of councillors attended many more meetings than had been the case before the wars. Interest in council business among the councillors was much higher than it had been before the wars.

The city council of Châlons-sur-Marne was a remarkably flexible institution. With a purely customary existence, unconstrained by formal constitutions or regulations, it was an admirable vehicle for expressing the communal mentality and aspirations of the inhabitants. Because the city was unencumbered by complex systems of voting regulations, replete with property qualifications and inner and outer councils, there was very little or none of the antioligarchical agitation one sees in other cities. The council was inclusive rather than exclusive; all elements of Châlonnais life were represented, or at least felt that they were.[17]

The council was also without significant rivals to its authority within Châlons. Châlons had no sovereign court, such as the parlements of Paris or Rouen, to meddle in the conduct of civic affairs. The four seigneurs of Châlons were for the most part interested merely in defending their own particular interests. The great exception to this came in the 1570s and 1580s when Bishop Clausse attempted to resuscitate his authority in the city in the interests of the Catholic League. By then, however, it was too

[17]Although the evidence for this assertion is inferential and contextual, it is strong nevertheless. Without a serious internal disturbance over thirty-five tumultuous years, given the strong communal identity, this explanation seems more likely than any other. As far as can be determined from the sources, councillors were drawn from the socioeconomic elite of the city, and there seems to have been no significant antielite agitation. Given the nature of the sixteenth-century society and the size of the city, elite and nonelite would have been tied together in a series of common bonds and institutions, such as parish organizations, guilds, confraternities, and the civic watch and militia. Compare this with Wolfgang Kaiser, *Marseille au temps des troubles, 1559–1596: Morphologies sociale et luttes des factions*, trans. Florence Chaix (Paris: Editions de l'Ecole des Hautes Etudes en Sciences Sociales, 1992), 312–18, 342; where much of the tension and conflict in Marseille is traced to animosity between the traditional elite of merchant-nobles, and a group of "second-rank" families who triumphed in the dictatorship of Charles de Casaulx.

late, and he was simply ignored and eventually excluded altogether from the city.

When Châlons found itself face to face with the crises and challenges of the Wars of Religion, it was governed by a council with great experience in civic government and which represented all the significant interests within the city: the clergy, royal officeholders, and the urban notability. Moreover, the council was animated by a dedication to the city's integrity and solidarity; this arose from the long struggle of the inhabitants to gain a voice in the conduct of the city's affairs. A primary question to be addressed, then, is how well this devotion to urban integrity and solidarity, as revealed in the actions of the city council, stood the test of thirty-five years of civil and religious war. Would Châlons be torn apart by confessional strife and political factionalism? Or would the councillors strive to maintain their city's integrity in pursuit of their own agenda in defiance of the forces that threatened France with dissolution and anarchy?

Chapter 3

The Community Defended:
Structure and Challenge

N *LES BONNES VILLES DE FRANCE*, Bernard Chevalier writes of the importance of a city's walls, "The *bonne ville* is identified by its rampart; it is limited by the rampart, which is the source of its strength, the secret of its power, and the symbol of its value."[1] Yet a physical structure by itself is nothing. To be effective, a city's defenses must be coordinated. There must be a chain of command, from the top down to those on the ramparts. There must be effective agreement on what constitutes a threat and how to counter it. Nowhere is the necessary congruence between structure and policy more apparent than in the realm of civic defense. What resources did the structure of civic defense in Châlons place at the council's disposal? What specific measures were taken to defend the city, and against what kinds of threats? How did the councillors use the defensive mechanisms at their disposal to pursue their agenda?

The wall that protected Châlons in the sixteenth century was essentially the same one constructed in the twelfth century. Yet a city wall is not constructed once and for all. It is in essence a living organism, undergoing continual change over time as it is "unceasingly remade, improved, or completed."[2] This was especially true of Châlons, for the city stood constantly in the path of invasions. The wall was all that stood between the city's survival and its ruin, and as the boundary between the city and the outside world it underwent constant renovation and improvement.

---

[1] Bernard Chevalier, *Les bonnes villes de France du XIVe au XVIe siècle* (Paris: Aubier Montaigne, 1982), 113.

[2] Chevalier, *Les bonnes villes de France*, 117.

In the sixteenth century Châlons' system of fortifications consisted of the wall as it had been rebuilt in the twelfth century, approximately 4,700 meters in length and enclosing approximately 113 hectares[3] (see fig. 3.1). The city was entered through one of six gates. In addition, there were five bastions and as many as sixty-six towers on the wall.[4] Châlons' situation on several islands was, from a military perspective, both a blessing and a problem. It was a blessing in that the rivers which surrounded the city provided a natural moat; it was a problem in that the same rivers which protected the city also eroded the foundations of the walls, necessitating constant repairs.[5] In addition, the rivers Mau and Nau which flowed through the city were potential weak spots where they broke the line of the wall. This problem was solved by the construction of three châteaux, spanning the rivers where they entered the city. On the north, where the Mau and the Nau are one, stood the château St. Antoine, next to the gate of the same name. On the south, the château du Marché stood guard over the Nau, and the château de Mauvilain over the Mau.

Maintaining this system of defenses was very expensive.[6] In the nature of things, the amount spent on fortifications varied greatly from year to year, depending on what needed to be done and the severity of the threat facing the city. Nor were military activities the only factors to be considered. In 1562, at the beginning of the Wars of Religion, for example, Thierry de l'Hôpital, sieur de Castel, the royal captain of Châlons, was commissioned to examine the walls and recomwmend measures needed simply to repair the damage of rain and floods.[7] There was always a certain amount of upkeep to do, regardless of the military situation.

In general, over the period of the Wars of Religion, the city's annual total expenditure averaged about 15,000 livres.[8] That a good portion of

---

[3]Georges Clause and Jean-Pierre Ravaux, *Histoire de Châlons-sur-Marne* (Le Coteau-Roanne: Horvath, 1983), 67.

[4]The information on the city's fortifications is taken primarily from Louis Grignon, *Topographie historique de la ville de Châlons-sur-Marne* (Châlons, 1889), 521. See also Sylvette Guilbert, "Les fortifications de Châlons-sur-Marne à la fin du Môyen Age," *Actes du 95e congrès national des sociétés savantes, Reims, 1970;* Section d'archéologie et d'histoire de l'art (Paris, 1974), 195–203, esp. 197.

[5]Guilbert, "Les fortifications," 196.

[6]The financial affairs of the city are treated in detail in chapter 4.

[7]AD Marne E suppt. 5247.

[8]The budgets of the city for the period of the Wars of Religion are contained in AD Marne E suppt. 4926, 4927 (formerly AC Châlons, CC 95–96).

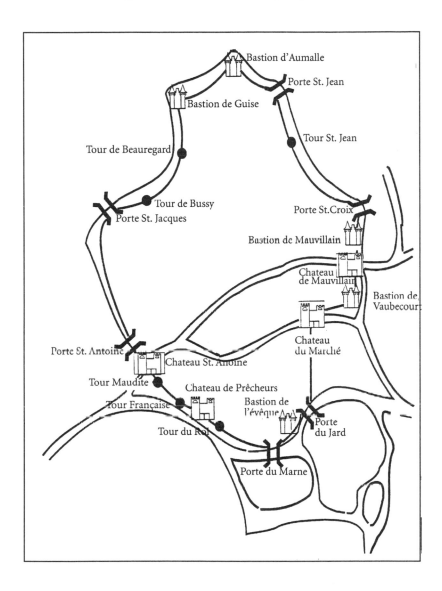

Fig. 3.1. Fortifications of Châlons in the Sixteenth Century

this was spent on fortifications is readily apparent. In 1563, for example, the year construction was begun on the bastion d'Aumale, the city's total expenditures came to 16,817 livres. The amount spent on fortifications was a staggering 14,305 livres, or 85 percent of the total.[9] This was not a typical year, for new construction was obviously more expensive than maintenance. In 1565, for instance, only 2,404 livres of a total 7,841 livres was spent on fortifications.[10] In general, usually somewhere between 50 and 75 percent of the city's total annual budget went to defend the city in any given year.

Year	Total expenditures (in livres)	Expenditures for fortifications (in livres)	Percent of Total spent on fortifications
1561	10,860	7,188	66.18%
1564	11,947	5,788	48.44%
1566	9,946	3,604	36.23%
1580	10,383	8,736	84.13%
1589	18,474	16,137	87.34%
1590	18,018	10,137	56.26%
1594	16,815	10,206	60.69%

Fig. 3.2. Expenditures on Fortifications for Selected Years

As one might expect, the city tended to spend the most money on the city's defenses when it felt the most threatened. From 1589 to 1594, when Châlons was an isolated and vulnerable royalist outpost in Champagne, expenditures on fortifications averaged about 11,000 livres out of average annual budgets of about 17,000 livres. In 1589, the council spent a record amount (for the period of the Wars of Religion, at least) of 16,813 livres out of a total budget of 18,474 livres.[11] Expenditure on fortifications was clearly the largest single item in the annual city budget.

So much for the fortifications. What of the human element? As Chevalier points out, "the defensive capacity of the *bonne ville* resides not so much in the might of its fortifications as in the number and resolution of

[9]AD Marne E suppt. 4926, fols. 357, 360.
[10]AD Marne E suppt. 4926, fols. 384, 392.
[11]AD Marne E suppt. 4927, fols. 22, 26.

its inhabitants, simple citizens who, of necessity, transform themselves into ardent defenders of their own hearths.... Facing a besieging army, the *bonne ville* defends itself by itself, with its own power...."[12]

How did Châlons defend itself? Who was in charge of the "simple citizens"? How were their orders carried out? The city council, as the only permanent institution with jurisdiction over the whole city, held ultimate responsibility for the security of Châlons. Nevertheless, the councillors did not act in a vacuum, for there were several other authorities who claimed a voice in the defense of Châlons: the royal captain, the bishop, garrison commanders, the governor and lieutenant-général of the province, and the king himself. Of these, the most immediate was the captain.

Over the course of the Wars of Religion, there were three different captains of Châlons: Thierry de l'Hôpital, sieur de Castel; his son Jean; and Hugues de Champagne, sieur de St. Mard. Jean de l'Hôpital does not figure at all in the history of Châlons, for he was killed in Flanders shortly after his father had resigned in his favor. There was a subsequent dispute over the post between Castel, the council's choice, and St. Mard—a dispute that St. Mard eventually won because of his support from Guise, the governor of Champagne.

In general, conciliar relations were much smoother with Castel than with St. Mard. There are several reasons for this. First, Castel seems not to have been at all interested in the governance of Châlons beyond his role as captain. In the decade 1559–1569, Castel attended only eighteen council meetings, and these were directly related to his function as captain. For example, Castel was at the council meeting of April 3, 1560, at which was read a letter from the king informing the town of his deliverance from the Conspiracy of Amboise. On Castel's advice, presumably, the council increased security, posting two archers at each gate.[13] Castel also served as the conduit for letters and instructions from the lieutenant-général and the governor.[14] In addition, he acted as what we might call a security consultant, as in 1568, when residents of the ban St. Pierre requested reopening of the Porte St. Jean. On the advice of Castel, the request was refused.[15]

---

[12]Chevalier, *Les bonnes villes de France*, 115.　　[13]AD Marne E suppt. 4785, fols. 20–21.

[14]On August 5, 1561, d'Espaulx wrote to Castel ordering the confiscation of all the weapons in the city; see AD Marne E suppt. 4785, fol. 50.

[15]AD Marne E suppt. 4786, fols. 87–88.

A similar case occurred in 1568. The council asked Castel's advice after they had received a letter from Lieutenant-Général Barbezieulx that commanded increased security. The captain recommended posting six arquebusiers at each gate.[16] In short, from the council's point of view Castel must have been a nearly ideal captain, appearing when he was needed but otherwise leaving the council in peace to govern the city.

In contrast, St. Mard sought to insinuate himself into the town's governance. Between 1574 and 1580 he attended no fewer than forty-one meetings of the city council. Of course, some of this is explained by the fact that these were turbulent years. Even so, St. Mard attended many meetings which did not deal directly with security and when there was no immediate threat to the town. As a result, there was a good deal of tension between the council and St. Mard. Several instances of this tension are examined in a later chapter; for now, two incidents will suffice as illustrations: In 1577, the captain drew up regulations for the guard without consulting the council; in 1580, he authorized construction on the walls and actually took bids for the work before the council found out and remonstrated to him.[17]

This tension was heightened by the perception that St. Mard had his own agenda, or rather that of his patron, the duc de Guise. St. Mard had secured the post with Guise's support, and the provincial governor had several times ordered the council to pay St. Mard substantial sums of money over and above his regular salary. Castel, on the other hand, served no agenda; rather, his agenda was that of the council: obedience to the king and preservation of the military integrity of Châlons. When Châlons threw off Guise's domination in 1588–1589, Castel once again resumed the position of captain.

Castel was also an outsider in that he apparently had little or no financial or political interest in Châlons beyond his captaincy. St. Mard, on the other hand, was the son of Guillaume de Champagne, seigneur de Varymont, a *receveur-général* in the élection of Châlons and longtime city councillor. No doubt it grated on the nerves of the other councillors to have the son of one of their colleagues order them around, with the backing of one of France's most powerful nobles. The more so since

---

[16]AD Marne E suppt. 4786, fols. 89–90.
[17]AD Marne E suppt. 4787, fols. 121–22; AD Marne E suppt. 4787, fols. 235–37.

Champagne's acquisition of the captaincy for his son was apparently one step in the family's bid for true *gentil* status.

By the sixteenth century the bishop of Châlons had been all but eliminated from the government of the town. On only one occasion during the Wars of Religion did the bishop try to reassert any control over the town's security. This too occurred during Guise's occupation, when Bishop Clausse obtained a commission from Guise which gave him control of the keys to the gates.[18] During those periods when Châlons played host to a garrison, the commander of the soldiers also interfered in the council's handling of security. The council's strained relations with the garrison commander, the sieur de Bussy, during the first War of Religion in 1562–1563 is noteworthy.

These tensions occurred to a greater or lesser extent virtually every time a garrison was stationed in Châlons. In 1586, Guise wrote to the council ordering them to "reinforce your guard, according to the orders of Captain Johannés"; in 1587, he wrote in the same vein concerning M. de Lenoncourt, "ung second moy mesme."[19] Lenoncourt proceeded to assign the password to the night watch and have the keys to the gates brought to him at night. The council decided to advise him of the city's practice in this regard, and to ask him to leave these functions to the council.[20]

As the commander of several hundred heavily armed aliens, the commander of the garrison was obviously a person to be reckoned with. Once the garrison was in the city, the council's range of options in dealing with the commander was severely limited. Nevertheless, the council did not always give in to the commander easily. Their major recourse was to ask to have the garrison removed, which they did ask innumerable times. When this request was refused, as it usually was, the only practical course was for the council to try to keep the commander and his soldiers happy. Thus, in 1575, when the soldiers under the command of a Captain Biraguc complained about their lodgings and food, St. Mard and his father were put in charge of satisfying them.[21] This pattern was repeated on several other

---

[18]AD Marne E suppt. 4787, fol. 168.

[19]Georges Hérelle, ed., *La Réforme et la Ligue en Champagne* (Paris: 1888–92), 1:136: "renforcer vos dictes gardes, selon et ainsy que vous dira le cappitaine Johannès"; AD Marne E suppt. 4789, fol. 2.

[20]AD Marne E suppt. 4789, fols. 4–5.

[21]AD Marne E suppt. 4787, fols. 45–46.

occasions, and the council each time satisfied the demands of the commander.[22]

No doubt the council's experience stood them in good stead in 1588–1589, when Châlons finally threw off Guise's domination and expelled de Rosne. The council clearly recognized that the town's defense required a garrison, but they insisted on the right to name the captains and their lieutenants, and had them swear an oath to the city.[23] Likewise, the overall commander of the garrison and royal governor, Philippe de Thomassin, had to swear to uphold the city's liberties and privileges, and the council emphasized that his position was only temporary.[24] When the council recognized that professional military assistance was essential, they obtained it in such a way as to preserve their overall control.

Over the period of this study, five provincial governors had jurisdiction over Châlons: François II de Clèves, duc de Nevers (governor, 1561–63); François de Lorraine, duc de Guise (appointed governor in February 1563, murdered February 24, 1563); Claude de Lorraine, duc d'Aumale (acting as governor for his young nephew Henri de Lorraine, duc de Guise, 1563–1567); Henri de Guise (governor, 1563–1588); and Louis de Gonzague, duc de Nevers (acting as governor for his son, Charles de Gonzague, duc de Rethelois, 1589–1595). Of these, the first Nevers died before the wars began in earnest and thus had little cause to intervene in Chalons' security, beyond writing to inquire about the state of the city and ordering the council to maintain calm.[25] D'Aumale, acting for his nephew after the murder of the elder Guise, presented a different situation. He figures in the history of Châlons mostly as the supporter of Bussy against the council during the first war in 1562–1563. In 1567, the young duc de Guise took over his *gouvernement* in his own right, remaining governor of Champagne until his death in 1588. Thus, in terms of length of tenure alone, Guise would have been the governor with the greatest impact on Châlons. It was not length of tenure alone which marked Guise's governorship of Champagne. For beginning as early as 1574, and more so after 1576 and especially after 1585, Guise imposed a virtual military occupation on Châlons, making the city into his military headquarters in Champagne in the cause of his family and the Catholic League. Guise naturally

---

[22]AD Marne E suppt. 4788, fols. 80, 105.   [23]AD Marne E suppt. 4789, fol. 42.
[24]AD Marne E suppt. 4789, fols. 70–71.   [25]Hérelle, *La Réforme*, 1:34–35, 38.

took a very strong interest in Châlons' military security, prescribing regulations for the city guard, posting garrisons in Châlons, installing his own man as captain, and attempting to restore the bishop's role in civic defense.[26]

In general, the governors' wishes and orders were mediated to the council through their subordinate, the lieutenant-général. For Champagne and Châlons during the Wars of Religion there were five lieutenants-généraux. Adolphe de Lyon, seigneur d'Espaulx, acted as lieutenant-général for Aumale and Guise until 1572. Succeeding him was Charles de la Rochefoucauld, sieur de Barbezieulx, lieutenant-général until 1579 when he was replaced by Joachim de Dinteville. Only during Dinteville's tenure were the governor and lieutenant-général not in accord. Even then, from 1580 to 1585, Guise and Dinteville maintained the fiction of cooperation in the service of the king. It was only after 1585 that the split became obvious.

From 1585 until the pacification of Champagne in 1594, there were three different lieutenants-généraux. Dinteville continued as the royalist appointee, while Mayenne, upon his assumption of the post of lieutenant-général of the kingdom in 1589, appointed as joint lieutenants-généraux de Rosne and Antoine de St. Paul. The council in Châlons was thus placed in a very difficult position. They were confronted with opposing authorities, both equally legitimate in their minds: the direct authority of the king as expressed through Dinteville and the delegated authority of the king as expressed through Guise, de Rosne, and St. Paul. Faced with Guise's dominance in Châlons, the council really had no choice but to go along with Guise's wishes and orders. Nevertheless, they continually emphasized their dual obedience to the king directly *and* to their governor *under the king*. When Guise died, their dilemma was solved—the conflicting authority had been removed and they awaited the king's appointment of a new governor.

Generally, the king left security arrangements in Châlons up to his appointees, the governor, the lieutenant-général, and the captain. Letters from the king to the council regarding security are very general, exhorting the city to "faire bonne garde," and "éviter toute surprise." This could

[26]AD Marne E suppt. 4787, fols. 1, 40

hardly have been otherwise. At several points the king (in each case, Henry III) took a direct interest in Châlons' security. One such occasion took place in the spring of 1585, when Guise and Dinteville confronted each other in Châlons. That Henry was concerned about the fate of Châlons is evident from his correspondence with Dinteville; indeed, it was through Dinteville, instead of through the council, that Henry attempted to thwart Guise.[27] Nevertheless, the king also communicated with the council in a letter specific to the occasion:

> although we recognize that ... you will not forget anything pertaining to the security of our city of Châlons, nevertheless, based on warnings given of the ill-will of some [i.e. Guise], we wished to write you this little letter to let you know that, if you have been heretofore careful to maintain and conserve your city in repose and tranquillity in our obedience, you must now be more careful and keep a closer guard than ever.[28]

More significant than this occasion were the events following Guise's murder at Blois in December 1588. Henry II, from then until his death in August 1589, took a keen interest in Châlons, his letters to the council becoming much more prescriptive and specific. In the same letter in which he explained the necessity of Guise's death, he requested that the council expel de Rosne. Shortly thereafter, the king requested weekly updates on the situation in Châlons. He also provided detailed and specific security arrangements for the city.[29] Following this period of crisis, relations between the king and the council reverted to their more normal course. Once the situation had stabilized somewhat, Henry III seemed content to leave Châlons' security in the hands of Louis de Gonzague, duc de Nevers, the new governor, Dinteville, the lieutenant-général, and Thomassin, the commander of the garrison. In general, relations between Henry IV and the council followed the same course: The machinery and the personnel

---

[27]Edouard de Barthélemy, *Correspondance inédite de M. de Dinteville, lieutenant-général au gouvernement de Champagne, 1579– 1586* (Arcis-sur-Aube, 1889), 84–92.

[28]Hérelle, *La Réforme,* 1:132: "encores que nous estimion que ... vous n'oublierez riens de ce qui pourra appartenir à la seureté de nostre ville de Chaalons, néantmoins, sur quelques advis qui nous sont donnez de la mauvaise volunté que ont aucuns, nous avons bien voullu vous escripre ce mot de lettre pour vous mander que, si vous avez été cydevant fort soigneux à mantenir et conserver lad. ville en repos et tranquilité soubz nostre obéissance, vous vous en rendez maintenant plus soigneux et y prenez garde de plus près que jamais."

[29]Hérelle, *La Réforme,* 1:155–57, 173–76.

(with the temporary exception of Nevers) continued, and Henry IV never had to become involved in Châlons' security as intimately as his predecessor.

The inhabitants of Châlons were organized into several different bodies for the security and defense of the city. First, there were the guards posted at the gates, or *gardes des portes*, to regulate access to the city. These were paid positions.[30] Since arrangements for this were a matter of custom, we are ignorant of how many were normally posted at each gate. In times of threat or crisis, the guard could be supplemented, as was the case in 1568, when extra guards were posted to keep out persons stricken with the plague.[31] Similarly, on February 23, 1585, the complement was increased to six during the day and four at night, and on March 15, to ten during the day.[32]

Control over the keys to the gates was a matter of the greatest importance. Whoever possessed the keys controlled access to the city and in effect controlled Châlons itself. Normally, control over the keys rested with the captain, and in his absence with his lieutenant, a regular member of the city council.[33] Custody of the keys was periodically a matter of contention. We have already seen how the council opposed the bishop's attempt to wrest this control from the council. It would also have seemed to be a sore point between the council and garrison commanders.[34]

Besides the gardes des portes, there was also a watch, or *guet*. In theory, all male adult inhabitants were subject to watch duty, although there were in fact a number of exemptions allowed. First, city councillors were exempt; next, the chapter and clergy claimed exemption, to which the

[30]In 1584 their wages were increased to 20 sous; see AD Marne E suppt. 4788, fols. 69–70. Châlons was perhaps different from many other cities in this respect. According to Chevalier, *Les bonnes villes de France*, 119, the *garde des portes* "was the affair of notables, since it demanded expensive armaments and implied great responsibility."

[31]AD Marne E suppt. 4786, fols. 93–94.

[32]AD Marne E suppt. 4788, fols. 75, 76.

[33]Edouard de Barthélemy, *Histoire de la ville de Châlons-sur-Marne et de ses institutions, des origines à 1848*, 2d ed. (Châlons, 1883), 79–80. In 1563, however, the council delegated custody of the keys to four "notables bourgeois," presumably on a rotating basis; see AD Marne E suppt. 4785, fol. 139. Precisely who had custody of the keys during the Wars of Religion is therefore uncertain.

[34]In 1563 Bussy, in declaring his displeasure with the council, declared "qu'à faulte de faire entrer quelques gens de guerre en ceste ville, il s'estoit délibéré de partir dès demain de ceste ville et délaisser ladite ville et les habitans d'icelle, et que jà il avoit renvoyé les clefz des portes au sr. de Castel, cappitaine de ceste ville" ; see AD Marne E suppt. 4785, fol. 116.

council was unalterably opposed. In addition, exemption could be claimed because of age or in recompense for other services.[35] According to Chevalier, watch duty tended to fall more heavily on the *menu peuple*.[36] Whether this was the case in Châlons, we can only guess. Watch duty, especially at night, was considered onerous, which is readily apparent from the council's nearly continual injunctions that the inhabitants perform their guard duty "en personne tant de jour que de nuict." That inhabitants tried to escape this duty in peacetime is readily comprehensible. In times of external threat or crisis the council redoubled its exhortations. The severity of threat may in fact be roughly gauged by the penalties imposed for dereliction, ranging from ten sous up to ten écus for the first offense and imprisonment for the second.[37]

The position of Châlonnais Huguenots vis-à-vis watch duty is somewhat ambiguous. Early in the wars, Huguenots were excluded from the *guet* and forced to pay for replacements on orders from the king.[38] This indeed might be seen as a justifiable precaution in an era when most towns succumbed to subterfuge rather than brute military force. How long this exclusion applied we do not know. We do know, however, that in 1580 the council proceeded against those derelict in their watch duty, whether they were Protestant or Catholic.[39] It seems that the Catholic councillors, by the time the first eruption of religious passion subsided, realized that their own native Huguenots posed no fifth-column threat to the security of the city.

---

[35]AD Marne E suppt. 4787, fol. 123; 4788, fols. 92, 118. Jacquemyn Grenelle requested exemption because of his age and offered to supply a substitute; see AD Marne E suppt. 4786, fol. 108. Jean Vallet, cleric and schoolmaster in St. Alpin, was granted an exemption "pour le service qu'il faict nuict et jour en lad. église"; see AD Marne E suppt. 4789, fol. 51. Inhabitants who were also soldiers were not exempt (AD Marne E suppt. 4789, fol. 76), nor were those with soldiers billeted in their houses; AD Marne E suppt. 4789, fol. 129. On the other hand, those for whom watch duty entailed undue financial hardship were given grain from the *hôpitaux* St. Lazaire and St. Esprit; see AD Marne E suppt. 4786, fols. 46–47).

[36]Chevalier, *Les bonnes villes de France*, 120.

[37]AD Marne, E suppt. 4789, fol. 146.

[38]Hérelle, *La Réforme*, 1:40.

[39]AD Marne E suppt. 4787, fol. 266. On the importance of the keys, see Albert Babeau, *La ville sous l'ancien régime*, 2 vols. (Paris, 1884), 2:4–7, 45. For civic militias in general, see Gaston Zeller, *Les institutions de la France au XVIe siècle* (Paris: Presses Universitaires, 1948), 47–49; Babeau, *La ville*, 2:21–22; Chevalier, *Les bonnes villes de France*, 121–22. For Châlons, see Barthélemy, *Histoire*, 2d ed., 81–86; Louis Barbat, *Histoire de la ville de Châlons-sur-Marne et de ses monuments depuis son origine jusqu'en 1855* (Châlons, 1865), 314.

Beyond his duty in the guet, every male inhabitant also served in the civic militia. The militia was organized in units called *cinquanteniers*, each cinquantenier corresponding to a district of the city. There were twenty-four cinquanteniers, each commanded by a captain, a lieutenant, an ensign, and a sergeant. The *rôle des cinquanteniers* drawn up in 1592 reveals a total of 1,366 men in the militia, each cinquantenier containing between 45 and 82 men. In addition, in 1592 the militia's ranks were augmented by 60 refugees. Each inhabitant was to supply his own equipment. The most common (and least expensive) weapon was the pike, followed by the sword, and finally arquebuses, of which there were 467. Naturally, the distribution of the arquebuses depended on the relative wealth of the neighborhood. The cinquantenier of Jean Baudier had no arquebuses for its 61 members, whereas that of François Hanotel had 39 arquebuses for 60 members.[40]

In times of crisis, the civic militia was Châlons' last line of defense, providing extra men to guard the walls,[41] or (usually in conjunction with garrison troops) for offensive operations—notably in the early 1590s, when Châlons was virtually alone as a royalist outpost in League-dominated Champagne. Each cinquantenier had its own muster point within the city, where each member was expected to meet at the sound of the tocsin.[42]

Besides being the city's last line of defense, the cinquanteniers served several other purposes within Châlons. They were in essence the city's umbrella military organization. Since each adult male served in the guet and the militia, the *capitaines cinquanteniers* were responsible for seeing that those in their companies actually performed their watch duty, for drawing up lists of those available for the guet, for punishing derelicts, and for the conduct of their men.[43]

The cinquanteniers also provided a convenient means for the council to keep its finger on the city's pulse. Following Dinteville's confrontation with Guise in Châlons in 1585, the council had the capitaines cinquanteniers report on the number of soldiers in their respective districts.[44] More

[40] AD Marne E suppt. 5241.
[41] AD Marne E suppt. 4786, fol. 113.
[42] AD Marne E suppt. 4789, fol. 76.
[43] AD Marne E suppt. 4786, fol. 98; 4788, fols. 79–80; 4789, fol. 51.
[44] AD Marne E suppt. 4788, fols. 78–79.

importantly perhaps, the cinquanteniers provided the council with a sample of the city's state of mind. In February 1577, when Châlons was being pressured by Barbezieulx and the cardinal de Guise to join the League, the council did not order a general assembly of the inhabitants to debate the issue; rather, each cinquantenier was to elect two or three men to consider the articles of the League.[45] The reluctance of these deputies to sign the League's oath no doubt played a large role in the council's reluctance, or rather, confirmed the councillors in their own predispositions.

In addition to the gardes des portes, the guet, and the compagnies cinquanteniers, there was also the *Compagnie des Arbalétriers*, or Company of the Crossbow. This was a sworn association or corporation of Châlonnais dedicated to the practice and use of the crossbow and, later on, the arquebus.[46] Founded by a charter from the dauphin (later Charles V) in 1357, it was what we might call a shooting club. Although there is no direct evidence for it, it is almost certain that the arbalétriers took part in the campaigns around Châlons alongside the militia and the garrison troops. The Compagnie des Arbalétriers figures in the council's conclusions on several occasions. In 1563, they requested exemption from watch duty.[47] In 1574, the king granted exemptions from the taille to the company's captain and the *roy des arquebusiers*, the winner of the company's annual competition.[48] In 1567, the company presented letters from the king granting them a practice field.[49] The council apparently gave them the use of the garden of the Jacobin monastery, for in 1575, the monks presented the council with a letter from Guise ordering the arbalétriers to practice elsewhere, to which the council replied that there was no other suitable place.[50] The arbalétriers seem not to have played a leading role in Châlons' security arrangements; rather, it seems that the company was more of a social club and auxiliary military force of amateur enthusiasts.

The city had possessed its own artillery since the early fifteenth century. The artillery was in the charge of six lieutenants and a *capitaine* or *garde de l'artillerie*, who was usually a councillor.[51] At the time of the Wars

---

[45]AD Marne E suppt. 4787, fol. 128.

[46]See Zeller, *Les insitutions*, 48–49; Chevalier, *Les bonnes villes de France*, 122–23; Babeau, *La ville*, 2:55–77; Barthélemy, *Histoire*, 2d ed., 88–94; Barbat, *Histoire*, 113–15.

[47]AD Marne E suppt. 4785, fols. 107–8.   [48]AD Marne E suppt. 4787, fol. 19.

[49]AD Marne E suppt. 4786, fol. 24.   [50]AD Marne E suppt. 4787, fol. 42

[51]Barthélemy, *Histoire*, 2d ed., 87–88; Barbat, *Histoire*, 124–25; AD Marne E suppt. 4788, fol. 103.

of Religion, the city possessed six pieces of varying size and power. The artillery was not normally kept mounted on the walls, but was stored in a warehouse. When the city was threatened, it was necessary to inspect, clean, and mount the artillery; and when the threat passed, the artillery was taken down.[52]

In addition to military threats, the security of Châlons was troubled by other crises as well. The two most common nonmilitary threats were the plague and poor vagrants (*povres vagabondz*). The measures implemented to confront both military and nonmilitary threats were substantially similar although in the case of military threats, more stringent precautions were implemented as well.

Security measures taken by the council when confronted with the plague and vagabondage may be characterized as either defensive or offensive. Defensive measures were those taken to keep undesirables out of the city, primarily by instructing the gardes des portes to be more careful about whom they let in, or by posting extra guards.[53] Offensive measures were designed to rid Châlons of plague victims and beggars already within the walls, usually by wholesale expulsion.[54] In all cases, a strict distinction was made between natives and foreigners (i.e., non-Châlonnais). The council recognized an obligation to its own sick or poor inhabitants, and made every effort to provide care for the sick and provision for the poor.[55]

When confronted with a military threat, the council implemented many of the same measures and supplemented them with more stringent precautions, such as furnishing the garde des portes with more specific instructions. The gardes might be instructed to let only twelve or fifteen soldiers into the city at any one time, or not to allow in anyone accompanied by six or more horses, or indeed not to admit anyone.[56] If it became

---

[52]AD Marne E suppt. 4785, fols. 76, 78; 4786, fols. 99–100; 4787, fols. 33, 77, 216–17; 4788, fol. 103.

[53]For instances regarding vagabonds, see AD Marne E suppt. 4788, fols. 35, 79–80, 96, 116–17. For the plague, see AD Marne E suppt. 4786, fols. 93–94. In several cases, the council ordered the *gardes* not to let in people from specific places because of the plague; see AD Marne E suppt. 4789, fol. 139. For a description of the measures taken against the plague in Châlons, see Guilbert, "A Châlons-sur-Marne," 1283–1300.

[54]For expulsion of vagabonds, see AD Marne E suppt. 4789, fol. 10; 4788, fols. 103, 117. For plague victims, see AD Marne E suppt. 4788, fols. 101–2.

[55]On July 27, 1586, the council ordered the expulsion of all beggars who had been in Châlons for less than six months; see AD Marne E suppt. 4788, fol. 103.

[56]AD Marne E suppt. 4787, fol. 220; 4789, fols. 92, 130.

impossible to guard sufficiently all the gates, several gates could be closed, usually over the objections of the inhabitants. Sometimes the councillors themselves personally supervised security at the gates, or required a daily report of all entries, and required the gardes to confiscate the arms of all entrants.[57]

The most detailed and complete list of security precautions taken by the council appeared in August 1578. It concerns the conciliar reaction to the presence of a regiment of infantry at Notre-Dame-l'Epine under the command of the same Bussy who had been commander of the garrison in Châlons in 1562 and 1563.[58] The measures taken by the council included closing all but two gates, posting twenty men to guard the gates that remained open, changing the keys to the gates, and commanding the gardes to keep the keys in their possession from the opening of the gates until their closing (presumably so the gates could be locked at a moment's notice). Each capitaine cinquantenier was to give the captain of the city a daily list of those entering the city, and all innkeepers were to present the captain with a daily roster of tenants. The walls and the *maison des poul-dres* were to be inspected at seven o'clock each morning, and a councillor was to be present at the hôtel de ville night and day. All foreigners were to leave their arms at the gate and no vagabonds were to be allowed inside. All these regulations were to be posted at the gates so no one could claim ignorance. These regulations were presented to Guise the day after they had been approved by the council. He endorsed them and added several more: The gardes des portes were not to admit more than ten soldiers per day, the houses of the city were to be searched for arms and men, and no arms were to be allowed to leave the city.[59]

Protecting the city from external menaces, whether the plague, vaga-bonds, or soldiers, was a fairly straightforward matter. The city merely shut itself off from the outside world, turtlelike, until the threat passed. During the Wars of Religion towns succumbed to internal subversion as well as to external military attack. How were these internal threats of sub-version handled at Châlons?

[57]AD Marne E suppt. 4789, fol. 37; 4788, fol. 77.
[58]AD Marne E suppt. 4785, fols. 164–65.
[59]AD Marne E suppt. 4787, fols. 165–66.

During the earlier part of the wars, the major threat seems to have come from the city's Huguenots. Object lessons abounded in the threat that Huguenots presented to cities all over France by opening city gates to Protestant commanders. The council enacted a series of measures to counter such a threat, ranging from expelling Protestant councillors to excluding Protestants from the guet. However, the council drew the line at ordering the expulsion of native Huguenots; in 1563 the council refused to accede to Bussy's request to do just this. To be sure, in 1562, the council imposed a discriminatory tax of four thousand livres on the city's Protestants. This was done on royal orders, and even then the council sought to moderate its effects by asking Bussy to apply the funds received from the previous seizure of Huguenot goods to this amount.[60] In 1580 the council also confiscated Huguenot arms. Again, the impetus for this order came from an outsider, Guise; there is some reason to question whether the spirit as well as the letter of the order was actually carried out. Several weeks later the council acted against those delinquent in watch duty, both Protestant and Catholic.[61]

Toleration of native Huguenots did not apply to foreigners (i.e. non-Châlonnais); several times the council acted against foreign Huguenots. At the very beginning of the wars in 1562, the council ordered the expulsion of foreign Protestants, that is, those who had lived in Châlons for less than a year.[62] This distinction between foreigners and natives was brought home once again in August 1589, in the aftermath of the assassination of Henry III. The council once again expelled all foreign Huguenots, but allowed natives to stay, provided they took an oath to the city and behaved themselves, "without causing any scandal or holding any assemblies or exercise of the said new religion."[63]

In short, the council's attitude towards Protestants was the same as its attitude towards the sick and the poor. The councillors recognized an obligation towards their own, but reserved the right to expel or discriminate against foreigners. Clearly, the council wished Châlons to be a com-

---

[60]AD Marne E suppt. 4785, fols. 94–95.

[61]AD Marne E suppt. 4787, fols. 264, 266.

[62]AD Marne E suppt. 4785, fols. 63–64.

[63]AD Marne E suppt. 4789, fol. 100: "sans faire aulcun scandale ou faire assemblée ou exercice de ladite nouvelle religion."

pletely Catholic city; they also wished Châlons to be plague- and beggar-free. But wishing could not make it so; in the hard light of reality, the councillors tolerated native Protestants, plague victims and beggars simply because they were Châlonnais.

After 1589, the major threat of subversion came not from the Huguenots, but from those Catholics who were partisans of the League. There was in fact some opposition within Châlons to the council's decisions to remain loyal to Henry III and to recognize Henry IV. Compounding this opposition was the presence of numerous Catholic refugees in Châlons, which presented the council with a more complex problem than the presence of Huguenots. They felt obligated to accept Catholic refugees from Leaguer towns in Champagne, but how could they be sure that no agents of the League would enter as well?

The basic procedure followed was to keep close track of foreigners, and to ensure that even if hostile elements were inside the walls, they could do no harm. Already in 1580 the city's innkeepers were instructed to report foreigners, and if possible, to seize their arms while they slept. In 1585, when Guise and Dinteville were contending over control of Châlons, all innkeepers and *taverniers* were ordered to report the names of their guests to the captain on pain of a fine of two écus, the arms of all entrants were to be seized at the gates, and arrivals of groups of twelve or more were to be reported to the captain.[64]

In 1588, 1589, and thereafter, even more aggressive measures were enacted. In June of 1588 the council appointed delegates to search the inns and houses of the city. These delegates were to take militia with them to expel any soldiers that might be found.[65] A similar search was ordered in March of 1589, and all foreigners and "disreputable persons" (*gens sans aveu*) were to leave town immediately "sur peine de la hart," and all refugees who had arrived since the previous Christmas were to register with the council on pain of expulsion and a twenty-écu fine.[66] In April, another search was conducted, and innkeepers and anyone else lodging guests were ordered to report their lodgers' names, *qualité*, and residence on pain of death.[67] In August, following the king's death, a survey of refugees was

[64]AD Marne E suppt. 4787, fol. 239; 4788, fol. 77.
[65]AD Marne E suppt. 4789, fols. 26–27.
[66]AD Marne E suppt. 4789, fol. 64.   [67]AD Marne E suppt. 4789, fol. 76.

ordered; and in December, communication with Reims was forbidden.[68] Press regulations were imposed to make sure "that nothing is printed against the honor of God, the service and honor of the king, and the public peace."[69] In February of 1591, it was forbidden on pain of death for anyone to go to or communicate with rebel towns, and all foreigners and vagabonds were once again expelled.[70] All newcomers were to be brought to the hôtel de ville, where a councillor (present from the opening to the closing of the gates) would search their persons and baggage.[71] All refugees had to register with the council, sign an oath of loyalty to the king, and declare whether they knew of any schemes against Châlons.[72]

Because bonnes villes prided themselves in their military self-sufficiency, the presence of a garrison was a tacit admission of the city's inadequacy. This was a blow to the city's pride and integrity as a bonne ville.[73] The city councillors of Châlons would therefore go to almost any lengths to keep the city free of garrisons, up to and including claiming a blanket exemption.[74] Nevertheless, when the threat was severe enough, the councillors swallowed their pride, put aside their apprehensions, and welcomed even invited—soldiers into Châlons. Such was the case in the summer of 1562, at the outbreak of the first war, when the city was threatened by a Huguenot army.[75] When the immediate threat was past, however, the council immediately requested the garrison's removal.[76] Robert Harding has aptly characterized this ambivalence in discussing relations between town councils and provincial governors: "When an immediate threat loomed, there was little the towns ... would not do for their governors. They requested garrisons, taxed themselves and the peasantry, pleaded with governors to reside and sent supplies or money to governors elsewhere. Then, as security returned, they resisted the governor's demands."[77]

The most notable example of the council's requesting a garrison in Châlons, instead of trying to avoid one at all costs, comes in 1588 and

---

[68]AD Marne E suppt. 4789, fols. 99, 123.
[69]AD Marne E suppt. 4789, fol. 124: "à ce qu'il ne s'imprime chose contre l'honneur de Dieu, la service et honneur du Roy et repos publicq."
[70]AD Marne E suppt. 4789, fol. 171.   [71]AD Marne E suppt. 4789, fols. 77–78, 90.
[72]AD Marne E suppt. 4789, fol. 90.   [73]Chevalier, *Les bonnes villes de France*, , 113.
[74]AD Marne E suppt. 4785, fol. 57.   [75]AD Marne E suppt. 4785, fol. 74.
[76]AD Marne E suppt. 4785, fol. 109.   [77]Harding, *Anatomy of a Power Elite*, 88.

1589, following the death of Guise and the expulsion of de Rosne. Even at this point, and throughout the succeeding years as the city was threatened by the Leaguer forces under St. Paul and de Rosne, the council assured itself of some degree of control over royal soldiers. The council appointed the captains of the four companies, one of whom was Castel. The other three were Claude Godet, seigneur de St. Hilaire; Claude Cuissotte, seigneur de Gizaulcourt; and François Godet, seigneur d'Omey. All were Châlonnais, the last two being former city councillors; the captains and the lieutenants swore an oath "to devote themselves faithfully to the guard and defense of the city."[78] The four hundred men raised for these companies came primarily from Châlons itself and from the surrounding countryside. The council was thereby seeking to obviate some of the worst abuses arising from the presence of soldiers within the city.

These safeguards reduced without eliminating the inevitable problems implicit in the presence of a garrison in Châlons. In May 1589 the council had to forbid the captains of the garrison from trying to command the gardes des portes.[79] The presence of Châlonnais in these companies posed a problem. When Châlonnais soldiers serving in the garrison requested exemption from their watch duty, the request was denied; if they could not come in person, they had to send replacements. This requirement was reiterated in January 1590. At the same time, those lodging soldiers in their houses were refused exemption as well.[80] In February 1590, when the garrison was reduced to three hundred men because of financial constraints, the council ordered that no more than four or five inhabitants could serve in each company.[81] After all, why should some be paid for doing what everyone else was required to do gratuitously?

It is clear that the security apparatus of Châlons-sur-Marne was central to the city's experiences during the Wars of Religion. Without a well-defined and smoothly functioning defense machinery, the city could not have pursued as independent a course as it did. How does Châlons' experience compare with that of other cities? The function of civic defensive

[78]AD Marne E suppt. 4789, fol. 42:"de bien et fidèlement s'employer ... à la garde et deffense de la ville."

[79]AD Marne E suppt. 4789, fol. 77.

[80]AD Marne E suppt. 4789, fols. 76, 129.

[81]AD Marne E suppt. 4789, fol. 132.

institutions is a question which has been little studied; we are therefore unable to theorize how typical Châlons' experience was.

Barbara Diefendorf has pointed out the role of the Parisian civic militia during the early years of the Wars of Religion in forming the Leaguer mentality. Because the Parisian militia was formed at the beginning of the period in response to religious violence, it had a somewhat ambiguous raison d'être: Was it a force to repress Huguenots, or a force to maintain order? Clearly, the captains of the militia thought the former. Frustrated by the royal government's wild swings between toleration and repression, "it is scarcely any wonder that after years of discontentment with kings who frustrated these aims, many of the militia officers rallied to a Catholic League that promised satisfaction."[82]

Unlike Paris, Châlons-sur-Marne entered the Wars of Religion with a long tradition of strong and clearly focused civic self-defense. The city councillors had inherited from their predecessors of the Hundred Years' War a relatively complete, flexible, and smoothly running machinery for the security of the city. Within living memory of some Châlonnais was the invasion of Charles V in 1544, when Châlons' military strength had apparently diverted the emperor from attacking the city to sacking and burning Epernay and Vitry instead.[83] Again, unlike Paris, there was no ambiguity as to the militia's function: it was there to defend the city. Thus, even if there had been militant Catholics of the type described by Diefendorf, the militia's institutional role was already well defined and it could not have been easily twisted to their own intolerant ends. The militia in particular and the whole defensive structure of the city in general served the agenda of the council throughout the Wars of Religion.

---

[82]Barbara Diefendorf, "The Background to the League: Civic Values in Paris at the Beginning of the Wars of Religion," paper presented at the Conference of the Society for French Historical Studies, Québec, March 1986.

[83]Maurice Poinsignon, *Histoire générale de la Champagne et de Brie*, 3 vols. (Paris: 1885, 1898; rpt. Paris: Guenégaud, 1974), 2:78–87; Clause and Ravaux, *Histoire*, 135; Barthélemy, *Histoire*, 2d ed., 270–71.

Chapter 4

Fiscal Impact of the Wars

HE FINANCIAL AFFAIRS OF CHÂLONS occupied more of the council's time than any other category of business. The town's finances are bewilderingly complex, and the documents are incomplete, which makes it impossible to paint a comprehensive picture of the fiscal impact of the Wars of Religion. Yet it is possible to gain an impressionistic view of the major elements of Châlons' finances and to discern the impact of the wars, at least in broad strokes. The basis of this sketch is the city's annual budgets or *comptes*, which detail revenues and expenditures. Yet, evidence for the major impact of the wars is not revealed in the comptes; it is found in the continued royal taxation, the demands to furnish supplies to passing armies, and the supporting of garrisons in the city. How did the disruptions of three decades of civil war affect the town's finances? Did fiscal considerations influence the councillors in their course of action?[1]

The fiscal organization of Châlons predated the political organization of the city council. Up until the fourteenth century, the four temporal seigneurs exercised complete fiscal control over their respective bans. Each ban had its own fiscal officers and machinery. The burdens placed on the city by the Hundred Years' War and the seigneurs' inability or unwillingness to coordinate their financial affairs led to the recognition that a city-wide fiscal structure was needed. Beginning in the second half of the

---

[1]On civic finances in general, see Roger Doucet, *Les institutions de la France au XVIe siècle*, 2 vols. (Paris: Picard, 1948), 1:380–93; Albert Babeau, *La ville sous l'ancien régime*, 2 vols. (Paris, 1884), 1:251–309; Gaston Zeller, *Les institutions de la France au XVIe siècle* (Paris: Presses Universitaires, 1948), 49–51; Bernard Chevalier, *Les bonnes villes de France du XIVe au XVIe siècle* (Paris: Aubier Montaigne, 1982), 210–17. For rudimentary descriptions of Châlons' fiscal system, see Edouard de Barthélemy, *Histoire de la ville de Châlons-sur-Marne et de ses institutions, des origines à 1848*, 2d ed. (Châlons, 1883), 97–110; Louis Barbat, *Histoire de la ville de Châlons-sur-Marne et de ses monuments depuis son origine jusqu'en 1855* (Châlons, 1865), 304–10.

fourteenth century, the kings of France granted various rights of *octroi* to the city as a whole. An octroi was a grant of permission to collect indirect taxes for the city's use on a wide variety of goods and services. The rights were granted for a limited time only; upon their expiration they had to be renewed or they would lapse. In 1375, the city assumed the basic fiscal organization it would maintain through the sixteenth century. In that year, a general assembly of the inhabitants confided the conduct of the city's financial affairs to a *receveur des deniers communs*. The receveur was elected at the city's annual general assembly on St. Martin's Day (November 11), and when the city council was first formed in the early fifteenth century, he was made an ex officio member. The council quickly assumed overall responsibility for the town's finances.

Châlons' fiscal procedure in the sixteenth century was really quite primitive. At the end of each year, the receveur presented to the city council his accounting of receipts and expenditures. There was no attempt at forming a provisory budget to project the city's affairs in advance; nor was there any ongoing auditing mechanism. Upon receiving the receveur's report or *compte,* the council delegated several of its members to examine it. Compounding this inefficient procedure was the fact that the receveur apparently made no distinction between his own money and the city's; he was not responsible for a continual accounting of his receipts and expenditures. As a result, he was personally responsible for any discrepancies. Therefore, upon his election the *receveur* was required to post a bond or *caution* of 2,000 livres to be held against the final settlement of his accounts.[2] The ensuing settlement of accounts was frequently a long and complex matter. In 1585, the council was still examining the accounts of receveur Michel Alfeston for the years 1582 and 1583; in what appears to have been the most difficult case of all, in 1577 the council was still trying to reconcile the accounts of Pierre François from 1563. This process became even more complicated when the receveur happened to die before his books were approved by the council. In 1579, the widow of Pierre Chastillon presented her husband's accounts for the years 1571 through 1574. In 1581, apparently in an attempt to bring some semblance of fiscal order to the city's confused affairs, the council ordered all receveurs for the

---

[2]AD Marne E suppt. 4785, fol. 55.

previous ten years, their widows, or their heirs, to bring their comptes to the council to be examined and cleared.[3]

In theory, the city's revenues were of two types: *deniers patrimoniaux* and *deniers d'octroi,* paralleling the division in royal finances between ordinary and extraordinary revenues.[4] The former were the revenues received from the property owned by the city, including rents on houses, gardens, and barns. Also included in this category were tolls on various bridges in the countryside around Châlons. Collection of these tolls was leased out to *fermiers,* who turned over a portion of the receipts to the receveur. Châlons owned the tolls on the bridges at Aulnay, Mathougues, Condé, and Tours-sur-Marne. The deniers patrimoniaux furnished but a small part of the city's revenues. In 1564, for example, revenue from these sources amounted to just under 390 livres. The city's total revenues for that year came to approximately 10,014 livres; the deniers patrimoniaux therefore provided 3.89 percent of the city's receipts[5] (fig. 4.1).

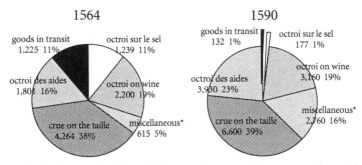

1564

goods in transit
1,225 11%

octroi sur le sel
1,239 11%

octroi des aides
1,801 16%

octroi on wine
2,200 19%

crue on the taille
4,264 38%

miscellaneous*
615 5%

1590

goods in transit
132 1%

octroi sur le sel
177 1%

octroi on wine
3,160 19%

octroi des aides
3,930 23%

miscellaneous*
2,760 16%

crue on the taille
6,600 39%

*includes the deniers patrimoniaux and other extraordinary or one-time payments to the council

Fig. 4.1. City Council Revenues in Livres Tournois

Although the bulk of the city's revenues came from the deniers d'octroi, no practical distinction was made between the two types of revenue: they were both included in the same compte. Octrois were assessed on a wide variety of goods, the most important being a levy of one-

---

[3]AD Marne E suppt. 4788, fol. 88; 4787, fol. 135; 4787, fols. 200–210, 217–18; 4788, fol. 14.

[4]On this distinction, see Zeller, *Les institutions,* 49–50; Chevalier, *Les bonnes,* 211.

[5]AD Marne E suppt. 4926, fols. 348–60. After 1579, the écu was introduced as a new money of account at the rate of 3 livres : 1 écu. For ease of comparison, I have converted all amounts given in écus to their equivalent values in livres tournois.

fourteenth of the value of retail wine sales in Châlons. Revenue from this source remained relatively constant throughout the Wars of Religion, accounting for between 18 percent and 29 percent of the city's income.

Octrois were also realized on the transit of many types of merchandise, including wheat and wine, through the city. From 1561 to 1589, revenue from this source remained relatively constant, providing 8 to 12 percent of the city's receipts. With the final rupture with the League and the Sixteen in 1589–1590 and Châlons' isolation in League-dominated Champagne, revenue from this source fell off drastically. In 1590, these octrois brought in less than 1 percent of the city's budget; in 1594, it was a little over 1 percent, and by 1596, it had still not fully recovered, accounting for just over 1 percent of the city's revenues[6] (fig. 4.1).

The city was also allowed to share in the royal monopoly on the sale of salt. Châlons was the site of a *grenier à sel,* or royal salt warehouse, and the city collected an octroi on the salt sold from its grenier.[7] Like the octroi on goods passing through Châlons, revenue from the octroi sur le sel remained constant until 1590, bringing in between 8 and 12 percent of the city's revenues. After 1590, revenue from this source fell off as well. In 1590, it brought in only 1 percent of the city's income; by 1596, it had recovered somewhat, accounting for 4.5 percent of the city's revenue.

The greatest revenue sources for the city in any given year were called *octrois,* but were in fact different from the octrois we have just examined in that they were not assessed directly on goods. One of these was the *octroi des aides,* by which the city received a rebate from the royal tax system. *Aides* were the major royal indirect taxes, collected on a variety of goods, usually at the rate of one sou per livre, or 5 percent.[8] The aides were generally farmed out; that is, the right to collect them was bought at auction. The city apparently bought up these leases, and whatever was left after sending the required amount to the royal treasury went into the city's coffers. In Châlons, aides were levied on a whole range of goods, including live animals, wood, charcoal, copper, iron, meat, fish, leather, wool, and

---

[6]The comptes for the period of the Wars of Religion are contained in AD Marne E suppt. 4926 and 4927 (formerly AC Châlons, CC 95–96).

[7]For a description of the *gabelle* and the salt distribution system, see Martin Wolfe, *The Fiscal System of Renaissance France* (New Haven: Yale University Press, 1972), 330–42.

[8]Wolfe, *Fiscal System,* 317–18.

draps (finished woolen cloth).[9] Revenue from the octrois des aides shows a gradual increase throughout the wars. In 1561, they accounted for only 13 percent of the city's revenue; by 1580, this had increased to 16 percent, and in 1594 to 34 percent.

The other major source of revenue was connected with the basic taxation unit of sixteenth-century France, the *élection*. (Châlons was the seat of both an élection and a *généralité*, the superior taxation jurisdiction.) This was a *crue*, or surtax, of two sous per livre on the *taille* (the major direct royal tax) paid in the élection of Châlons. Henry II had granted this crue to Châlons in 1553 to be used for the city's fortifications.[10] In subsequent years, it became exceedingly important to the city, usually accounting for up to 40 or 45 percent of the city's annual revenues. From 1589 to 1596, the amount brought in by this octroi remained steady at 6,600 livres (2,200 écus), representing a nominal increase over previous years, but in relative terms, a decline from about 40 percent of the city's receipts to about 31 percent.

Managing the octrois occupied a great deal of the council's time and energy. Since the octrois were temporary grants only, they had to be renewed or they would be lost. To complicate this state of affairs, the octrois had been granted to the city at different times and for different durations; the council was almost continually involved in securing the renewal of one octroi or another. In 1561, procureur Charles François was sent to court to solicit the duc de Nevers' aid in renewing the octroi des aides; he was successful and the octroi was renewed for three years.[11] In 1562, the council sent its *greffier,* or clerk, Ambroise Jacobé, to court to renew the octroi sur le sel.[12] In 1563, François obtained the renewal of the octroi of two sous per livre of the taille for four years and of the octroi of merchandise passing through Châlons.[13] Obtaining the requisite renewals was an ongoing and complicated process.

The actual collection of the city's octrois was leased to the highest bidder who was said to have bought the *ferme* (farm) of that particular octroi. Selling and managing these fermes also occupied the council's time

---

[9]AD Marne E suppt. 4927, fols. 70–71, has a complete list of the items on which *aides* were collected.

[10]AD Marne E suppt. 4838.   [11]AD Marne E suppt. 4785, fols. 42–43, 47–48.

[12]AD Marne E suppt. 4785, fol. 73.   [13]AD Marne E suppt. 4785, fol. 125.

and energy. The fermes were generally sold to inhabitants of Châlons for periods of one to three years.[14] In 1578, the council clashed with the trésoriers-généraux of the généralité over the sale of the ferme of the octroi on retail wine sales. The trésoriers announced in December that they, and not the council, would sell the ferme. The council remonstrated, apparently to no effect, since on December 27 the trésoriers announced that they would sell the ferme that afternoon. The procureur and other councillors went to the sale to protest and were authorized by the council to buy the ferme for up to 3,000 livres (1,000 écus). Councillor Claude Lignage eventually bought it for three years for 2,580 livres on behalf of the city. The trésoriers refused to recognize this transaction, however, and the matter was eventually turned over to the duc de Guise for adjudication; we do not know the results.[15]

The council was also continually confronted by refusals to pay the octrois and requests for exemption or reduction in their amount. For example, in 1560, the merchants of Vitry refused to pay the octroi on their wheat passing through Châlons. In 1567, the *grenetier à sel* (the official in charge of the grenier) refused to turn the octroi sur le sel over to the city until the council paid his wages. In 1564, the mendicant orders requested exemption from the octroi on retail wine sales. In 1575, Marc de Berlize requested exemption from the same octroi for three years because his house had burned down; his request was refused.[16] In 1567, the city's taverniers offered to buy exemption from the *ferme de fourrage* for 340 livres. The council sold them a year's exemption for 100 livres. When it expired, the taverniers offered to pay 600 livres for a complete exemption; the council agreed, but stated that they did it only because they needed the money right away, and that this action was not to be construed as a precedent for others.[17]

Administration of the octrois was also subject to verification by the Chambre des Comptes in Paris, the sovereign accounting tribunal for most of France. Thus, in 1568 Pierre Maupeou, a procureur in the

---

[14]In 1580, Quentin Caillot bought the *ferme des aides* and the *ferme des vins*; see AD Marne E suppt. 4787, fol 272.

[15]AD Marne E suppt. 4787, fols. 176–80, 182–83.

[16]AD Marne E suppt. 4785, fol. 74.

[17]AD Marne E suppt. 4785, fols. 18, 22–23, 44, 168; AD Marne E suppt. 4786, fols. 26, 29, 63–64.

Chambre des Comptes, wrote to the council to have the letters renewing the octrois verified. In 1575, former receveur Pierre François was summoned to the Chambre des Comptes regarding his compte for 1562. In 1582, councillor Charles Gorlier was sent to Paris with the city's records to settle accounts with the Chambre des Comptes.[18]

What can we conclude about the impact of the wars on the city's revenue as revealed in the annual comptes? First, the confusion of wartime disrupted the working of the fiscal machinery to a certain extent. In 1567, the council explained that the renewal of the city's octrois could not be verified in the Chambre des Comptes because of the "present troubles." In 1575, when former receveur François was summoned to the Chambre des Comptes to settle his accounts for 1562, the council instructed him to explain that payments to soldiers were responsible for any possible discrepancies.[19] Later on, in the late 1580s and 1590s, the process of renewing octrois seems to have broken down entirely as the country slid towards anarchy, for there is no mention in the council's records of renewing the octrois. The city seems to have gone on collecting the octrois without the usual renewals and verifications.

This leads us to the question of how the wars affected the actual amount of money that the city collected. In general, the city's revenues remained relatively constant until the late 1580s. From 1590 on, however, when Châlons was virtually the only royalist city in Champagne, there occurred a dramatic shift in the sources of revenue, even though the total amount remained relatively stable. For one thing, revenue from the bridge tolls of the deniers patrimoniaux suffered from disorder and warfare in the countryside. Thus, from 1590 through 1596, the council received no revenue from the bridges at Tours-sur-Marne and Mathougues because they had been destroyed on Dinteville's orders.[20] The reduction in deniers patrimoniaux, however, was insignificant, since these provided but a small part of the city's receipts.

The greatest impact of the wars was on the deniers d'octroi; although here, again, revenues were quite stable until 1590. The greatest disruption

---

[18]AD Marne E suppt. 4786, fol. 73; AD Marne E suppt. 4787, fol. 67; AD Marne E suppt. 4788, fol. 30.

[19]AD Marne E suppt. 4786, fol. 40; AD Marne E suppt. 4787, fol. 69.

[20]AD Marne E suppt. 4927, fol. 37.

involved octrois which were realized from regional commercial inter-course. For example, revenue from the octroi sur le sel, which depended on the sales from the grenier in Châlons to the countryside, dropped from 1,311 livres in 1589 to 177 livres in 1590. The same is true of the octrois on merchandise passing through Châlons: In 1580, the city realized 885 livres from this source; in 1589, it received only 120 livres.[21]

The resulting shortfall was offset by those sources of revenue which were not at the mercy of disorder and warfare in the countryside, or *plat pays*. The octroi of one-fourteenth on retail wine sales in the city, for example, remained constant throughout the period, regularly accounting for upwards of 20 percent of the city's income. Revenue from the octroi des aides increased from 2,451 livres in 1580 to 3,267 livres in 1589. In 1594, this increased further still to 7,161 livres, or 34 percent of the city's revenues, whereas in previous years this source had typically provided Châlons with 20 to 30 percent of its receipts. The same is true, though less dramatically, of the octroi of two sous per livre of the taille. This sum increased from 1,005 livres in 1580 to 6,600 livres in 1589 and thereafter.[22]

What appears to have happened, then, is that the royal taxation juris-dictions in Châlons, the élection and the généralité, stepped in to make up the city's shortfall in revenue from its other sources. The revenues which remained constant (the octroi on retail wine sales) and those which increased (the octroi des aides and the octroi of two sous per livre of the taille) were both relatively immune to disorder and warfare. In particular, these two octrois were both entirely under the control of the officials of the élection and the généralité. So when the revenues subject to the disrup-tions of endemic warfare dropped off after 1589, royal fiscal officials plugged the gap by increasing the city's revenues from those sources that were under their control and were not so subject to disruption.

The picture on the expenditure side of the city budgets is a good deal simpler. As mentioned in the previous chapter, the city's expenses for for-tifications were the largest single item in any given year. This accounted for anywhere between 50 and 75 percent of the total, and in the nature of things, fluctuated greatly.

---

[21]AD Marne E suppt. 4927, fols. 3, 19, 20.
[22]AD Marne E suppt. 4927, fols. 1, 2, 18, 29, 35, 49, 61.

Among the fixed costs appearing in the comptes were the yearly sala-
ries paid to the officers of the city, ranging from 40 sous for the *trompette*
to 90 livres for the captain. This amount was normally around 300 livres
annually; in 1580, however, it jumped to 597 livres, due to extra payments
of 300 livres to captain St. Mard, apparently on Guise's orders.[23] After
1589, the amount needed to pay the city's officers dropped by about 100
livres annually; since captain Castel had found gainful employment as a
garrison captain in Châlons, the council no longer paid the salary of the
captain of the city.[24]

Also among the fixed costs of the city was the *taillon* or "little taille."
This was a surtax on the taille, instituted by Henry II and intended to pay
for food and supplies for royal armies.[25] Apparently, the city council paid
Châlons' assessment out of its regular revenues. The amount of the taillon
remained quite stable at around 400 livres annually until 1589, when it
ballooned to 1,035 livres. Thereafter, it leveled off at about 850 livres.[26]

From 1589 on, we see a new item in the expenditure side of the
comptes: interest payments on *rentes*, or annuities sold by the city council
to pay for its garrison. In 1589, this interest amounted to 468 livres; by
1596 it had almost doubled to 867 livres.[27]

Among the most unpredictable expenses that faced the council was
the cost of receptions and gifts for visiting dignitaries. When Charles IX
and Catherine de Médicis visited Châlons for several days on their tour of
the kingdom in 1564, the council spent 2,649 livres on gifts and receptions, or 22 percent of the year's revenues of 11,947 livres.[28] Likewise, in
1571 the council spent 2,183 livres on gifts and receptions for an entry of
their governor, the duc de Guise. Included in this amount was a payment
of 1,905 livres to the city's goldsmiths.

Managing the city's business, especially the octrois, required a certain
investment of money as well as time. There were always numerous trips
taken by councillors on city business, whether to court to remonstrate
with the king; to Paris to visit the Chambre des Comptes, Cour des Aides,
or Parlement; or to Reims or Troyes to consult with the councillors of

---

[23]AD Marne E suppt. 4927, fol. 10.   [24]AD Marne E suppt. 4927, fols. 24–25.
[25]Wolfe, *Fiscal System*, 305.   [26]AD Marne E suppt. 4927, fols. 22, 40, 53, 65.
[27]AD Marne E suppt. 4927, fols. 23, 41, 85–86.
[28]AD Marne E suppt. 4926, fols, 370, 374; AD Marne E suppt. 4764.

those cities on matters of mutual interest. Not only was there the cost of the travel itself, but the appropriate fees had to be paid and gifts bought. Thus in 1561 procureur Charles François was reimbursed 95 livres for a trip to court to have the octroi des aides renewed. In that year, such expenses came to 756 livres, or 7 percent of the city's budget.[29]

If we look simply at the formal comptes of Châlons' receveurs, we might conclude that the city adjusted rather well to the fiscal stringencies of the period and that the impact of the wars was minimal. Over the period of the Wars of Religion, the budget of Châlons approximately doubled, rising from about 10,000 livres annually to about 20,000 livres. On the revenue side, the increases came in the octroi des aides and the octroi of two sous per livre of the taille. On the expenditure side, by far the greatest increase came from larger costs for fortifications. On the whole, the two sides roughly balanced: in some years the city ran a slight surplus, in some a slight deficit.

This picture of a financially solvent city is quite misleading, however. The major fiscal impact of the wars does not show up in the formal comptes of the receveurs. It is to be found in continued royal taxation, the furnishing of supplies (*munitions*) to soldiers in transit to or from the major theaters of war, and the payment of garrisons within Châlons itself.

The total fiscal impact of these burdens is impossible to ascertain precisely; the state of the documents simply does not permit it. Of necessity, therefore, these observations are impressionistic and at times anecdotal. If we cannot arrive at a close analysis of Châlons' financial burdens, we can at least obtain some idea of what demands the city faced and the expedients resorted to in order to meet those demands.

Martin Wolfe has written that from 1588 to 1594, "the royal fiscal system lay smashed in pieces, some large, some tiny."[30] It seems, however, that most individual pieces continued to function without central coordination of the system, or, in the words of a recent study of the royal financial system: "The League War of 1589–98 had had a less disruptive effect on the French direct tax system than one might think. The local tax bureaucracy continued to function throughout the war without the sanction of a strong central government. The tax system provided both sides

[29]AD Marne E suppt. 4926, fols. 322–23, 327.
[30]Wolfe, *Fiscal System*, 213.

with substantial revenues during the war, helping to prolong hostilities."[31] This certainly seems to have been the case in Châlons, for royal taxation continued uninterrupted during the wars. As the seat of a généralité and an élection, royal tax officials were on the spot; even if taxes could not be collected from the countryside, they could still be collected from the area under the city's control. In Châlons, one looks in vain for any evidence of the collapse of the royal fiscal system.

The major royal direct tax was the taille. Various authorities have claimed that towns were generally exempt from the taille, that it was considered a "peasants' tax."[32] This is a matter of some confusion, since not all towns were exempt at all times. Although several historians of Châlons have stated that the city was exempt from the taille, during the Wars of Religion the city received no such exemption.[33] Throughout the period, the inhabitants of the city were assessed between 2,500 and 8,000 livres in any given year.[34]

The taille was an *impôt de répartition*. That is, each taxation district was assessed a lump sum to be divided among its taxpayers. It was not an *impôt de quotité*, or rate tax, where each taxpayer paid a predetermined portion of his income.[35] The city council had a profound interest, therefore, in reducing the amount the city was assessed: every reduction in the total assessment meant lower taxes for all. Requests for decreases in the assessment of the taille are a recurring feature in the council's records.[36]

In addition to the taille, Châlons was subject to other royal taxes. Besides the taillon or "little taille," there was the *solde pour 50,000 gens de pied* (also called the *subvention des villes closes*), first assessed by Francis I in 1543 to raise money for the royal army.[37] Châlons was assessed this tax

---

[31]James B. Collins, *The Fiscal Limits of Absolutism: Direct Taxation in Early Seventeenth-Century France* (Berkeley: University of California Press, 1988), 67.

[32]Zeller, *Les institutions,* 256. On the other hand, Roger Doucet, *Les institutions de la France au XVIe siècle.* 2 vols. (Paris: Picard, 1948), 1:390, implies that exemption from the *taille* was somewhat more exceptional. Wolfe, *Fiscal System,* 311, states that "all the important towns were probably exempt from the taille."

[33]As regards Châlons, both Barthélemy, *Histoire,* 2d ed., 106, and Barbat, *Histoire,* 307, state that the city was exempt; a claim belied by the existence of the taille assessments.

[34]The taille registers are in AD Marne E suppt. 4845–4873.

[35]Wolfe, *Fiscal System,* 305.

[36]AD Marne E suppt. 4786, fols. 79–80, 84–85; 4787, fols. 2–3, 82–83.

[37]Wolfe, *Fiscal System,* 115–16.

(ranging between 2,500 and 7,500 livres) in 1569, 1574, 1575, 1576, 1579, 1582, and 1584 through 1588.[38] As was the case with the taille, the council continually remonstrated, requesting reductions in the city's assessment.[39]

Besides continued royal taxation, Châlons was also subject to demands to supply food to royal armies and to German mercenary reiters in transit to or from the theaters of war. Because these munitions were usually supplied in kind—grain, bread, meat, and wine—it is impossible to gauge their cost, but it must have been substantial. These demands also came when the city was least able to meet them: the times when such armies were present around Châlons were the times when the city's expenses for fortifications and garrisons were highest. These demands were concentrated in, but not limited to, the duration of the wars. When each war ended, the reiters were sent back to Germany under royal escort. They therefore required supplies from Châlons when traveling in either direction.

In general, the council made every effort to meet the demands made on them. Even though the consequences of not doing so were too horrible to be risked, the city was not always able to fulfill its obligations, even when the council was forced to its last resort, confiscation of grain from Protestants and the *hôpitaux* of the city. Faced with an order to supply two hundred thousand loaves of bread to the king's army camped at Vitry in 1567, the council searched the Huguenots' houses for grain. However, to protect their fellow inhabitants, regardless of religion, they first warned the Huguenots of the impending searches. As a result, the searches did not yield enough grain to meet the demand. The council then confiscated grain from the Hôpital St. Jacques, the Hôtel Dieu, the Abbey of Toussaints, and various merchants. Still, the council could collect only 560 *setiers*, not enough to supply the requested bread. Finally, the council informed D'Espaulx, the lieutenant-général of Champagne, that it could not supply the requested amount.[40]

---

[38]AD Marne E suppt. 4840. Châlons' assessment for both the *taille* and the *solde pour 50, 000 gens de pied* belies the statement of Wolfe, *Fiscal System*, 311, that the *solde* was "a sort of substitute for tailles.... there seems to be ground for believing that towns paying soldes did not pay tailles."

[39]AD Marne E suppt. 4787, fols. 70, 185.

[40]AD Marne E suppt. 4786, fols. 46–50. For a thorough discussion of the burdens imposed by supplying armies in Dauphiné, see L. Scott Van Doren, "War, Taxes, and Social Protest: The Challenge to Authority in Sixteenth-Century Dauphiné" (Ph.D. diss., Harvard University, 1970), 120–30.

During those periods when Châlons played host to a garrison, the council was ultimately responsible for paying the soldiers. When the garrison was imposed upon an unwilling city, the council paid the soldiers grudgingly, continually requesting their removal. In 1562, the council voted to see whether the companies stationed in Châlons had a full complement; why should they pay for soldiers who were not present?[41] In 1563, when the soldiers requested money to buy food, the council refused on the grounds that it had not requested the garrison. In 1575, the council refused to supply any more food before the soldiers paid for what they had already consumed.[42]

The council's ultimate goal was the complete removal of the garrison; failing this, they tried to shift the financial burden away from themselves. Thus, in 1575 the council asked the duc de Guise to remove the garrison, or at least to provide a "règlement certain" for its provision. Guise responded by empowering the council to requisition supplies from the *plat pays*.[43]

If the councillors begrudged the presence of the soldiers, the garrison nevertheless had to be paid. The council walked a tightrope in this respect. They wanted to pay the minimum amount possible, but the potential consequences of a horde of unpaid and hungry soldiers within the city were such that payment could not be escaped altogether. When paying the soldiers was inevitable, the council raised the necessary money through confiscations, loans, and subscriptions. In 1562, the council seized the possessions of Huguenot refugees to pay Bussy's soldiers. They also borrowed 1,055 livres from an Orléannais merchant to pay the soldiers. In October, they raised a voluntary contribution of 1,200 livres: 100 livres from each of six *élus* (officials of the élection) and 600 livres from Guillaume de Champagne, receveur-général of the généralité.[44]

From 1589 on, when Châlons was garrisoned at the council's instigation, the attitude of the councillors was somewhat different. They no longer requested the soldiers' removal; indeed, the soldiers were necessary

---

[41]AD Marne E suppt. 4785, fols. 89–90. See also Van Doren, "War, Taxes," 130–39.
[42]AD Marne E suppt. 4785, fol. 124; AD Marne E suppt. 4787, fols. 47–48, 52–53.
[43]AD Marne E suppt. 4785, fols. 56–57, 60–61.
[44]AD Marne E suppt. 4785, fols. 84–88; AD Marne E suppt. 4785, fol. 90; AD Marne E suppt. 4785, fol. 100.

to protect the city from the Leaguers under St. Paul and de Rosne. The council thus made every effort to pay the soldiers in full and on time. In a sense, Châlons' isolated and vulnerable position in Leaguer Champagne aided the council's efforts to solicit help from the royal fiscal system in paying for the garrison. Since the major royalist outpost in the province, preserving Châlons' security became a matter of priority for the royal fiscal bureaucracy. The council was aided in its efforts to gain financial assistance from this source because the royal fiscal jurisdictions were based in Châlons. Thus, immediately following de Rosne's expulsion in late 1589, the council asked for and received 3,600 livres from the trésoriers-généraux of the généralité.[45]

To make up the remainder of the amount required, the council resorted to a series of expedients. It borrowed substantial sums from individuals, including its own members. It sold rentes against the revenues of the city. It short-circuited the royal fiscal machinery in effect by collecting direct taxes itself: in February 1589 the councillors ordered a list made of all those who could contribute—those who had paid 3 livres or more in the last assessment of the taille. In this manner the council raised over 16,000 livres. In April an additional tax was imposed on those who had paid more than 30 livres in the last taille. Receipts from the grenier à sel were assigned directly to the payment of the garrison. In July, the councillors contributed 60 livres each to be used to pay the soldiers. A gold buffet belonging to Madame de Guise was seized and melted down. Dinteville agreed to buy 18,000 livres worth of grain from the city's storehouses, enabling the proceeds to be used to pay the garrison. Eventually, the soldiers were paid in grain rather than cash.[46]

Even with all these improvised sources of revenue, the council still had difficulty meeting the garrison's payroll, for the amount needed was significant. Each of the six company captains was paid 100 livres per month, the lieutenants 56 livres, the ensigns 36 livres, and each soldier 12 livres per month. When one includes the administrative officers of the city (two *commissaires* at 40 livres per month and two *contrôleurs* at 10 livres per

---

[45]AD Marne E suppt. 4788, fols. 45–46. The council made several similar requests at later dates, receiving, for example, 5810 livres in August 1589; see AD Marne E suppt. 4788, fol. 110. In 1590, the *trésoriers* were unable to supply any more money; see AD Marne E suppt. 4788, fols. 132–33.

[46]AD Marne E suppt. 4788, fols. 47, 52, 60, 61, 62–63, 69, 70, 94, 109, 121, 126, 133–34, 135.

month) and 150 livres per month for expenses, the total cost of the garrison to the city each month was almost 8,400 livres.[47] In these years, the council lived from hand to mouth: expenses ate up revenues faster than revenues could be raised.[48] That the exigencies of the years between 1589 and 1594 saddled the city with significant debt is obvious; the extent of that debt is difficult if not impossible to calculate, and its duration is beyond the scope of this study.

What then can we say about the financial impact of the Wars of Religion in Châlons and about the influence of fiscal considerations on the council's course of action? As mentioned, the true measure of the wars on the city's finances cannot be definitively determined from the annual comptes of the receveurs. Nevertheless, although the city's revenues remained relatively stable, there was a significant shift in the sources of these revenues away from those more subject to disorder in the countryside to those under the control of royal fiscal officials. Those expenditures revealed in the comptes also remained relatively constant, the lion's share in any one year going into the city's fortifications.

The major financial burdens of the period—supplying passing armies with *munitions* and supporting garrisons—do not show up in the comptes. Their impact was great, though impossible to calculate precisely.

Politically, it is likely that financial considerations played a minor but contributory role in the city council's decisions to remain loyal to the crown and aloof from the League. In a negative sense, adherence to the League had little to offer the city in the way of fiscal recompense. Those areas under Leaguer control paid no less tax; it was simply diverted to another destination.[49] In a positive sense, the council recognized that the crown was still the source of largesse. Indeed, Châlons was well rewarded for its loyalty after 1588. A grateful Henry III transferred to Châlons numerous royal courts and jurisdictions from rebellious cities: the greniers à sel from Sezanne and Epernay, the *Cour des monnaies* from Troyes, the *siège présidial* from Vitry, and a portion of the Parlement of Paris. The

---

[47]AD Marne E suppt. 4788, fols. 57–58.

[48]In February 1590 the garrison captains told the council that the soldiers were growing impatient. For the previous two months they had received only 4 livres each. The council responded by reducing the garrison by half, from six hundred to three hundred men; see AD Marne E suppt. 4788, fols. 130–32.

[49]Wolfe, *Fiscal System*, 188.

economic impact of these translations was indirect but real nevertheless. Each new bureaucracy brought with it salaried officials and employment for Châlonnais avocats and procureurs.

Old habits die hard; the councillors clearly preferred their known and traditional obligations and revenues to unknown and unforeseeable ones at the hands of the League. Many of the costs associated with the wars were inescapable; had Châlons been a Leaguer town, the council would still have had to maintain its fortifications, support garrisons, and furnish supplies to passing armies. There was therefore no fiscal incentive to join the League. On the contrary, the royal government seemed better able to aid the city. The fiscal circumstances of the city only confirmed the councillors in the course to which they were already predisposed.

Interview between Henry III and the duke of Guise
(detail of painting by P. C. Comte)

Part 2

Châlons during the

Wars of Religion

Chapter 5

The Community Challenged, 1560–1576

1560–1567

B Y THE EARLY 1560s, it was clear that France was heading towards civil religious war. The government of the sickly boy-king Francis II, thoroughly dominated by his ultra-Catholic Guise in-laws, was coming face to face with a growing and militant Protestant movement that drew its strength from a large segment of the military nobility and the urban middle class. In March 1560, a group of Protestant noblemen, with the tacit support of the Prince de Condé (a prince of the blood royal and the leading noble Huguenot) and at least the acquiescence of John Calvin, attempted to capture the court at Amboise, ostensibly to rescue the young king from his evil advisors. The plot ultimately failed; a number of the conspirators were executed and Condé himself was sentenced to death, only to be reprieved by the death of the king in December.

The "Tumult of Amboise" was followed in May by the Edict of Romorantin, which was singularly repressive of the Huguenots. Following the death of Francis II and the accession of his brother Charles IX, the queen mother and regent, Catherine de Médicis, attempted a policy of balance and reconciliation between the religious parties. She sponsored a theological conference at Poissy, and through the Edict of St. Germain in 1562, granted the Huguenots limited toleration, but these efforts were defeated by the heat of religious passion. All over France, Catholics and Protestants clashed in violent confrontations. The most notorious of these, and the one which signaled the outbreak of civil war, occurred on March 1, 1562, in the Champenois town of Vassy. The duc de Guise and his entourage were spending the night there on their way to the Guises' ancestral home at Joinville when they were awakened by the sound of a Huguenot worship service. A confrontation ensued in which a number of Huguenots were killed. This Massacre of Vassy was followed by a similar event at Sens in April, by Protestant coups in Troyes, Lyon, Angers, Tours, and Blois, and by Condé's seizure of Orléans. Earlier, on March 16 following his "triumph" at Vassy, Guise had entered Paris as a conquering hero, to the wild acclamations of Parisian Catholics.

Clearly, religious passions within France were at a feverish level. What was the experience of Châlons during this tumultuous period? As A. N. Galpern has written, "the Châlonnais seemed to have learned to endure one another," and, "if France had been Châlons writ large, perhaps civil war would not have begun."[1] Indeed, from the very beginning of the religious wars, certain characteristics of a conciliar mentality are made manifest in the minutes and actions of the city council. The council was reluctant to persecute native Huguenots; indeed, there was a desire to protect them from powerful outsiders. When discriminatory measures were unavoidable, they were virtually always undertaken at the instigation of outsiders, and to the greatest extent possible their effects were mitigated by the council and were relatively mild by the standards of the time. And the council was committed to a civic agenda that maintained the council's integrity and freedom of action.

Châlons remained peaceful in the period between the failure of the conspiracy of Amboise in 1560 and the first civil war, as witnessed by the council's reply to a letter from the duc de la Rochefoucauld, lieutenant-général of Champagne, in November 1560, requesting a report on the state of "police" in the city. The council replied that "there has been no commotion in this city, and at present there is no appearance that there will be in the future."[2] Châlons apparently remained peaceful over the next six months. In fact, there is no hint at all of the tensions and conflicts which were about to drive France into civil war.

The first evidence of religious division in Châlons came in the council meeting of January 15, 1561, when it came to the council's attention that a

---

[1] A. N. Galpern, *The Religions of the People in Sixteenth-Century Champagne,* Harvard Historical Studies, 92 (Cambridge, Mass: Harvard University Press, 1976),151–152, 179.

[2] AD Marne, E suppt. 4785, fol. 34: "qu'il n'y a eu par cy devant aulcun tumulte, sédition ou émotion populaire en icelle ville, et n'y a de présent apparence qu'il en doibve subvenir à l'avenir."

Master Henry Maurroy "has made known many times in his sermons that there have been conventicles and secret assemblies and other things ill-suited to the honor and welfare of this city and its inhabitants, the said conventicles and assemblies being forbidden by the royal Edict of Romorantin following the Conspiracy of Amboise." The council resolved to question Maurroy about his statements, particularly how he knew about these assemblies and what proof he had of them.[3] Nothing further is heard of the matter, so we must assume that Maurroy was exaggerating the situation. Significantly, to judge by its own words, the council was not so concerned about the possible existence of heresy in Châlons as about "the honor and welfare of this city and its inhabitants."

The first hint of any real trouble in Châlons appears in the spring of 1561 when, on June 2, the duc de Nevers, governor of Champagne, requested information from the council concerning a recent disturbance in the city. The council replied that all was under control and that the trouble had been caused by a preacher staying with Jacques Langault, a grenetier à sel and city councillor. Langault maintained that "the alleged preacher was a physician whom he had invited from the city of Strasbourg to treat his wife." The council also recorded, at the insistence of two of its members, Guillaume de Champagne and Nicolas Braulx, that "they have heard that the said Langault had caused up to sixty armed men to come into his house."[4] Again, nothing further is recorded about this matter, and we may safely discount these assertions as scare tactics, the more so since Champagne and Braulx were often in the vanguard of anti-Protestant measures. Furthermore, Langault himself continued to sit on the council.

Nevertheless, even if the assertions of Maurroy, Champagne, and Braulx were exaggerated, the Huguenots in Châlons were on the move. The preacher/physician mentioned above was almost certainly Pierre Fornelet, Châlons' first pastor sent from Geneva via Neufchâtel. On October 6 he wrote letters to Calvin in Geneva and to his colleagues in Neufchâtel

---

[3]AD Marne, E suppt. 4785, fol. 37.

[4]AD Marne, E suppt. 4785, fol. 47: "ledit Langault a dict que icelluy que on disoit estre prédicant estoit ung médecin qu'il avoit fact venir de la ville de Strassbourg pour penser et médicamenter sa femme, nous a esté requis par les srs. de Champaigne et N. Braulx en fere mention en ces présentes conclusions, et encores de ce qu'ils ont dict que ledit Langault avoir faict venir gens d'armes en sa maison jusques au nombre de soixante."

about the great growth in the church in Châlons and the surrounding countryside:

> The first assembly, which was held with great difficulty had twelve people. We had another one this evening where there were hardly less than a thousand people. We baptize and bury our dead in a Christian manner and are thinking about celebrating the Lord's Supper in order to fully declare ourselves a Church of Christ.[5]

> There are fully fifteen villages around here which desire the holy ministry of the Gospel, but through lack of pastors stay in that state.[6]

An early example of external pressures on the council came in August 1561, when the king and Adolphe D'Espaulx, his lieutenant in Champagne, wrote to Thierry de l'Hôpital, sieur de Castel and captain of Châlons, ordering him to confiscate all the arms in the possession of the inhabitants, "in order to preserve the repose and tranquillity of our subjects and to prevent any trouble or sedition among them."[7] It is important to realize that this was not done because of any trouble in Châlons, but as a result of national policy. A royal edict of July 1561 had prohibited any assemblies, public or private, "where preaching and the administration of the sacraments takes place in any form other than that received in the Catholic Church."[8]

A further threat to the city's integrity and another example of outside interference in Châlons' affairs occurred in November, when the bishop of Châlons, Jérôme Bourgeois (a militant Catholic and ally of the Guises) used armed force to prevent Huguenots from attending the city's annual general assembly on St. Martin's Day (November 11). The Huguenots complained to the duc de Nevers, who subsequently demanded an explanation from the bishop and from the sieur de Castel, captain of the city.

---

[5]"Lettre de Pierre Fornelet à Neuchâtel du 6 octobre, 1561," *Bulletin de la Société de l'histoire du protestantisme Français*, XII [1863], 361–66: "La première assemblée qui fut faicte, à grande difficulté, fut de douze personnes. Nous en avons faict aujourd'huy une en la nuict, là où il n'y avoit guère moins de mille personnes. Nous baptisons et enterrons chrestiennement noz morts, et sommes en délibération de célébrer la saincte cène, pour déclairer que nous sommes une église de Christ entièrement."

[6]"Lettre de Pierre Fornelet à Calvin du 6 octobre, 1561," *Bulletin de la Société de l'histoire du Protestantisme Français*, XIV [1866], 364–67: "il y a bien quinze villages par deça qui désirent le sainct ministère de l'Evangile, mais par faute de pasteurs y demeurent là."

[7]Georges Hérelle, ed. *La Réforme et la Ligue en Champagne*, vol. 1, *Lettres*; vol. 2, *Pièces diverses* (Paris, 1888-92). 1:33.

[8]Jean Mariéjol, *La Réforme et la Ligue* (Paris: Hachette, 1904), 45.

The bishop's role in governing the town had long been reduced to perfunctory and ceremonial functions, and the council clearly resented any attempts to expand episcopal authority, quite apart from the fact that the bishop's actions were unpalatable in themselves.[9]

At the same time, the council itself was displaying its rather equivocal attitudes towards the town's Huguenots. On January 13, 1562, Charles François, procureur of Châlons, reported to the council that he had heard "that several of the inhabitants of this city are seeking to obtain a temple." The council declared that "they had not intended and did not intend … to ask for a temple in the name of the inhabitants," and that if such a request is ever presented, it will be opposed by the council.[10] Strong language indeed. However, it is surely significant that present at this council meeting were four of the five Huguenot councillors who were later expelled from the council. Furthermore, they continued to attend right up until the other councillors refused to deliberate with them, indicating at least their acquiescence in this matter. After all, such was the law of the land, even under the new and more tolerant edict of January. The request was only a rumor and all councillors, Protestant and Catholic, seemed concerned to live as peaceably as possible and not to attract outside attention or interference in their affairs.[11]

---

[9]Hérelle, *La Réforme*, 1:34–35. Bourgeois' militant Catholicism is evidenced by several incidents. In December 1561, shortly after the St. Martin's assembly, Bourgeois traveled to Vassy, a Protestant stronghold in his diocese. There he engaged in a debate with the Huguenot pastor, Jean Gravelle, concerning the apostolic succession of bishops. He then traveled on to Joinville, the ancestral seat of the Guise family, presumably to report to the duke. He subsequently asked the king to empower the Guises to punish the Huguenots of Vassy; see Ernest Grosjean, *Implantation de la Réforme en France vue et vécue depuis Châlons-sur-Marne, 1561–1598* (Châlons, 1979), 9–10. At Easter in 1564, he intervened to stop a procession of the clergy which "se faisait par tout le clergé, depuis la cathédrale jusque sur le marché, en chantant le psaume *Confitimeni Dominus*, et se terminait par un repas que l'abus avoit rendu crapuleux"; see *Histoire du diocèse de Châlons-sur-Marne par D. François, religieux bénédictin de la congrégation de Saint-Vanne*, MS vol. in Bibliothèque Municipale de Châlons-sur-Marne, Fonds Ancien, 1851, 121.

[10]AD Marne, E suppt. 4785, fol. 55: "Le procureur de lad. ville a dict avoir eu advertissment que plusieurs habitans de lad. ville poursuivoient ung temple, dont n'a esté communicqué aux gouverneurs de lad. ville.… Les assistans ont déclaré qu'ilz n'avoient entendu et n'entendoient en général ny en particulier avoir baillé charge, mandement ou procuration pour demander aulcun temple au nom desd. habitans."

[11]Similarly, in remonstrating against an order to garrison a company of soldiers in the town, the council states that "jusques à présent n'y a occasion d'y asseoir et mectre garnison, tant pour n'estre bruict de guerres au pays que pour n'y avoir eu d'émotion ny tumulte notable en icelle, ny recherche de ceulx de l'ancienne contre ceulx de la nouvelle"; see AD Marne, E suppt. 4785, fol. 57.

On March 31, 1562, the city council of Châlons took the harshest measure yet against Châlonnais Huguenots when they expelled five Protestant councillors because "they have separated themselves from the rest of the council by religion."[12] This was followed over the next six months by the exclusion of Protestants from the watch, by the flight of a number of Protestants from the town, and by the seizure and sale of the exiles' property. Yet when these actions are put into their national context of massacres, coups, and civil war, they seem very mild indeed. By contemporary standards, Châlons was a model of tranquillity.[13]

The purging of the council was to a large degree a result of external demands and circumstances. This was a time when the council was coming under the conflicting and irreconcilable demands of powerful outside parties, with the result that no matter what the council did, someone important would be displeased. The conflicting pressures on the council are evident from two letters received in April 1562, on the eve of the first civil war. On April 19, the duc de Nevers wrote to Castel concerning "sedition in Châlons, even by the priests," and asked him to "maintain affairs with the greatest docility and amity possible."[14] Several days later, Castel received a letter from Bishop Bourgeois in which he informs the captain of his intention to make the Protestants "reel" (l'on les veulle souller). Bishop Bourgeois also tells Castel that "Monseigneur the cardinal de Lorraine is coming to Châlons tomorrow, or Wednesday at the latest, and Monseigneur de Lorraine will arrive soon thereafter, for he is leaving Paris today, and his company, which is around Châlons, awaits him at our expense."[15] Here indeed is reason for the council to take action against their Protestants. No one would wish for a repetition of Vassy or Sens. Yet the action

---

[12]AD, Marne, E suppt. 4785, fol. 61: "les autres dessus nommez ont déclaré qu'ilz n'entendoient et ne voulloient délibérer avec eulx ny en leur présence pour ce qu'ilz s'estoient séparez d'eulx par religion."

[13]Hérelle, *La Réforme*, 1:40–41; AD Marne, E suppt. 4785, fol.85. By way of contrast and context, J.H.M. Salmon, *Society in Crisis: France in the Sixteenth Century* (London: St. Martins, 1975), 135–36, mentions that besides the massacres at Vassy and Sens already mentioned, some fifty Huguenots were massacred at Cahors, and two hundred at Tours. Galpern, *Religions of the People*, 170–72, indicates that in Troyes, gangs of ruffians roamed the streets beating up those who refused to kiss a rosary, Huguenot children were forcibly baptized in the Catholic church, Huguenot couples were forced to undergo a Catholic marriage ceremony, and Catholic soldiers murdered Protestants and pillaged their houses with impunity.

[14]Hérelle, *La Réforme*, 1:38.   [15]Hérelle, *La Réforme*, 1:39.

they took, the expulsion of the five councillors, was a far cry from the violence and discord experienced by other towns.

On May 27, the council declared:

> There come daily Huguenot foreigners to live in this town to increase the number of the said city. Be advised if we obtain letters from the king to constrain them to leave this city and to return them to their own country and villages.[16]

Harsh words, but notice what is missing. The council does not do this on its own authority; it will not act without letters from the king. Moreover, it is not directed at native Huguenots, only "foreigners" who have lived in Châlons for less than a year. The council was obviously prepared to tolerate native Protestants if they had to, but not outsiders.

As if being surrounded by the Guises was not enough, there were also German mercenaries or reiters, posted at Tours-sur-Marne, about twenty miles from Châlons, and the area was threatened by the Huguenot chief in Champagne, Antoine de Croy, prince de Porcien, who had spent the spring pillaging the Champenois countryside.[17] The wonder, then, is not that action was taken against the Protestants, but that it was not more severe. The fact that on July 18 the council felt it necessary to lodge two or three hundred soldiers in the city is a testimony to the seriousness of that threat.[18]

In this atmosphere, it is hardly surprising that a number of Châlonnais Protestants decided to go into exile, mostly to Strasbourg. On July 14, six Protestant families requested permission to go into exile. They were followed by a number of other families in September and October, including those of Pastor Fornelet and four of the five councillors purged in

---

[16]AD Marne, E suppt. 4785, fol. 63: "Il vient journellement des estrangiers huguenotz demourer en ceste ville pour accroistre le nombre de ceulx de lad. ville. Soit advisé si l'on obtiendra lettres du Roy pour les contraindre à sortir hores de ladicte ville et les renvoyer en leurs pays et villages."

[17]For Porcien's career, see Claude Haton, *Mémoires contenant le récit des événements accomplis de 1553 à 1583, principalement dans la Champagne et la Brie*, 2 vols. , ed. Felix Bourquelot (Paris: Documents inédits sur l'histoire de France, 1857), 269–73; Maurice Poinsignon, *Histoire générale de la Champagne et de Brie*, 3 vols. (Paris, 1885, 1898; rpt. Paris: Guenégaud, 1974), 2:176–77. Regarding the *reitres*, on June 23, the council was ordered by the king to send to Tours-sur-Marne, about twenty miles from Châlons, forty *setiers* of oats, six *queues* of wine, four cattle, and twenty sheep to feed them; see AD Marne, E suppt. 4785, fol. 71.

[18]AD Marne, E suppt. 4785, fol. 74.

March.[19] The fact that most of these refugees waited until September or October to leave Châlons is important, for it took a great deal to drive them out. Indeed, they were not driven out by threats from within Châlons, but by the clear potential for persecution imposed from without. It seems that exile was a precautionary measure rather than a desperate flight to save one's life.

The summer of 1562 had seen substantial commotion in Châlons, not between Protestant and Catholic, but between soldier and burgher, "foreigner" and Châlonnais—or more specifically, between Antoine de Clermont, sieur de Bussy, the royal governor, and the city council. Bussy and the council clashed on two different but related fronts: Bussy's attempts to garrison the town, and his desire to have the council pursue a harder line against the Huguenots. In both cases, Bussy's wishes ran directly contrary to those of the council. The two issues were related, in Bussy's mind at least, because the presence of Huguenots in Châlons constituted a potential fifth column. The relationship between the governor and the council got off to a rocky start when, not a month after the council had agreed to lodge three hundred soldiers in the city, Bussy demanded that three more companies be placed in the city because "those of the new opinion are near this city in great number and threaten to surprise it." The council demurred: additional soldiers would worsen the plague, which "grows each day." Besides, the men already in the city are sufficient to guarantee its security; if Bussy wants more, he can station them in the "petites villes et villages" around Châlons. Furthermore, the city just cannot afford to pay any more soldiers; as it is, they have had to borrow money from the bishop to pay those already in town.[20]

On August 25, Bussy ordered the sale of the property of the Huguenots who had fled. Already on August 12, he announced to the council that he had seized several boatloads of grain belonging to Protestants. The council acquiesced in these acts for several reasons. First, it was legally authorized by royal letters patent of July 25 that ordered the seizure of

---

[19]Hérelle, *La Réforme*, 2:41–42. On Châlonnais refugees, see Roger Zuber, "Les Champenois réfugiés à Strasbourg et l'Eglise réformée de Châlons," *Mémoires de la Société d'agriculture, commerce, sciences et des arts du département de la Marne*, 1964, 31–55; Grosjean, *Implantation de la Réforme*, 35–36.

[20]AD Marne, E suppt. 4785, fol. 82.

exiles' property for the sustenance of royal troops.[21] Second, the council desperately needed money, most of all to pay the soldiers already in the town. They had already borrowed money from the bishop, they had tried to raise voluntary contributions, and finally obtained a tariff of five sols per muid of wine sold in the city.[22]

In addition, there were other military expenses: the repair and maintenance of the walls, the setting up of artillery, and an increase in the number of guards at the gates. Further yet, measures needed to be taken against the plague which had struck Champagne that summer.[23] In short, the sale of the exiles' property must have seemed a heaven-sent expedient. Already, the soldiers were making known their displeasure at the arrears in their wages. On August 25, the council asked Bussy to punish the soldiers who had stolen and sold the furniture from the house of Pierre Billet, then in Strasbourg.[24] The councillors knew that more of the same, if not worse, lay in store unless they could find a way to pay the soldiers.

Even the selling of the exiles' property had its problems, for Bussy and the council proceeded to argue over who should administer the funds obtained therefrom. The council wanted the funds applied to the town's affairs, while Bussy wanted them to go into a general war chest, administered by himself. The council finally relented at the insistence of two councillors, Guillaume de Champagne and Gilles Godet, but made it very clear that it was against the better judgment of the majority.[25]

At the same meeting on August 31, Bussy ordered a "list and catalogue" of Huguenots living in the town. The council declared that "in truth it does not know the number ... of those of the new opinion, and cannot in good conscience comply...."[26] They asked Bussy to content himself with a list already compiled of the Huguenots who had gone into exile. At the next council meeting, on September 4, instead of the usual list of those present, we find the following statement:

> Council held in the chambre de ville in the hôtel of the Holy Spirit by those in attendance in the presence of the clerk and the procureur of the

[21]AD Marne, E suppt. 4785, fols. 82–83; Grosjean, *Implantation de la Réforme*, 36.
[22]AD Marne, E suppt. 4785, fols. 76, 81
[23]See Haton, *Mémoires contenant*, 332–33.
[24]AD Marne, E suppt. 4785, fol. 82.
[25]AD Marne, E suppt. 4785, fol. 87.
[26]AD Marne, E suppt. 4785, fol. 87: "les gens du conseil ne sçavent à la verité le nombre et cathalogue de ceux de lad. nouvelle oppinion et ne le peuvent déclarer en plaine conscience."

city, who are enjoined to sign the conclusions which are arrived at by the said council for the integrity of this city and that from now on those present at the council will not be named until otherwise ordered.[27]

Evidently, as a measure of protection from Bussy and the garrison, the councillors deemed it wise to hold their meetings incognito.

Bussy continued his attempt to increase the number of soldiers in the city. Finally the council ran out of patience, concluding to remonstrate with Bussy, reminding him of the great expenses endured by the city over the last three months,

> as much for arming and guarding the city as for subsidizing the company that they have supported for two months, the total for each month coming to 2,151 livres 15 sols, and more, for mounting and equipping the artillery of the king and of the city, putting gabions on the platforms and furnishing them with adequate numbers of shovels, picks, hoes, and baskets, paying for dispatches to Court, advancing money to the captains for raising infantry, refreshing the supplies of powder and other expenses ordered either by Seigneur D'Espaulx or by the Seigeur de Bussy, without counting the feeding of the poor and treatment of the plague-stricken, which over the last four months comes to more than 1,000 livres per month.[28]

The royal governor also persisted in his hard line towards Châlonnais Protestants. On November 25, the council agreed in principle to the expulsion of the Huguenots from the city, and on December 27, delegates were appointed to interview the parish clergy and make a list.[29] Even now, however, the council insisted on retaining control of this process; Bussy was to

---

[27]AD Marne, E suppt. 4785, fol. 88: "Conseil tenu en la chambre de la ville en l'hostel du St. Esprit par les assistans aud. conseil en presence du greffier et du procureur de lad. ville ausquelz a esté enjoinct signer les conclusions qui sont faictes par led. conseil pour la probité d'icelle et que doresnavant ne seroit nommez les noms des assistans audict conseil jusques ad ce que aultrement en soit ordonné."

[28]AD Marne, E suppt. 4785, fol. 97:"tant pour eulx armer et garder ladite ville que pour soldoyer la compaignie qu'ilz ont deffrayée par deux mois, montant icelle somme par chacun desdits mois à 2151 livres 15 sols, et encores pour monster et équiper l'artillerie du Roy et de la ville, faire gabions sur les plattes formes, et eulx fournir de bon nombre de paesles, picz, hoyaulx et hottes, payer voyages de postes en court, advancer deniers aux capitaines pour lever les compaignies de gens de pied, rafreschissement de pouldres et aultres fraiz à eulx ordonner tant par les seigneur Despaulx que par ledit sr. de Bussy, sans y comprendre la nouriture des pauvres et traictement des pestifiérez dès et depuis quatre mois, revenant à mil livres tournois et plus par chacun mois."

[29]AD Marne, E suppt. 4785, fols. 102, 106.

be furnished only with an extract of the list. Nor should we make too much of this measure, for the expulsion was never actually carried out. What probably happened was that the council dragged its feet, and the war ended before such a list could be made. There is also a good deal of circumstantial evidence to suggest that the council felt threatened enough by the course of the war to feel compelled to give in to Bussy for the security of the town. That autumn Porcien had returned and resumed pillaging the country "between the Meuse and the Marne," sacking abbeys and villages in the vicinity of Ste. Menehould, about thirty miles from Châlons.[30] Late October saw the arrival of German reiters in Champagne on their way to reinforce Condé's army and the arrival of the cardinal de Lorraine in Châlons on his way to the Council of Trent.[31] Doubtless, the council felt extreme pressure to go along with Bussy.

The position of the Huguenots who remained in the city during the war may be exemplified by an incident concerning that year's St. Martin's assembly. In 1562, the register informs us, the assembly was held in the Jacobin convent instead of in the episcopal palace, because Madame de Nevers was lodged there, and "those of the new opinion will not be admitted there."[32] The clear implication is that Protestants were still allowed to attend the assembly, and further, that its location was changed in order to accommodate them.

The first War of Religion ended with the Edict of Amboise on March 19, 1563. The nature of warfare in the sixteenth century precluded contemporaries from believing that the war was really over, and in fact hostilities did continue, especially since both sides had cause to feel themselves betrayed by the edict.

On April 7, Bussy informed the council that he "has had warning that there is a mass of men in the village of Bricquenay who intend to attack Châlons after Easter and that to prevent them, it is expedient to put the company of Captain D'Estrées in the city for eight or twelve days." The council clearly did not believe him, for they concluded to send delegates

---

[30]Poinsignon, *Histoire générale*, 2:177–78.

[31]AD Marne, E suppt. 4785, fol. 95; Poinsignon, *Histoire générale*, 2:179–80.

[32]AD Marne, E suppt. 4785, fol. 101: "en icelle ne seront admis ceulx de la nouvelle opinion...."

"to make a faithful report of the assembly, if there is one ... and should it turn out that there is certain danger, the city will do its duty."[33]

Ten days later, Bussy made the same request in view of the passage of homeward-bound German reiters under the escort of the Prince de Porcien. The council again demurred, preferring to send messengers to ascertain the route of the reiters.[34] For Bussy, this was the last straw. He informed the council that "for lack of having some soldiers enter the city, he has decided to leave tomorrow, abandoning the city and its inhabitants, and that he had returned the keys to the gates to Seigneur Castel, captain of this city."[35] Despite conciliatory gestures on the part of the council, Bussy prohibited the council from meeting "on pain of their lives," and wrote to the queen complaining of the council's intransigence.[36] Catherine apparently turned the matter over to the duc d'Aumale, brother of the late duc de Guise, who was acting as governor of Champagne for his nephew, the young duc de Guise, named to replace his murdered father, who in turn had replaced the injured duc de Nevers. D'Aumale in turn wrote in the harshest terms to the council:

> Messieurs, I have just been informed of the scandalous act which took place in your city to Monsieur de Bussy d'Amboise, lieutenant of the king. I find it so strange, as does the queen, that if you do not repair this incredibly great fault by such great obedience as is due him, I hope, being there, as I soon will be, to give the order that the king commanded me and impose the punishment that such seditious acts merit; and for this reason be sure to do the same among yourselves, that each content himself in all docility and obedience to the said Bussy, with such respect as is due him.[37]

[33]AD Marne, E suppt. 4785, fol. 112: "pour faire rapport fidèle de l'assemblé si aulcun s'en faicte aud. lieu ... et où il adviendra advertissement du certain danger la ville fera son debvoir."

[34]AD Marne, E suppt. 4785, fols. 115–16.

[35]AD Marne, E suppt. 4785, fol. 116:"qu'à faulte de faire entrer quelques gens de guerre en ceste ville, il s'estoit délibéré de partir dès demain de ceste ville et délaisser ladite ville et las habitans d'icelle, et que jà il avoit renvoyé les clefz de portes au sr de Castel, cappitaine de ceste ville."

[36]Hérelle, *La Réforme,*1:49 n.

[37]Hérelle, *La Réforme,* 1:48–49: "Messieurs, je viens d'estre adverty de l'acte scandaleux qui a esté faicte en vostre ville à Monsieur de Bussy d'Amboise, lieutenant du Roy en icelle; que je trouve si estrange, comme aussy faict la Royne, que sy vous ne réparez ceste faulte merveilleusement grande par une grande obéissance que vous luy debvez, j'espère, estant de par delà comme je seray bien tost, y donner l'ordre que le Roy m'a commandé avec ung tel chastiment que telz faictz séditieux le méritent; et pour ceste cause regardez de faire en sorte parmy vous qu'ung chascun se puisse contenir en toute doulceur et obéissance audict sieur de Bussy avec ung tel respect qu'il luy est deub."

The council, suitably chastened, sent a committee to Bussy to inform him that they were "greatly sorry to have offended him" ("grandement marry de l'avoir offensé") and somewhat disingenuously asked what had so upset him.[38] Bussy, in turn, authorized the council to meet again. However, on April 29, when he requested the posting of one hundred soldiers in the city, the council stated that Châlons had always been exempt from garrisons, but that they would nevertheless obey if Bussy would produce written orders from the king or d'Aumale. Besides, they added, "because, thanks to God, the foreign forces are distant from this city, and the inhabitants of the city are in union and accord, we cannot understand why the garrison should be posted in this city."[39] Bussy retorted that his orders were verbal. The matter was finally settled when d'Aumale himself, during a visit to Châlons in early May, ordered four companies of infantry stationed in the city.

Meanwhile, having heard of the Edict of Amboise, the Châlonnais refugees in Strasbourg returned home. Of the twenty-one families who left Châlons in 1562, all but one (the family of Pastor Piere Fornelet) returned in the spring of 1563. There is some evidence of tension upon their return. When the five purged councillors attempted to resume their places on the council, the other councillors refused to readmit them. They appealed to the bailli of Vermandois, who ruled in their favor. Charles François, the procureur of Châlons, then appealed the case to the Parlement of Paris. The issue was not finally settled until May of 1564, when Charles IX, visiting Châlons on his tour of the kingdom, ordered the councillors reinstated.[40]

Here, again, we have prima facie evidence of religious intolerance in the city council. There is, however, compelling evidence to suggest that the

---

[38]AD Marne, E suppt. 4785, fol. 117:

[39]AD Marne, E suppt. 4785, fol. 119:"grâce à Dieu, les forces estrangières son esloingées de lad. ville, les habitants de lad. ville sont en bonne union et accord, et ne se peuvent expliquer pourquoy lad. garnison doibve estre assise en lad. ville."

[40]Hérelle, La Réforme, 2:44–48. For an instructive contrast, see L. Scott Van Doren, "War, Taxes, and Social Protest: The Challenge to Authority in Sixteenth-Century Dauphiné" (Ph.D. diss. Harvard University, 1970), 37–50, on the events of 1560 in the Dauphinois town of Valence. Here, confronted with a large and militant Protestant community, the Catholic city council continually requested its repression, even at the cost of the suspension of its powers and the military occupation of the duc de Guise's stand-in, Maugiron.

council was pushed in this direction by the duc d'Aumale. On October 23, 1563, François declared that

> following certain letters of the king and his mother the queen, the said plaintiffs had been suspended from the said council during the troubles, and since Monseigneur d'Aumale ... had ordered that the suspension continue, he commanded and enjoined the council of the said city not to admit the said plaintiffs to the said council.[41]

Very early in the Wars of Religion, then, certain elements of the council's mentality are apparent: first, Châlons had indeed arrived at some sort of modus vivendi with its native Huguenots; second, such confessional hostility as did take place was nonviolent and rather mild by contemporary standards; and third, the impulse for such persecution came from external sources—the Bishop, Bussy, d'Aumale, or the course and conduct of the war.

1567–1576

THE PATTERN OF ACTIONS AND ATTITUDES exhibited by the council during the civil war of 1562–1563 was continued through the wars that occurred between 1567 and 1576. In the intervening years, Châlons reverted to its customary course of existence. The reinstated Protestant councillors continued to sit on the council and there were no further actions taken against the town's Huguenots.[42] During this period, the Huguenot church of Châlons seems to have reconstituted itself, albeit not legally, for the Edict of Amboise permitted Protestant worship in only one town per bailliage. Nevertheless, it seems likely that the refugees who had recently returned from Strasbourg met unofficially, even though they lacked a pastor, Pierre Fornelet having availed himself of the protection of Henri-Robert de la Marck, duc de Bouillon, in Sedan, where he spent the rest of his life and where he died, in 1604.[43] The Protestants of Châlons sent a lay representa-

---

[41]AD Marne, E suppt. 4785, fol. 122: "suyvant certaines lectres clauses du Roy et de la Royne sa mère, lesdictz demandeurs avoient esté suspenduz dudict Conseil durant lesd. troubles, et depuis, par ordonnance de Monseigneur le duc d'Aumalle ... avoit esté par luy ordonné que lad. suspension tiendroit, commandé et enjoinct à ceulx du Conseil de lad. ville ne admectre lesd. demandeurs aud. Conseil."

[42]The minutes of the council again record those in attendance beginning November 13, 1564. Michel le Caussonier, J. Beschefer, Pierre le Duc, Claude Billet, and J. Langault, all expelled earlier, resumed their places and continued to attend.

[43]Grosjean, *Implantation de la Réforme*, 47.

tive to the provincial synod at La Ferté-sous-Jouarre in April 1564. At this assembly the Châlonnais church reserved the right to recall Fornelet as its pastor at such time as the church could be officially reestablished. Though Fornelet never resumed his duties in Châlons, the church was clearly active again and planning for the time when it could freely assemble once more.[44] It is significant that during this interwar period the city council, although it must have been aware of the Huguenots' activities in contravention of the Edict of Amboise, never requested the church's suppression. In fact, the minutes are completely silent about any religious contention in the city.

The first echo of the events which were to plunge France into another civil war is found in a letter from D'Espaulx to the council, read at the meeting of July 31, 1566, in which he orders it to pay extra attention to the security of the city.[45] This letter resulted from Spain's efforts, through the emperor, to detach Metz from France in 1565, thus threatening the northeastern frontier, and the iconoclastic fury which swept the Netherlands and parts of northern France in the summer of 1566.[46]

Events did not really begin to heat up until the summer of 1567 with Alba's march along France's eastern frontier, shadowed on the French side by a royal army under the command of D'Andelot.[47] In July, Condé and Coligny left court over a dispute regarding the command of the army and proposed amendments to the peace of Amboise inimical to the Huguenots. In this general atmosphere of suspicion, Huguenot synods meeting at Chatillon-sur-Loing and Valéry prepared for war, the more so since the king had hired six thousand Swiss mercenaries who had just entered France.[48]

The failure of the Huguenot plot to seize the court at Meaux on September 26–28 marked the opening of hostilities in the second civil war. Condé's strategy was to seize the crossings on the Seine above Paris, thus preventing the capital's resupply, and then to take it by siege. This strategy

[44]Grosjean, *Implantation de la Réforme,* 46.

[45]AD Marne, E suppt. 4786, fol. 17.

[46]James W. Thompson, *The Wars of Religion in France, 1559–1576* (Chicago: University of Chicago Press, 1909), 300–303.

[47]Mariéjol, *La Réforme et la Ligue,* 94; J.H.M. Salmon, *Society in Crisis,* 169.

[48]Salmon, *Society in Crisis,* 169; Poinsignon, *Histoire générale,* 2:196–97; on the Swiss, see Thompson, *Wars of Religion,* 318.

was foiled by the Huguenot defeat at St. Denis on October 10. Following the battle, the Huguenot army retreated eastward through Brie and Champagne in order to effect a rendezvous with the reiters of John Casimir of the Palatinate. The army retreated in two columns: one, under Coligny, via Brie-Comte-Robert, Montereau, Port Renard, Courlon, Bray-sur-Seine, Nogent, Provins, and Sens; the other, under Condé, via Villecendrier, Villenauxe-la-grande, Sézanne, and Epernay (about thirty miles downstream from Châlons).[49] Meanwhile, they were pursued by the royal army under the duc d'Anjou.

Châlons, meanwhile, was feeling the repercussions of this new war. On October 2, Barbezieulx informed the council of his intention to lodge five hundred men in Châlons under the command of a Captain Lahure. At the same meeting some forty Huguenots requested the council to ask Barbezieulx's permission to leave the city, leaving behind their wives, children, and property.[50] The council agreed to intercede with Barbezieulx on their behalf. Their request was repeated in fuller detail on October 3, when they requested Barbezieulx's permission (he was then present in Châlons) to go into their fields and about their affairs. They also requested the release from prison of two of their coreligionists, Jacques Roussel and Jacques de Bar.[51] Again the council concluded that it would do what it could on their behalf. Apparently none of the Huguenots contemplated fleeing the country entirely, as they had in 1562. Clearly, they were not panicked. This may have resulted from their opinion that this war was bound to be of short duration and were determined not to have their lives disrupted as had happened in 1562–1563, and perhaps they had acquired a measure of confidence in their Catholic neighbors, based on their experience in the first war, that they would not be subject to undue harassment.

Subsequent events seem to prove that their confidence was well founded. With the retreat of the Huguenot forces through Champagne, Châlons became a strategic focal point and its retention in royal hands a matter of some importance. On October 25, Guise, in his capacity as governor of Champagne, wrote to the council asking what steps they had

[49]On the campaigns of the war, see Salmon, *Society in Crisis,* 170–72; Mariéjol, *La Réforme et la Ligue,* 97–98; and Thompson, *Wars of Religion,* 326–44. On the retreat, see Poinsignon, *Histoire générale,* 2:200–201; Haton, *Mémoires contenant,* 1:462–88.

[50]AD Marne, E suppt. 4786, fol. 36.   [51]AD Marne, E suppt. 4786, fol. 37.

taken regarding their Huguenots. On December 3, D'Espaulx asked to lodge two more companies in the city. And on December 19 came an order to supply two hundred thousand loaves of bread to the royal army camped nearby.[52] The city was already hard pressed to meet its financial commitments to the three companies garrisoned in Châlons; this new imposition clearly forced the council to its last resort: the confiscation of grain belonging to Huguenots. Clearly, this conclusion was intended primarily for D'Espaulx's ears, for at the same meeting, the council also "concluded, that the procureur of the city present himself at the homes of those of the said religion and inform them of the peril to their property, especially their grains, wine, and other foodstuffs."[53] At the next council meeting on December 26, the deputies appointed to conduct the searches reported, not surprisingly, "that they had transported themselves to the houses of those of the new religion to seize the grain located in their houses to aid in the supply of two hundred thousand loaves ordered supplied by the inhabitants to the army, and ... found only very small quantities in the houses of those of the said religion."[54] The Huguenots were not the only ones to have their grain seized. The council also confiscated the grain stored in the Hôpital St. Jacques, the Hôtel Dieu, the abbey of Toussaints, and by various merchants. Still, the 560 setiers of grain collected was not enough and the council decided to remonstrate that it was impossible to meet the demands placed upon them. [55]

Meanwhile, the Huguenot forces had arrived in the vicinity, leisurely pursued by the royal army under Anjou. On December 27 the duke arrived in the vicinity of Châlons with his army of fifty thousand men.[56] A forward guard under the command of the comte de Brissac encountered a Huguenot force at the château of Sarry, just upstream from Châlons, and forced the defenders to retreat to Notre-Dame L'Epine before breaking off pursuit.[57] Condé, meanwhile, managed to escape via Possesse across the

---

[52]AD Marne, E suppt. 4786, fols. 40, 45–46.   [53]AD Marne, E suppt. 4786, fol. 47.

[54]AD Marne, E suppt. 4786, fol. 48: "Les deputez du Conseil se sont transportez ès maisons de ceulx de la religion nouvelle pour prandre les blefz qui ilz se trouveroient en leurs maison pour ayder à la fourniture de deux cens mil pains ordonnez ausd. habitans fournir pour la nouriture d'icelle armée, et ne s'en est trouvé que bien petite quantité és maisons et greniers d'aucuns particuliers de lad. religion."

[55]AD Marne, E suppt. 4786, fol. 48.   [56]Poinsignon, *Histoire générale*, 2:204.

[57]Poinsignon, *Histoire générale*, 2:204; Mariéjol, *La Réforme et la Ligue*, 99.

Meuse to Pont-à-Mousson where he and Coligny at last effected their rendez-vous with John Casimir on January 11, and from where they retreated into Burgundy.[58] At the same time, Anjou established his camp at Vitry, from where he continued to exact provisions from the towns of the region.[59]

For all intents and purposes the war in Champagne was now over. In February, the royal army left its camp near Troyes to return to Paris. Condé, meanwhile, joined forces with a Huguenot army from the south in laying siege to Chartres. The war was formally ended with the Peace of Longjumeau on March 23, 1568.

The Peace of Longjumeau satisfied both sides even less than had the Peace of Amboise in 1563, and from its inception it was apparent that it was no more than a truce forced upon the antagonists because of their lack of funds. In the south and west, Huguenot strongholds refused to admit their royal captains. Protestants were alarmed by the course of events in the Netherlands, where Horn and Egmont had been executed in June and where a proposed invasion led by the Prince of Orange was postponed due to a lack of funds. In addition, Orange's brother, Louis of Nassau, had suffered a severe defeat at Jemmingen in July. In France, the cardinal de Lorraine now possessed the strongest voice on the king's council, where he advocated increased cooperation with Spain in the Netherlands, hoping to avoid war with Philip II. At the same time, local Catholic Leagues were forming for the defense of the Church, especially in Burgundy under the influence of Tavannes, but also in Anjou, Beauvais, Berry, and Maine. In Champagne, the League manifested itself primarily in Troyes where twenty-eight members of the clergy swore an oath "des associés de la ligue chrestienne et roiale." The Troyes city council, however, refused to subscribe.[60]

The transitory nature of the Peace of Longjumeau and the tensions that were soon to lead to another civil war were evident in Châlons. The dissatisfaction of Châlonnais Huguenots with the peace is clear from the minutes of the council meeting of April 27, where it was brought to the council's attention that some Huguenots "are employing insolent proposi-

---

[58]Mariéjol, *La Réforme et la Ligue*, 99; Poinsignon, 2:204.
[59]Poinsignon, *Histoire générale*, 2:05; Hérelle, *La Réforme*, 1:53–54.
[60]Poinsignon, *Histoire générale*, 2:207.

tions and threats, which present the danger of sedition to which it is necessary to provide a remedy." The remedy settled on was to inform the distant bailli of Vermandois in Laon and not to take any immediate action.[61]

Apparently the specter of renewed war prompted a number of Huguenots to leave Châlons, for on July 25 D'Espaulx wrote to Castel: "I have seen from your letter that those of the Religion from Châlons, Troyes, and Reims are leaving these cities; I do not know what causes them to do this because I do not see at all that they have any occasion to do it; and I believe that since they are doing it, they have something up their sleeve."[62] A similar letter from Guise on July 27 exhorts Castel: "If you can discover to what end all this leads, do not fail to send to me and continue to advise me of what you can learn regarding their schemes."[63] Who, if anybody, left and where they went, is unknown. It is possible that no one left Châlons at this time. In the past, those desiring to leave had requested the council's permission. In the summer of 1568, no such requests were recorded.

The third civil war was occasioned by the crown's attempted arrest of Condé and Coligny at the former's château at Noyers on August 23 and by the concurrent revocation of the Edict of Longjumeau. The two Huguenot leaders managed to escape and made their way to La Rochelle, arriving on September 19. The main actions of this war were carried on in the west, notably Condé's defeat and death at Jarnac on March 13, 1569, and Coligny's defeat at Moncontour on October 3. The war affected Champagne and Châlons chiefly through the passage of troops on their way to the lower Loire. Once again Châlons played host to a garrison of soldiers and was constantly requested to admit more troops. Once again the guard of the gates and walls was increased, artillery was mounted, and powder was stored.

The first real threat to Châlons came in December 1568, with the invasion of William of Orange from the Low Countries in support of his Huguenot brethren in fulfilment of a secret treaty signed with Condé in August. On December 10, the council heard that Orange's men were encamped just outside the city in the villages of Grandes-Loges, La Veuve, and Juvigny. They voted to ask a Captain Jacques of one of the regiments

---

[61]AD Marne, E suppt. 4786, fols. 80–81.   [62]Hérelle, *La Réforme,* 1:57.

[63]Hérelle, *La Réforme,* 1:58: "Si vous pouvez descouvrir à quelle fin tend cela, vous ne fauldrez de le me mander et continuer à m'advertir de ce que pourrez apprendre de leurs desseings."

of the comte de Boissons and commander of the city in Barbezieulx's absence, to bring into Châlons the infantry companies stationed in the villages of Mathouges, Aulnay, Fagnières, Coolus, and Compertrix.[64] Needless to say, the council's invitation reflects the intensity of the perceived threat.

Orange was in the area attempting to link up with a force of reiters under Wolfgang of Bavaria, duke of Zweibrucken (Deux-Ponts). To prevent this, a royal army was sent to Château Thierry under Aumale's command. Despite Aumale's efforts, the Protestant commanders linked forces and crossed the Seine above Bar and proceeded from there to the Loire to join Condé.[65]

The council's alarm at the presence of Orange's men soon faded. On Christmas Day, the Seigneur D'Aultry, commander of Châlons in Barbezieulx's absence, asked to bring more soldiers into town in order to avoid being surprised, as had happened at Vitry. The council demurred since the enemy had already withdrawn.[66] D'Aultry repeated his request on December 29, only to receive the same reply, with the additional observation that the troops would be better lodged in the Barrois or Perthois.[67] Nevertheless, the council did not feel completely secure, for on January 2 they asked D'Aultry to seek out and expel foreign Huguenots or to "s'assurer de leurs personnes" and to draw up a list of foreign (non-Châlonnais) Catholics to assist with guarding the walls.[68]

The apprehension with which the council regarded soldiers, especially reiters, becomes evident in January as well. On January 7, Aumale wrote to Castel ordering him to permit the passage through Châlons of two regiments of reiters. Castel relayed his instructions to the council on the thirteenth. The council agreed to this passage, but took the precaution of posting arquebusiers in the windows of the houses along the route.[69]

After the passage of Orange and Zweibrucken, the main action of the war was carried out in the west. Châlons was not again threatened by the actual conduct of the war, but once more reverted to its role as supplier of

[64]AD Marne, E suppt. 4786, fol. 116.
[65]Thompson, *Wars of Religion*, 373–74; Mariéjol, *La Réforme et la Ligue*, 108–109.
[66]AD Marne, E suppt. 4786, fol. 119.   [67]AD Marne, E suppt. 4786, fol. 120.
[68]AD Marne, E suppt. 4786, fol. 122.
[69]Hérelle, *La Réforme*, 1: 61; AD Marne, E suppt. 4786, fol. 124.

money and food to the royal armies. Unfortunately, there is a gap in the council minutes after May 1569, so we do not know the council's reaction to the royal victories of Jarnac and Moncontour.

This time, a number of Châlonnais Huguenots did go into exile, most of them, as in 1562–1563, to Strasbourg. Only seven families felt compelled to seek refuge in the Alsatian city. Among these were the families of Jacques Beschefer, Claude Billet, and Pierre Margaine, veterans of the earlier exile. They arrived in two groups, one in late September and the other in early October, following the revocation of the Edict of Longjumeau, when Protestant worship again became illegal throughout France. Nevertheless, as we have seen, many—perhaps most—Châlonnais Huguenots preferred to remain at home, trusting their Catholic relatives and neighbors. Again, as in 1563, those who did leave returned home immediately following the Edict of St. Germain on August 8, 1570.[70]

The Edict of St. Germain was the most favorable peace granted to the Huguenots thus far. It established liberty of conscience throughout France, freedom of worship on estates of seigneurs possessing powers of high justice, and wherever it had been established before the war as well as in two cities in each province. It granted a blanket amnesty, gave Huguenots the right to hold public office, and granted them the four towns of La Rochelle, Cognac, Montauban, and La Charité.[71]

Information on Châlons-sur-Marne during the years between 1569 and 1574 is scarce because there is an unfortunate lacuna in the livres des conclusions of the city council, although some information is available from other sources. It is apparent that Huguenot worship was soon reestablished. At a regional synod held at Blacy, near Vitry, in August 1571 and presided over by none other than Pierre Fornelet, the list of delegates includes Robert de Renty, described as pastor at Châlons, and Anthoine d'Apremont, a lay elder.[72]

It is also apparent that while religious passions continued unabated elsewhere in France, in Châlons the councillors retained the attitudes that they had held since the beginning of the wars. Early in 1572, D'Espaulx wrote to Castel regarding rumors of armed Huguenot assemblies: "These

[70]Zuber, "Les Champenois réfugiés," 49–53.
[71]Mariéjol, 113; Salmon, *Society in Crisis*, 176–77.
[72]Grosjean, *Implantation de la Réforme*, 51–52.

assemblies would not occur unless they wanted to take or surprise some place. You know the doubt which I have always had and still have of your city: I found it very strange that you sent me no information of the assemblies."[73] In the absence of further information, one may speculate that the city councillors were not as alarmed by these purported assemblies as was D'Espaulx, and let them continue, if indeed they took place at all. The "doubt" in which D'Espaulx held Châlons is obviously a reference to their record of tolerance and moderation or, in his eyes, their prevarication and lack of principle.

The St. Bartholomew's Day Massacre has been the subject of an enormous amount of historical literature.[74] Among the questions addressed have been the motivation for it, the complicity of the king and the queen mother, its magnitude, its nature (whether primarily religious, social, or economic), and its spread to the provinces. It is not necessary for our purposes to deal with all its aspects here. There was no St. Bartholomew's Day massacre in Châlons. Although we lack detailed information on Châlons in the years 1569 through 1574, this assertion is beyond doubt. No contemporary sources refer to any trouble in Châlons. In fact, the only direct evidence we have of the period makes the opposite point. An account written by a bourgeois of Strasbourg who had been in Paris at the time of the massacre informs us that "at Châlons they told the Huguenots to remain peaceful, and promised to protect them; but [the Huguenots] did not believe it, and as many as were able fled by water."[75] Whether they did not believe the promise of protection, or doubted the Châlonnais' ability to fulfil their promise is not clear.

---

[73]Hérelle, *La Reforme*, 1:72: "Ces assemblées ne se font poinct qu'ilz n'aient envye de prendre ou surprendre quelque chose. Vous sçavez le doubte que j'ay toujours eu et que j'ay encore de vostre ville: j'ay trouvé bien estrange que vous ne m'en ayez faict nul advertissement."

[74]For a small sample of the literature on the massacre, see N[icola] M[ary] Sutherland, *The Massacre of St. Bartholomew and the European Conflict* (London: Macmillan, 1973); Janine Garrisson-Estèbe, *Tocsin pour un massacre, la saison des St-Barthélemy* (Paris: Le Centurion, 1968); Ilja Mieck, "Die Bartolomäusnacht als Forschungsproblem: Kritische Bestandaufnahme und neue Aspekte," *Historische Zeitschrifte* 216 (1973): 73–110; Natalie Z. Davis, "The Rites of Violence" in idem, *Society and Culture in Early Modern France* (Stanford: Stanford University Press, 1975).

[75]"À Châlons on doit avoir dit aux huguenots de se tenir tranquilles, et on a promis de les protéger; mais ils se méfient et s'enfuient par eau et tant qu'ils peuvent." Rodolphe Reuss, ed., "Un nouveau récit de la Saint-Barthélemy par un bourgeois de Strasbourg," *Bulletin de la Société de l'Histoire du Protestantisme Français* 22 (1873): 380.

The question of why there was no massacre in Châlons is badly put. In fact, cities which did experience a massacre are in the minority. It is more appropriate to ask why certain cities did experience a massacre. Philip Benedict has enumerated five variables upon which the likelihood of a massacre depended:

> the manner in which the news of the events in Paris was first relayed to the city; the extent of the influence wielded by Catholic noblemen bent on violence; the depth of anti-Protestant sentiment among the mass of the urban population (this being chiefly a function of the city's experience over the preceding decade of civil war and of the size and aggressiveness of the local Protestant community); the ability of the Huguenots to defend themselves against threats to their safety; and the behaviour of the local officials when faced with confusing or contradictory reports arriving from Paris.[76]

As regards the first two of these variables in Châlons, we are unfortunately ignorant. Over the first decade of civil war, Châlons remained relatively tranquil and the mass of the urban population displayed little anti-Protestant sentiment. This, as Benedict says, was a function of the city's experience. Although we cannot say with certainty how many Huguenots lived in Châlons, clearly there were not very many. In addition, Châlons had never been the object of a Protestant coup, attempted or successful, as had many cities which did experience massacres in 1572, such as Rouen, Lyon, Orléans, and Troyes. Thus there was no vicious cycle of suspicion and hostility.

As to the Châlonnais Huguenots' ability to defend themselves, they were clearly in the minority and unlikely to have chosen a course of physical resistance. Rather, as our anonymous source tells us, they preferred to flee rather than stay and take their chances. The archives of Strasbourg reveal no Châlonnais refugees arriving the summer or autumn of 1572. Strasbourg no longer accepted any but the most notable refugees;[77] furthermore, because of Champagne's proximity to Paris, the news of the massacre must have arrived quickly, allowing little time for premeditated flight such as had occurred in 1562 and 1568. And, as our anonymous

---

[76]Philip Benedict, "The Saint Bartholomew's Massacres in the Provinces," *The Historical Journal* 21, no. 2 (1978), 223, 224.

[77]Zuber, "Les Champenois réfugiés," 40.

Strasbourgeois source tells us, "the routes into Germany are very insecure, because of the disorderly bands uniting everywhere and, without the passport of the duc d'Aumale it would not have been possible to pass through because one was frequently obliged to verify oneself."[78]

Although we have no concrete evidence of the behavior of local officials faced with news of the Parisian massacre and contradictory and confusing royal orders, some speculation is possible. Based on their conduct and actions over the previous decade, one must conclude that the powers in Châlons, notably in the council, interpreted the events and royal orders in a way that most suited their own attitudes and preconceptions. They may have behaved like Jean Harouys, the mayor of Nantes, who, upon receiving a letter from the duc de Montpensier commanding a massacre, ignored it and a week later read to an assembly of the city both it and a royal letter ordering him to maintain calm.[79] Alternatively , there was in Châlons no arch-Catholic royal captain or lieutenant governor to put his interpretation on royal wishes in defiance of municipal policy. Such incidents did occur in Angers and Saumur, where the lieutenant-général Monsoreau initiated massacres immediately upon instruction from Puyguillard, the provincial governor.[80]

Châlons' experience in the massacres of 1572 may be seen as lying between the extremes represented by the other major towns of Champagne, Troyes, and Reims. From the outset, Troyes had had a larger and more militant Protestant movement than Châlons. There had been incidents of iconoclasm and confessional violence throughout the 1550s and 1560s. In April of 1562, Troyen Huguenots attempted to seize control of the city. Troyes, therefore, had suffered Huguenot activism and Catholic resentment, which Châlons had not.

When we turn to the events of 1572, we see several other of Benedict's criteria for a massacre. Upon the outbreak of the massacre in Paris, a deputy of the city council of Troyes, Pierre Belin, was in Paris on town business. From the beginning, Belin had been one of the staunchest of

[78]*BSHPF,* 22:380: "les routes d'Allemagne sont très peu sûres, à cause de bandes désordonnées qui se réunissent partout et, sans le passeport du duc d'Aumale il n'aurait jamais réussi à passer car il a été plusieurs fois obligé de se légitimer."

[79]Benedict, *St. Bartholomew's Massacres,* 217.

[80]Benedict, *St. Bartholomew's Massacres,* 216.

Catholics and Guisards among the Troyen notables. He wrote to the mayor, Pierre Nevelet, informing him of the Parisian massacre. On August 27, after having consulted with Guise, he again wrote to Nevelet of the king's intention to exterminate the Protestants and concluded his letter saying "I believe that you have received letters to carry out the execution of his will." The bailli proceeded to imprison over thirty Huguenots who were subsequently murdered with the complicity of a recently returned Belin. Thus, the first news of the massacre to reach Troyes came from the arch-Guisard Belin and came to officials who were willing to carry out what they believed to be the king's wishes, despite subsequent letters to the contrary.[81]

The other major Champenois city, Reims, bears a superficial resemblance to Châlons.[82] The site of French coronations since Clovis, Reims had remained entirely peaceful throughout the first decade of civil war. Unlike Châlons, however, this seems to be because there were very few Protestants in Reims. This in turn is probably a result of the overpowering influence of the Guises. The duc de Guise's brother Charles, cardinal de Lorraine, was archbishop of Reims and kept a close watch on the events there. The Rémois seem to have shared a very strong attachment to the religion that provided the city with its ceremonial and symbolic raison d'être. In 1572, only two men perished.[83] Thus, while Reims does bear a superficial resemblance to Châlons, its reputation arose for entirely different reasons. The Reformation in Reims was so insignificant as to constitute no threat at all, and its adherents so few as to be hardly worth exterminating.[84]

The war precipitated by the St. Bartholomew's Day Massacre was centered largely on the siege of La Rochelle and ended in June 1573, although hostilities did continue in the south. Champagne and Châlons remained relatively untroubled during this war, the only threat occurring when a

---

[81]For Troyes, see Galpern, 112–17, 126–31, 152–57, 163–72, 177–78; Benedict, *St. Bartholomew's Massacre*, 216–17, 219; Poinsignon, *Histoire générale*, 2:139, 221–23.

[82]For Reims, see Galpern, 136–37, 167; Edouard Henry, *La Réforme et la Ligue en Champagne et à Reims* (St. Nicolas, 1867), 13–33.

[83]Poinsignon, *Histoire générale*, 2:223.

[84]Benedict, *St. Bartholomew's Massacre*, 224. For similar cases where the identity of a city was closely linked to Catholic orthodoxy, see Diefendorf, *Beneath the Cross*, 48, and Mack Holt, "Wine, Community and Reformation in Sixteenth-Century Burgundy," *Past and Present* 138 (1993): 58–93, esp. 72.

force of reiters invaded Bassigny in April. As it turned out, the Germans were defeated at Choiseul in May without threatening Châlons.[85]

Civil war began anew in early 1574 with Condé's escape from court and the machinations of the duc d'Alençon, the king's younger brother. Although not in a major theater of the war, Châlons once again was hard pressed by demands for money and the passage of German mercenaries employed by both the crown and the Huguenots and the armies sent to prevent the Germans' entry into France.

The war was formally concluded by the Peace of Beaulieu, or of Monsieur (after Alençon), on May 6, 1576. This was by far the most generous peace given the Huguenots thus far. Protestant worship was allowed throughout France except in Paris and wherever the royal court happened to be at the time. The king disavowed the St. Bartholomew's Day Massacre, and its victims were rehabilitated. The Huguenots received eight secure towns and were permitted to hold royal offices once again. Condé regained the governorship of Picardy, Navarre received Guyenne, and Alençon added to his holdings the appanages of Anjou, Touraine, and Berry.[86]

As in the previous wars, the peace was harder on Châlons than the war had been. John Casimir of the Palatinate refused to withdraw his reiters, who had been in the employ of Condé, until he received all the back payment due him, four months' wages for his soldiers, and a war indemnity, the sum of which came to 3,600,000 livres.[87] These reiters pillaged their way through southern Champagne and the Seine valley throughout May and June.[88] Meanwhile, the king's reiters followed the Marne through Meaux and arrived in the vicinity of Châlons towards the end of May.[89]

The council was fully informed of their imminent arrival and on May 21 asked Guise to distance them from the city. The duke replied:

Messieurs,
I have done everything possible regarding the fact of which you wrote me concerning the reiters, and know of no other resolution from the king,

[85]Poinsignon, *Histoire générale*, 2:225–26; Hérelle, *La Réforme*, 1:74–75.

[86]Thompson, *Wars of Religion*, 516–17; Mariéjol, *La Réforme et la Ligue*, 171–72; Poinsignon, *Histoire générale*, 2:243–44.

[87]Thompson, *Wars of Religion*, 521; Mariéjol, *La Réforme et la Ligue*, 171–72.

[88]Poinsignon, *Histoire générale*, 2:244–46.

[89]Poinsignon, *Histoire générale*, 2:246.

other than that he has sent men to administer their provisions and to distance them from you. I am very sorry not to have been able to do more for the relief of the poor people, but the necessity is so great that it is impossible to satisfy everyone. Believe that I will do everything I can, desiring nothing else than to see them out of this kingdom.[90]

In a subsequent letter Guise discharged Châlons from supplying the reiters, but the council was clearly worried about more than their storehouses.[91] One of the administrators of whom Guise wrote was the sieur de Mondreville, who then became the object of the council's remonstrances. He wrote to the council on June 3:

> Messieurs and good friends,
> You have every occasion to complain of the pillaging of the reiters. For my part, I am so tired of seeing subjects of the king molested and treated as the prey of foreigners that I would like to withdraw rather than remain any longer a spectator of such miseries. But for you to complain about me and the promise I made to you, you could not be more wrong. For I did not promise to prevent them entirely from roaming, only to withdraw them four or five leagues from your city, in order that they would not cut your grain ... which I have done.[92]

And again on June 15:

> I beg you to believe that ... I have forgotten nothing of what I thought I was able to do to help dislodge the three cornettes of reiters. But seeing that they are continually temporizing, thinking that they will receive

---

[90]AD Marne, E suppt. 4787, fols. 91, 92: "Messieurs, j'ay faict tout ce qui m'a esté possible pour le faict dont m'avez escript touchant les reistres et n'en ay sceu encore aultre résolucion du Roy, sinon qu'il a envoyé gens pour leur faire administrer vivres et les esloigner de voz quartiers. Je suis bien marry de ne pouvoir en cela mieulx faire pour le soulagement du pauvre peuple, mais la nécessité est si grande partout qu'il est impossible de pouvoir contenter chacun. Croyez que je m'y employeray en tout ce que je pourray, ne désirant rien tant que les veoir hors de ce royaume."

[91]AD Marne, E suppt. 4787, fol. 96; Hérelle, La Réforme, 1:93–94.

[92]Hérelle, La Réforme, 1:91–92: "Messieurs et bien bons amys, vous avez toutes les occasions de vous plaindre des pilleries ordinaires que font les reistres; de ma part, je suis sy ennuyé de veoir molester les subjectz du Roy et traicter comme s'ilz estoient donnez en proye aus estrangiers, que j'ayme myeulx me retirer que demeurer plus longtemps spectateur de telles misères. Mais de vous plaindre de moy et de la promesse que je vous ay faicte, vous auriez tous les tors du monde. Car je ne vous ay pas promis de les empescher de courir absolument, ains, sans plus, de les retirer à quatre ou cinq lieues de vostre ville, affin qu'ilz ne coupassent vos bleds ... ce que j'ay faict...."

money from the king, I believe that this is the cause of their longer stay near Châlons, to my very great regret, and not less to yours, I reckon.[93]

On July 11, the council was warned that eight cornettes of reiters were moving closer to Châlons. The council concluded to ask the king and Guise to remove them and to write to the colonels of the reiters and ask them

> to return to the poor people the animals seized today by their troops, being almost all the animals of the villages around this city. And to have them understand the despair of the poor people and that there is no longer any means of checking it, and that if some of them [the reiters] are attacked ... it will be to the regret of those of this city, who wish to accommodate the said colonels and governors of the said troops to the best of their ability."[94]

Apparently their reply was unsatisfactory, for on July 14 the council wrote again:

> The colonels are to be asked to distance their troops from this city in order that the pauvre peuple be able to harvest their crops, the time for which passes from day to day, and that if they do not withdraw, the despairing people of this country may be forced by their despair to assemble themselves and do something worse than has heretofore happened.[95]

Tensions continued to mount as more letters and remonstrances were fired back and forth and as the council increased security measures within

[93]Hérelle, *La Réforme,*1:94–95:"je vous prye croire que ... je n'oubliay rien de ce que je pensois pouvoir ayder à faire desloger les trois cornettes de reistres. Mais voyant que continuellement ilz temporisoient, pensant recepvoir l'argent que le Roy leur a envoyé à Chaallons, j'ay pensé que cela seroit encores cause de les faire sesjourner dadvantaige près dud. Chaallons, à mon tresgrand regret néantmoins, et au vostre, comme j'estime."

[94]AD Marne, E suppt. 4787, fol. 100: "de faire rendre au povre peuple les bestes qui ont esté enlevées par ceux de leurs trouppes, qui est quasi ce qui est de touttes bettes ès villages de l'environ de ladite ville. Et si leur fera l'on entendre le désespoir où est le povre people qu'il n'y a plus de moyen de le retenir, et que s'il s'advenoit que aulcuns des leurs en faisant courses ou aultrement fussent attacquez, ce seroit au regret de ceux de ladite ville qui désireroient accommoder lesdits collonelz et gouverneurs desdites troupes de tous biens s'ilz en avoient le moyen."

[95]AD Marne, E suppt. 4787, fol. 102: "Et seront lesdits srs. collonelz pryez d'esloigner leurs trouppes de ladite ville affin que le povre peuple ayt le moyen de faire les moissons, la sayson desquelles se passe de jour à aultre, et que s'ilz n'eslongnent ladite ville, le peuple dudit pays qui jà est comme désespoir pourroit estre contraint par désespoir s'assembler et faire chose pire que celle qui jà est advenue."

the city. On July 18, the council received a letter from the council of Reims warning of the approach of soldiers from that direction.[96] On the twenty-second, a delegation, which included Bishop Clausse, was sent to court to ask the king to remove the reiters.[97] On August 7, Clausse reported on his visit to court and the council was told that the reiters were virtually out of control and that they would not obey the orders of Guise or of Schomberg, their commander. As a last resort, the council decided on a personal appeal to Guise through Fleurant de Pigaille, *sergent à cheval* at the Chatelet, "given his acquaintance and easy access to the house of Monseigneur de Guise."[98] Finally, on August 9, the storm broke. The immediate occasion was an interview between Ambloff, the reiters' colonel and Schomberg's brother, and a peasant who had come to seek redress for his father's murder and who was accompanied by a delegation from the city. Ambloff received the delegation and counseled the aggrieved peasant to be patient, observing that "in wartime one cannot demand or have recourse to justice." Upon hearing this, the peasant pulled out his dagger and stabbed Ambloff, saying, "Here's war for you, since justice has no place." A skirmish followed, in which thirty soldiers were killed.[99]

The council recognized the gravity of these events and immediately took steps to control the fallout. The next day, August 10, the council appointed a commission of six councillors to draw up a report of the events of August 9 to be presented to the duc de Guise. The purpose of this report was to "excuse the city regarding the tumultuous events against the will of the community of the inhabitants."[100] The council's concern over how these events would appear at court was apparently quite justified, for on August 17 they received a letter from the king ordering his officers to punish the "principaulx coulpables."[101] It is clear from the context of the letter that the king held the town, and not the reiters, responsible. The king wrote again on August 16 (the letter was read at the council meeting

[96]AD Marne, E suppt. 4787, fol. 102.   [97]AD Marne, E suppt. 4787, fol. 104.

[98]AD Marne, E suppt. 4787, fol. 105: "attendu la connaissance et entrée qu'il a en la maison de monseigneur de Guise."

[99]"En temps de guerre, il ne faut réclamer ni avoir recours à la justice.… Voilà donc la guerre, puisque la justice n'a point lieu"; see Haton, *Mémoires contenant,* 2:860; Poinsignon, *Histoire générale,* 2:246–48.

[100]AD Marne, E suppt. 4787, fol. 106: "pour excuser lad. ville touchant led. faict advenu tumultuairement contre le gré de la communauté desd. habitans."

[101]AD Marne, E suppt. 4787, fols. 107–108; Hérelle, *La Réforme,* 1: 99–100.

on August 23) ordering the council not to allow any of those suspected of participating in the violence to leave town.[102] On the twenty-fifth, the council was informed by the duc de Guise that the reiters were finally leaving, but also that the king was sending a lieutenant of the *prévost de l'hôtel* to render justice in the affair of August 9.[103] Guise interceded on behalf of the Châlonnais in a letter to "Monsieur de Toutevaye, lieutenant de Monsieur le Grand Prévost de l'hostel du Roy":

> Monsieur le Lieutenant,
> I believe you have now finished the investigation into the events at Châlons touching Mondreville. And, assuring me that he will charge no one of the said city, I pray you, inasmuch as they are good subjects of the king, to treat them so graciously that they will continue in their accustomed fidelity and obedience. You know how important this place is, one of the principal ones in Champagne; I will not say anything more to you about it.... Monsieur le Lieutenant, they are the king's good subjects. I recommend them to you.[104]

We have no certain knowledge of the outcome of this matter. There is no record of any punishment, and the affair seems to have faded away on its own with the departure of the reiters. Its significance lies in its demonstration of Châlonnais communal solidarity against a clear threat. The council as a whole was determined to put the best face on events. Religion did not enter into it at all. These were the primarily Catholic subjects of a royally held town clashing with soldiers in the employ of their own Catholic king. What mattered to the councillors was not their religion, but their conduct and the threat they presented.

The city councillors of Châlons-sur-Marne had pursued remarkably persistent policies from the outbreak of the religious wars. Often in the face of powerful outsiders such as Bussy and d'Aumale and to the best of their ability, within the structures of power in which they operated, they

---

[102]AD Marne, E suppt. 4787, fols. 108–109; Hérelle, *La Réforme*, 1:100–101.

[103]AD Marne, E suppt. 4787, fol. 109; Hérelle, *La Réforme*, 1:101–102.

[104]Hérelle, *La Réforme*, 1:103–4: "Monsieur le Lieutenant, je croy que maintenant aurez achevé le procédure pour le faict advenu à Chaallons touchant Mondreville. Et m'asseurant qu'il ne s'en trouve chargez aucuns de lad. ville, je vous prie, d'aultant qu'ils sont fort bons subjectz du Roy, les voulloir traicter si gracieusement que cela leur donne occasion de continuer en leur fidélité et obéissance acoustumée. Vous sçavez de quelle importance est ceste place, l'une des principalles de Champaigne; qui me gardera vous en dire davantaige.... Monsieur le Lieutenant, ilz son bons subgectz au Roy. Je les vous recommande."

managed to maintain the integrity of their council, protect, as far as possible, their Huguenot fellow-inhabitants, and pursue the policies that were, in their minds, in the best interests of the city. From 1576 onward, however, the situation facing the city council was further complicated by the formation of successive Catholic Leagues whose goals often deviated from royal wishes and the agenda of the city council. Moreover, the chief of these leagues was the duc de Guise himself, governor of the province of Champagne, who was in a position to exert great pressure on the city council of Châlons to subscribe to the Leagues' goals. How would the council respond to this division of loyalties and this challenge to both its integrity and autonomy, and that of the city as a whole?

Chapter 6

The Community Subdued, 1576–1588

ROM 1576 ON, the national political picture was complicated by the growth of a Catholic party that defined itself largely in opposition to royal policy. First manifested in 1576, in protest against the Peace of Monsieur, this Catholic League became a serious rival to royal authority only after 1584, when the death of Henry III's younger brother, the duc d'Anjou (formerly d'Alençon), made the Protestant Henry of Navarre the heir presumptive. The Catholic League was orchestrated by members of the Guise family. At first it was led by the brothers Henri, duc de Guise, and Louis, cardinal de Guise. Following their deaths on the king's orders in 1588, the leadership was taken over by their brother, the duc de Mayenne, and their cousin, Charles III, head of the senior branch of the Guise family and ruler of the independent duchy of Lorraine.

Henry III's attitude towards the Catholic League fluctuated between accommodation, capitulation, and repression, according to the parties' relative strength and the political exigencies of the moment. Henry alternated between outlawing all political associations, such as the League, and capitulating to the League's demands as a tactical maneuver. Biding his time, he waited for a propitious moment to escape the tutelage of the Guises and the League.

From 1576 on, and especially after 1585, national politics became increasingly fractious. It was not a case any longer of a Catholic king versus his Protestant subjects. Rather, there were now three major parties involved: the Catholic League, the Huguenots under their leader Henry of Navarre, and royalist Catholics, caught between the Scylla and Charybdis of the religious parties. French Catholics were put to the ultimate test of being forced to choose between their king and their religion. In the process, France drifted perilously close to the precipice of anarchy and dissolution. It now remains to be seen how the city council of royalist and Catholic Châlons responded to these problems.

The Peace of Monsieur of 1576 and its generous treatment of the Huguenots and their commanders provoked a harsh reaction among many Catholics, resulting ultimately in the foundation of the Catholic League. This League, under the leadership of the duc de Guise, was designed to secure the preservation of the Catholic Church and the extirpation of heresy. Although there had been local leagues of both Huguenots and Catholics as early as 1563, this was the first effort at organizing a Catholic League on a national scale. The occasion for this League first arose in Picardy in 1576. Condé had been restored to the governorship of Picardy by the Edict of Beaulieu. D'Humières, governor of the town of Péronne, refused to turn the town over to Condé, forming an association to prevent Condé from taking possession of the province, and taking his appeal to a national audience:

> It is long since time to prevent and divert the heretics' scheming and conspiracies by a holy and Christian League, a complete understanding and cooperation of all good, loyal, and faithful subjects of the king, which is today the true and only way that God has put into our hands to restore holy service and obedience to His Majesty.[1]

Guise seized the opportunity presented by this discontent to publish a manifesto for a national Catholic League of princes, seigneurs, and Catholic *gentilshommes* "to establish the whole law of God, to restore and retain the holy service of this law according to the form and manner of the Holy Catholic, Apostolic, and Roman Church." The associates swore "complete and prompt obedience and service to him who shall be chosen chief."[2] The name of this "chief" was not divulged; there could be little doubt, however, that it was to be Henri of Guise.

---

[1]Jean Mariéjol, *La Réforme et la Ligue* (Paris: Hachette, 1904), 174: "Il est désormais plus que longtemps d'empescher et détourner leurs finesses et conspirations par une sainte et chrétienne union, parfaite intelligence et correspondance de tous les fidèles loyaux et bons sujets du roi, qui est aujourd'hui le vrai et seul moyen que Dieu nous a réservé entre nos mains pour restaurer son saint service et obéissance de sa Majesté."

[2]Mariéjol, *La Réforme,* 175–76: "d'establir la loy de Dieu en son entier, remettre et retenir le sainct service d'iceluy selon la forme et manière de la saincte Eglise catholique, apostolique et romaine.... toute prompte obeyssance et service au chef qui sera député."

King Henry III sought to defuse this challenge to royal authority by calling a meeting of the Estates General at Blois in November 1576. The king hoped that the Estates would deal primarily with matters of administrative and fiscal reform. However, Huguenot deputies boycotted the assembly, so it was almost completely dominated by the League. Henry allowed himself to be persuaded to renew the war against heresy. However, the Estates refused to grant him the funds necessary for this undertaking; thus by the end of the assembly, in February 1577, Henry III was committed to renew civil war but without the fiscal ability to pursue it. At the same time, the king sought to co-opt the League in his interests by having himself declared chief in place of Guise. He wrote to the provincial governors ordering them to encourage their local leagues and succeeded in having the League's oath modified to contain a stronger acknowledgment of royal authority.[3]

The six-month-long war provoked by the declarations of the king and the Estates was conducted primarily in the south and west and is unremarkable for any great campaigns. The war was ended in September 1577 with the Peace of Bergerac, later confirmed by the Edict of Poitiers. The peace settlement reduced somewhat the privileges gained by the Huguenots the previous year, restricting Protestant worship to the towns they actually held and to one additional town per bailliage. From the king's point of view, however, the most important aspect of the peace was that it outlawed all political associations, including especially the Catholic League.[4]

It is against this background of confusion and impending dissolution that events in Châlons must be viewed. Furthermore, the governor of Champagne was none other than Guise himself, and in the events of August 1576 the duke had both secured the withdrawal of the reiters and sought to moderate royal displeasure against the town. In this context it is not surprising that the Châlons city council would want to fall in line with Guise's wishes. On September 20, 1576, the council asked Barbezieulx, the

---

[3] J. H. M. Salmon, *Society in Crisis: France in the Sixteenth Century* (London: St. Martins, 1975), 202. For the modified oath, see Claude Haton, *Mémoires contenant le récit des événements accomplis de 1553, à 1583 principalement dans la Champagne et la Brie*, 2 vols., ed. F. Bourquelot (Paris: Documents inédits sur l'histoire de France, 1857), 2:1154.

[4] Salmon, *Society in Crisis*, 203.

lieutenant-général of Champagne, to prohibit Protestant worship in Châlons until, or unless, the king ordered otherwise.[5] Barbezieulx agreed to turn the request over to the king, apparently also referring the request to Guise. On September 28, the duc de Guise wrote to the council:

> And as for the Huguenot preachings taking place in your town ... I cannot tell you any thing else, except that you well know that you must permit and endure them, without a command to the contrary from the king or myself, to whom you have addressed nothing up to now.[6]

This statement, while certainly conforming to the letter of the Edict of Beaulieu, clearly implies that the council had only to address the king directly to obtain the prohibition of Huguenot worship, and even if the king should not grant it, Guise himself may.

To this end, the council orchestrated two petitions to be sent to the king, one in the name of the four seigneurs of Châlons and the other in the name of the inhabitants. Since these documents penetrate to the heart of religious attitudes within Châlons, it is worthwhile to examine them in some detail. In fact, they are less unequivocal than might appear at first glance.

The petition of the seigneurs, namely "Cosme Clausse, bishop/count of Châlons and commendatory abbot of St. Pierre-aux-Monts of the said Châlons, Louis de Clèves, abbot of Toussaints en l'Isle; ... and the dean, canons, and chapter of the church of the said Châlons," presented the request to outlaw Protestant worship in legal and practical—rather than religious—terms:

> without their [the seigneurs'] permission and authority, nothing may be attempted or innovated by anyone of any estate whatsoever to establish here a new form of police, even to exercise or spread new doctrine publicly or privately to the prejudice of their rights and those of the republic of Châlons; nevertheless ... some private individuals, foreign and native, have introduced into this city an unknown man and have had him preach and sow this new doctrine in a certain private house, ... in the temporal ban and seigneurie of our lord bishop, without the leave and

---

[5]AD Marne E Suppt. 4787, fol. 110.

[6]Georges Hérelle, ed., *La Réforme et la Ligue en Champagne*, vol. 1, *Lettres*; vol. 2, *Pièces diverses* (Paris, 1888-92), 1:102–3: "Et quant aux presches dont me parlez, qui se font en lad. ville, je ne puis vous en dire autre chose, sinon que vous sçavez bien si vous les debviez permectre et endurer sans commandement du Roy ou de moy, à qui vous n'en avez jamais rien mandé jusques à maintenant."

permission of the petitioners, and without presenting this man for examination, not knowing what is his doctrine and manner of living.... Also, inasmuch as by your edict of pacification [Edict of Beaulieu] of the troubles of this kingdom, the permission of the seigneurs of the places in which one wishes to establish the exercise of the so-called new religion is required.... may it please Your Majesty to prohibit the exercise of the so-called new religion.[7]

Thus the requested prohibition is a matter of feudal rights and public order rather than one of religious persecution.

The petition in the name of the inhabitants of Châlons, signed by the greffier of the council, requests the same thing, but in even more equivocal language and for somewhat different reasons:

Sire: Your very humble and obedient subjects ... remonstrate ... that, under the shadow of your last edict of pacification some private individuals in the said Châlons, in number about thirty, people of low condition, and who had a short time previously abjured the so-called reformed religion, have endeavored since then to establish worship within this city ... and have incited many like-minded, many of whom have never been inhabitants and many others who have voluntarily been absent for a long time and declared their residence in other places, and have not been taxed as residents of Châlons ... and who brag of bringing here ... many from the cities of Sedan, Jametz, and other places; from which one may easily foresee that if this worship continues in this city of Châlons, one of the principal keys and fortresses of your Kingdom,... the city will in a short time be filled with foreigners, sectarians of the so-called religion, a real means (under pretext of the said worship and

[7]Hérelle, *La Réforme*, 1:104–6. "sans leur permission et authorité ne doibt estre aucune chose attentée ou innovée par aucunes personnes de quelqu'estat que ce soit pour y establir une nouvelle forme de vivre en la police, mesmes y exercer et semer nouvelle doctrine publicquement ou en particulier, au prejudice de leurs droictz et de la republique dudict Chaalons; ce néantmoins sont advertys que depuis quelques jours en ça aucuns particuliers, tant dudict Chaalons que forains, ont introduict en ladicte ville ung homme incogneu, et veullent le faire prescher et semer nouvelle doctrine en quelque maison particulière dudict Chaalons, au ban temporel et seigneurie dudict Sr Evesque, sans avoir pris ne demandé le congé et permission desdictz supplians, et sans avoir présenté ledict homme à l'examen, ne congnoistre quelle est sa doctrine et manière de vivre.... Aussy, d'autant que par vostre eedict de la pacification des troubles advenuz en ce royaume et requis le consentement des seigneurs propriétaires de lieux esquelz on veult establir l'exercice de la nouvelle religion prétendue.... Ce considiré, Sire, et afin d'obvier à plusieurs aultres inconvéniens qui de ce en peuvent ensuyvir, vous plaise faire défensce ausdictz particuliers, à leurdict homme et tous aultres qu'il appartiendra, de ne prescher ne faire prescher en ladicte ville de Chaalons, et de n'y faire aucun exercice de ladicte nouvelle prétendue religion."

assemblies) for plotting secretly some sinister enterprise against this city, and likewise for surprising it in an instant at the first sign of a renewal of trouble.... May it please Your Majesty to interdict and forbid to all within this city of Châlons the public exercise of the said religion, or at least to provide for the eminent peril to your city by assigning the said worship for those of the said religion living here ... to another place. ...[8]

This petition, like the first, presents the request as a matter of public safety and convenience. Significantly, the council clearly distinguished between native and foreign Huguenots; clearly, the danger came from the latter, but the only way to obviate it was to deal with the former. Although the council would like to see this, it was most important that Protestant worship not occur within city walls; hence the provision for worship outside the city. Again, what seems to have concerned the council was not so much their own Huguenots (many of whom had given up their rights by abjuring or leaving the city), but the possibility of imported troublemakers from "Sedan, Jametz, and other places." And since there were few native Huguenots, and those were of "low condition," the easiest solution seemed to be to abolish Protestant worship altogether.

Taken in isolation, these documents might seem to indicate Catholic militancy. Upon closer examination of their contents and context, however, we see that this is not necessarily the case. These documents fall short of requesting persecution of Huguenots as heretics. Furthermore, the

---

[8]Hérelle, *La Réforme*, 1:106–8: "Sire, Voz treshumbles et obéissans subjetcz ... vous remonstrent ... que, soubz umbre de vostre eedict dernier de pacification, aucuns particulliers dudict Chaalons, au nombre de trente ou environ, gens de basse condicion et lesquelz auroint peu auparavant abjuré la relligion prétendue refformée, auroient entrepris puis naguères de dresser ung presche au dedans de ladicte ville et, pour favoriser leur entreprise, suscyté plusieurs leurs semblables, aucuns desquelz n'ont oncques esté tenuz pour habitans, et les aultres s'en seroient dès longtemps auparavant retirez voluntairment et faict déclaration de leurs habitations en aultres lieux; à l'occasion de quoy n'auroient esté imposez audict Chaalons aux tailles, emprunctz et contributions que lesdictz supplians y ont supporté ... et lesquelz particulliers se vantent d'y faire venir et introduire plusieurs qui sont ès villes de Sedain, Jamectz et aultre lieux; en quoy l'on peult aysément préveoir que, ledict presche se continuant en ladicte ville de Chaalons, laquelle, pour estre sur la frontière de Champaigne, l'une de principales clefz et forteresses de Vostre Royaume,... sera en bref temps remplye d'estrangers, sectateurs de ladicte prétendue religion, vray moyen pour, soubz prétexte desdictes presches et assemblées, faire et machiner secrètement quelque sinistre entreprise sur icelle ville, et mesmement pour la surprendre en ung instant au premier bouillon d'ung renouvellement de troubles.... Plaise à Vostre Majesté interdire et deffendre du tout audedans de ladicte ville de Chaalons l'exercice publicq de ladicte religion, ou bien pourveoir au péril éminant de vostre ville par assignation dudict presche pour ceulx de ladicte religion y demeurans comme dessus en autre lieu ou par aultre moyen expédient que Vostredicte Majesté sçaura mieulx adviser."

conditions under which the requests were made lead one to question just how representative they are of the council's attitude towards the city's Huguenots. Guise was still the governor of Champagne, and it was Guise who had intervened on the town's behalf in the aftermath of the clash with the reiters. It is therefore not surprising that the councillors would attempt to placate their governor by requesting what they knew to be his wishes. This is not to say that the seigneurs and councillors were indulging in a cynical attempt to curry favor with Guise. No doubt they sincerely wished Châlons to be a totally Catholic city. They nevertheless avoided requesting prohibition of Protestant worship on religious grounds, but confined their petitions to matters of feudal rights and public security. In addition, in their petition, the councillors built in a "fall back" position: In the event that Protestant worship was not outlawed altogether, that it should at least be conducted outside the city's walls. These petitions are illustrative of an ambiguous attitude towards Châlonnais Huguenots; on the one hand, the Catholic councillors clearly preferred a completely Catholic city; on the other, they were reluctant to persecute their fellow inhabitants on purely religious grounds. In any event, these petitions proved fruitless.[9]

Between 1576 and 1588, Châlons-sur-Marne increasingly came under the domination of the duc de Guise as part of his plans to consolidate his power base in eastern France. Between 1576 and 1585, he sought to dominate Châlons first through the city's adherence to the League, and then through appointing his clients to positions of power within the city. From 1585, when the Treaty of Nemours granted him the city as *place de sûreté*, until his death in 1588, Châlons was under virtual military occupation by Guise.

Like other cities of Champagne, Châlons was extremely hesitant to swear to the articles of the Leaguer oath. In Provins, where the three estates assembled separately to consider the matter, each estate waited for one of the others to take the lead, with the result that the articles were never ratified. The baron de Rosne, charged with securing the city's

[9]Hérelle, *La Réforme*, 1:108–9: In a decree dated November 2, the king ,"désirant que son eedit de pacifffication soit observé,… a ordonné que ceulx de la religion prétendue réformée qui seront habitans et demourans actuellement dedans ladicte ville de Chaalons y auront exercice de leurdicte religion pour eux seulement, et pour les forains qui y passeront, lors de leurdicte passaige aussy seulement … avec les conditions portées par ledict eedict de pacification, auquel Sa Majesté ne veult permectre qu'il soit rien innovée."

allegiance to the League, informed the estates, falsely, that Sézanne and Meaux had already subscribed. The delegates of the estates of Provins told de Rosne that the League seemed to be "something new, something never employed in France, nor ever heard of." Furthermore, they were waiting to hear what their deputies at the estates in Blois thought of the proposed League.[10] Troyes, solicited by Barbezieulx, proved equally hesitant, sending envoys to Reims, Châlons, and Sens to find out what those cities had done. Even the presence of Guise himself could not secure the council's subscription. Reims, like Troyes, refused to sign the articles without first knowing that other cities had already done so.[11]

Châlons was similarly solicited to sign the articles by Barbezieulx, lieutenant-général of Champagne. In a letter written at Troyes on February 9, 1577, and discussed in the council meeting of February 21, Barbezieulx requested the council to send two or three deputies to Troyes, "with the express power to deliver the adherence of the three estates ... to the association as is required and necessary."[12] The council responded by ordering each cinquantenier to elect two or three men to consider the matter at a special general assembly, to be held on February 28. On the appointed day, however, there were not enough present to deliberate and the meeting was postponed until March 5, and then again until March 10. On this date, the deputies of the cinquanteniers reported that many "refused outright to sign the articles, and that they themselves would not do so unless the council signed first."[13] Since nobody took the initiative, the League in Châlons was stillborn, as it was in most of the towns of the province, indeed in all of France. In Champagne, only Sens and Chaumont adhered to the League. In short, according to the duc de Nevers, the League in Champagne "was half-assed" ("n'alla qu'à une fesse"),[14] and according to Claude Haton, "nobody wanted to partake of it" ("personne n'en voulut manger").[15]

---

[10]Haton, *Mémoires contenant*, 2:886–87: "laditte ligue estoit une chose novelle, de laquelle on n'avoit jamais usé en France ni ouy parler. ...."

[11]Maurice Poinsignon, *Histoire générale de la Champagne et de Brie*, 3 vols. (Paris, 1885, 1898; rpt. Paris: Guenégaud, 1974), 2:257.

[12]"ayans pouvoir espécial de délivrer la tuition desd. trois estats ... de lad. association comme il sera requis et nécessaire"; see Hérelle, *La Réforme*, 1:110–12; AD Marne E suppt. 4787, fols. 124, 127.

[13]AD Marne E Suppt. fols. 124–28.   [14]Quoted in Poinsignon, *Histoire générale*, 2:258.

[15]Haton, *Mémoires contenant*, 2:885.

This hesitancy is subject to several interpretations. It has been seen as a refusal to subscribe to a corrupted League, that is, one headed by the king rather than Guise. In this view, the refusal of the towns to sign is seen as a rebuff toward Henry III.[16] This seems overly subtle and doctrinaire. Why should we not believe the deputies of the estates of Provins when they said simply that in their view the League was a novelty and an unnecessary one at that? Subscribing to the articles of a League of "princes, seigneurs, and Catholic gentilshommes" would have placed the cities under the thumb of the people from whom they had the most to fear. In addition, it seems obvious that by 1577 the state of affairs had not yet progressed (or deteriorated) to the point where such a League could be seen as necessary except by those unalterably opposed to royal policy or to those allied to the House of Guise.

Having been rebuffed in his efforts to have Châlons adhere to the League, Guise then sought to exercise his influence over the town through the town's captain, Hugues de Champagne, seigneur de St. Mard. In 1574, Guise had secured St. Mard's appointment in place of Thierry de l'Hôpital, seigneur du Castel, in a bitter confrontation. Clearly, the councillors preferred Castel, although St. Mard was the son of Guillaume de Champagne, a receveur général des finances, échevin, and long-time city councillor.[17] The council agreed to turn the matter over to the arbitration of Guise, as governor of the province. Guise judged in favor of St. Mard, thus placing one of his dependents in a strategic position. St. Mard and the council frequently found themselves at loggerheads. In the meeting of January 12, 1578, St. Mard presented a commission from Guise ordering the council to turn over to the captain funds earmarked for fortifications.[18] And on January 30, 1579, Guise ordered the council to pay St. Mard two hundred livres over and above his regular yearly salary of one hundred livres. This matter was not resolved until August, when St. Mard presented another

---

[16]Poinsignon, *Histoire générale*, 2:258.

[17]Thierry de l'Hôpital had apparently resigned in favor of his son Jean. When the latter died in Flanders in 1574, Thierry received royal letters confirming his resumption of the post. Guillaume de Champagne, meanwhile, had secured the appointment for his own son Hugues from Guise, the governor of Champagne; see Edouard de Barthélemy, *Histoire de la ville de Châlons-sur-Marne et de ses institutions, des origines à 1848*, 1st ed. (Châlons-sur-Marne, 1854), 287, and AD Marne E suppt. 4787, fols. 8, 11.

[18]AD Marne E Suppt. 4787, fol. 141.

letter from Guise ordering the payment of 66²/3 écus (or two hundred livres), with the proviso that the money was to be used for the city's fortifications.[19]

The contention between the council and the captain extended beyond finances. Clearly, St. Mard believed that he alone was in charge of the defense of the city. In the council session of January 24, 1577, it came to the councillors' attention that St. Mard had drawn up and published guard regulations without consulting them, and delegates were sent to consult with St. Mard.[20] On April 12, 1578, St. Mard complained to the council that the inhabitants were derelict in performing their guard duty.[21]

Guise's influence over Châlons was also exerted through Bishop Cosme Clausse. Clausse took a more active interest in city affairs than his predecessors, and he attended many more council sessions. In September 1578, Clausse presented the council with a commission from Guise for the security of the town. From the council's point of view the most contentious item in this commission was the provision that the keys to the gates be returned to the bishop every night. The council remonstrated to Guise that this was contrary to the customs and practice of the city.[22]

Guise's desire to dominate Châlons is also evident from the constant stream of letters exhorting the council to "faire bonne garde," and by his physical presence in Châlons no less than three times between April 1577 and August 1578, including, in May 1578, a conference between Guise, the duc de Lorraine, and "other princes of the house of Lorraine."[23]

The king sought to counter Guise's growing control of Champagne with appointments of his own. Upon Barbezieulx's resignation as lieutenant-général in late 1579, the king appointed in his place Joachim de Dinteville.[24] Despite the fact that they were working at cross-purposes, the governor Guise and the lieutenant-général Dinteville maintained the polite fiction that they were working together in the king's service. Dinteville, meanwhile, was trying to efface Guise's influence in Champagne and particularly in Châlons. This was to remain roughly the situation until 1585, when the polite fiction ended and Guise imposed a virtual occupation upon Châlons. In the meantime, the councillors of

[19]AD Marne E suppt. 4787, fols. 182, 199.   [20]AD Marne E suppt. 4787, fols. 121–22.
[21]AD Marne E suppt. 4787, fol. 148.   [22]AD Marne E suppt. 4787, fols. 166–68.
[23]AD Marne E suppt. 4787, fols. 130, 152, 165.   [24]AD Marne E suppt. 4787, fol. 221.

Châlons found themselves in the middle of a delicate and undeclared power struggle.

The fact that Champagne was not a major theater of either of the two civil wars in the late 1570s and early 1580s did not mean that the province or Châlons was insulated from the wars' effects. As in the previous wars, Châlons was faced with the passage of soldiers. On August 1, 1578, the council was informed of the arrival of a regiment of infantry at Notre-Dame-L'Epine under the command of their old nemesis Bussy. The councillors responded by sending the procureur and greffier to the commander with a gift of wine and a request to make sure that his soldiers "se comportaient modestement."[25] Later that month, the council instituted far-reaching security measures.[26] The annual St. Martin's assembly had to be postponed because of the presence of soldiers nearby, and in January 1580 St. Mard informed the council that upwards of a thousand cavalry were to be lodged in nearby Fagnières, Compertrix, and St. Gibrien.[27] To this latter news, the council responded by increasing the guard and giving instructions to the gardes des portes not to allow more than twelve or fifteen soldiers inside the town at any one time. In July, Châlons was threatened by the passage of reiters, and the council sent representatives to both the commander and the royal escort, asking them to avoid Châlons.[28] In December, Châlons found itself to be on the route of soldiers returning from Anjou's campaigns in the Netherlands.[29] The nearly constant presence or threat of the presence of soldiers on their way to or from the theaters of war forced the council to maintain the city in a nearly constant state of alert. There were endless exhortations from Dinteville, Guise, and the king to "faire bonne garde."

Internal relations between Châlonnais Huguenots and Catholics were also affected by this constant state of preparedness. The council found itself having to institute regulations clearly against their will. On July 5, 1580, the king wrote to Guise ordering him to have all the cities in his jurisdiction confiscate the arms of the Huguenots. Guise then wrote to the same effect to Dinteville, who sent both letters on to the council.[30] Yet at the end of the month, we find the council ordering proceedings against all

[25]AD Marne E suppt. 4787, fol. 164.   [26]AD Marne E suppt. 4787, fol. 164.
[27]AD Marne E suppt. 4787, fol. 220.   [28]AD Marne E suppt. 4787, fol. 266.
[29]AD Marne E suppt. 4787, fol. 282.   [30]AD Marne E suppt. 4787, fol. 262.

inhabitants—Protestant or Catholic—who refused to do their guard duty. Stranger still, at the same session, the Huguenots asked to have their arms returned to them, to which the council replied that they could not do so until the order confiscating their arms was rescinded or countermanded.[31] Thus, it appears that the council complied with the letter of the order to confiscate Huguenot arms, but at the same time, encouraged and even forced Huguenots to do their share in guarding the city.

Besides the presence of transient soldiers, a continual state of heightened security, and unpalatable orders regarding Châlonnais Protestants, the city faced yet another threat: the infestation of the countryside by brigands and undisciplined soldiers. Claude Haton of Provins provides a vivid description of them: "all exiles, vagabonds, thieves, renouncers of God and old debts, remnants of war, leftovers of the gallows, diseased, dying of hunger, they took without fear to the fields to pillage, beat, and ruin the people of the towns and villages who fell into their hands in the places where they lodged, and by the wayside."[32] Soldiers sent out to suppress the brigands more often than not joined forces with them; and where the authorities did manage to capture the soldiers, the gens de justice were often so intimidated that they let the troublemakers go.[33] These bandits were the subject of an extensive correspondence between Guise and the Châlonnais council over the next several years.[34]

Object lessons in the dangers of this situation abounded. For example, in July 1581, the town of Broyes-lez-Sézanne in Brie closed its gates to the army of the duc d'Anjou on its way to the Netherlands. The commander, monsieur de Tevalle, went to negotiate with the city authorities for lodging or at least for supplies. While negotiating, he was killed by a rifle shot by a barber of the town:

> This death so aroused the spirits of the soldiers that they took the town by force and massacred all the men and women they could find, without sparing anyone save the baroness and her servants, who were imprisoned

[31]AD Marne E suppt. 4787, fol. 267.

[32]Haton, *Mémoires contenant*, 2:937: "tous bannis, vacabons, volleurs, meurtriers, renieurs de Dieu et de vielles debtes, remenans de guerre, reste de gibet, massacreurs, vérollez, gens mourrans de faim, se meirent aux champs, pour aller piller battre et ruyner les hommes des villes et villages qui tomboient en leurs mains ès lieux où ils logeoient et par les chemins, sans crainte aulcune."

[33]Poinsignon, *Histoire générale*, 2:261–62.

[34]Hérelle, *La Réforme*, 1:112–13, 128–30; AD Marne E suppt. 4787, fol. 279.

in the Château of Esternay. The soldiers, not content with having massacred and pillaged the town, set fire to it at the four corners and in the
middle, burning the château, the churches, and houses, of which only
fourteen remained whole. The barber who had fired the shot was thrown
alive into the flames where he ended his days in great agony; and this
done the soldiers abandoned the town and went elsewhere.[35]

During these last two civil wars, religion had become a merely inci-
dental factor in the struggles of national power politics. Guise negotiated
for support from the Calvinist Elector Palatine and enlisted many Huguenots in the army under his command.[36] The king, caught between the fac-
tion of the Guises and the ambitions of his brother in the Netherlands,
looked for support wherever he could find it. However, religion was rein-
fused into the conflict when, on June 10, 1584, the king's younger brother,
the duc d'Anjou, died. Now, the most legitimate heir to the throne was the
Huguenot leader, Henry of Navarre. The prospect of a heretic king threw
all purely political calculations into disarray. Catholics, who were horrified
at the thought of further war, were equally horrified by the specter of a
Protestant monarch. Guise seized the opportunity to revive the moribund
League of 1576. He spent the summer of 1584 consolidating his aristo-
cratic support in Champagne, while his brother Mayenne did the same in
Burgundy, and his cousins Mercoeur, Elbeuf, and Aumale did so in Brit-
tany, Normandy, and Picardy respectively.[37] The League of 1584 was more
effective than its predecessor of 1576. Rather than a set of general and
loosely focused aspirations, it had as its raison d'être a concrete and seemingly attainable goal: the exclusion of the Protestant Navarre from the
succession.

In promoting the League, Guise relied on the assistance of Philip II of
Spain, formalized in the Treaty of Joinville, signed in January 1585. Faced
with this powerful array of forces, the king prevaricated, hoping that some
unforeseen development would eventually rescue royal authority.

---

[35]Haton, *Mémoires contenant*, 2:1065: "Cette mort eschauffa tellement le courage desditz gens de
guerre, qu'ilz par force se rendirent maistres du bourg et y massacrèrent tous hommes et femmes qu'ilz
eurent à la rencontre, sans pardonner à personne qu'à la baronne et sa servante, qui furent menées pri-
sonnières au chasteau d'Esternay. Ilz de guerre, non contens d'avoir massacré et pillé ledit bourg, y
allumèrent le feu ès quatre coings et au milieu, qui brusla le chasteau, les églises et les maisons, dont il
ne resta entières que quatorze. Le barbier qui avoit fait le coup fut par eux tout vif jetté dedans le feu,
où il finit ses jours à grand destresse, et, ce faict, l'abandonnèrent et allèrent aultant avant."
[36]Salmon, *Society in Crisis*, 204–5.   [37]Salmon, *Society in Crisis*, 236.

Catherine, on the other hand, realizing the League's preponderance of force, sought to negotiate, and went in search of the duc de Guise. Guise led the queen mother on a merry chase through Champagne in the spring of 1585, finally stopping at Epernay long enough for Catherine to catch up and engage in preliminary negotiations. What emerged from these negotiations in July was the Treaty of Nemours, or the king's total capitulation to the League. The king agreed to revoke all previous edicts of pacification and toleration and dismiss all Huguenots from high office. In addition, the treaty expelled all Protestant pastors from France in the space of one month and all recalcitrant Huguenots within six months. Further, Guise was given as security for five years the towns of Mezières, St. Dizier, Toul, Verdun, and Châlons-sur-Marne.[38]

The grant of Châlons-sur-Marne to Guise as a security town was in fact little more than recognition of a fait accompli. As we have seen, from 1576 Guise sought to control the town through his position as governor of Champagne, through the alliance of Bishop Clausse, and through the placing of his men, such as St. Mard, in positions of authority within Châlons. Nothing in the intervening years had weakened that hold; if anything, it was stronger in 1584 than in 1580. Meanwhile, Guise and Dinteville had continued their cautious pas de deux, each protesting their loyalty and service to the king while at the same time trying to counter the other's influence. This appearance of cooperation was increasingly impossible to maintain, and matters came to a head in March 1585.

Already on March 8, the king had written to the council of Châlons:

> You have not neglected anything pertaining to the security of our city of Châlons; nevertheless, based on warnings we have received of the ill will of some [i.e. Guise] we wanted to write this word to you to order that if you have hitherto been careful to maintain and conserve the city in peace and tranquillity under our obedience, you must now render yourselves even more careful and guard your city more closely than ever, in order that it may not be surprised to the prejudice of our service and the security of your property and lives.[39]

---

[38]Salmon, *Society in Crisis*, 238 ; Mariéjol, *La Réforme,* 237–38; Poinsignon, *Histoire générale,* 2:280–84; Edouard Henry, *La réforme et la ligue en Champagne et à Reims* (St. Nicolas, 1867), 81.

[39]"vous n'oublierez riens de ce qui pourra appartenir à la seureté de nostre ville de Chaalons, néantmoins, sur quelques advis qui nous sont donnez de la mauvaise volunté que ont aucuns, nous avons biens voullu vous escripre ce mot de lettre pour vous mander que, si vous avez esté cydevant fort

At the same time, the king was writing to Dinteville to warn all the cities of Champagne "that the evil is definitely increasing and that the mask has been virtually cast aside," and that Dinteville was to assure himself of Reims, Troyes, Châlons, Montereau, Langres, and Sens, which were the principal cities and particularly threatened.[40] Dinteville also wrote to the council in Châlons exhorting them "to advise him as continually as possible of the state of the city. Meanwhile, the city was receiving the same instructions from Guise.[41]

Thus the council was buffeted from both sides with letters exhorting the same course of action, but for different purposes: the king and Dinteville for preserving royal authority, and Guise for establishing his military headquarters in Châlons.[42] The council responded by further heightening the town's security. Significantly, the council chose to report their actions to Dinteville rather than to Guise.[43]

The fate of Châlons was effectively sealed by the king's unwillingness or inability to supply Dinteville with sufficient military force for the task at hand. Guise, on the other hand, acted decisively and with force, arriving in Châlons on March 21 with a force of four thousand men because, according to Dinteville, he realized that Châlons would not submit voluntarily.[44]

Meanwhile, the king was still pressing Dinteville to assure himself of Châlons. Leaving Troyes on March 20 with fifteen or sixteen men, Dinteville arrived in Châlons on the twenty-first, at roughly the same time as Guise, but by a different gate. The two met and discussed the situation. Dinteville reported this discussion to the king, indicating that Guise protested that "to his [Guise's] very great regret and displeasure ... for the

---

soigneux à maintenir et conserver lad. ville en repos et tranquilité soubz nostre obéissance, vous vous en rendez maintenant plus soigneux et y prenez garde de plus près que jamais, à ce qu'il n'y puisse estre faict aucune surprise au préjudice de nostre service et seureté de voz biens et vies"; see Hérelle, *La Réforme*, 1:132; AD Marne E suppt. 4788, fol. 76.

[40]"que le mal commence décidément et que le masque est quasi levé." Edouard de Barthélemy, ed., *Correspondance de M. de Dinteville* (Arcis-sur-Aube, 1880), 84–85.

[41]Hérelle, *La Réforme*, 1:133–34; AD Marne E Suppt. 4788, fol. 77.

[42]Salmon, *Society in Crisis*, 238; Henry, *La réforme et la ligue*, 76–77; Edouard de Barthélemy, *Histoire*, 2d ed. (Châlons-sur-Marne, 1883), 290.

[43]AD Marne E suppt. 4788, fol. 77. The keys to the gates and grills were changed, all innkeepers were ordered to report their lodgers to the council, the arms of all newcomers were to be seized at the gates, and no more than twelve people were to be allowed through the gates at any one time.

[44]Barthélemy, *Histoire*, 2d ed., 291, n.1.

preservation of his person, he had been constrained, as the first law of nature teaches everyone, to take the course to which he found himself reduced (which caused him more grief than he has met with under your reign)." The interview was cordial, but Dinteville, in a very inferior position, was forced to withdraw from Châlons the next day, leaving the town to Guise.[45]

The councillors seem not to have been very pleased with this course of events. They had been more or less duped by the captain, Guise's man St. Mard, who had prevailed upon them to welcome Guise when he arrived, thus leaving Dinteville to enter the town unheralded. On March 22, "aulcuns de la ville" went to Dinteville to explain what had happened and to excuse themselves:

> It was not due to their negligence, because following His Majesty's letters and mine [Dinteville's] they guarded the city as well as anyone could desire, which was all the commandment they had received. Moreover, not having received any revocation of the powers of their governor [Guise] they did not dare to comport themselves in this place other than as they had done in the past. I answered them that I could as yet judge nothing of Monseigneur de Guise's intentions, but that I could assure them that His Majesty would not revoke any of his protection.[46]

The same day, March 22, the council convened an extraordinary committee for security affairs to advise the council what to do. The council, faced with the military presence of their governor, decided on the better part of valour and acquiesced in Guise's occupation, for on March 24, the

---

[45]"À son très grand regret et desplaisir ... pour la conservation de sa personne il auroit esté contraint comme la première loy de nature l'enseignoit à ung chascun, prendre le party auquel il se trouvoit reduit qui luy estoit d'aultant plus grief qu'il se rencontroit soubs vostre règne." Barthélemy, *Correspondance de Dinteville*, 85–92; Poinsignon, *Histoire générale*, 2:279; Henry, *La réforme et la ligue*, 68–70; Barthélemy, *Histoire*, 2d ed., 290–91. Dinteville wrote to the king of these events, "indubitablement le sort en est jeté et le Rubicon passé, de sorte que sans la grâce spéciale de Dieu ... la décision ne se peult faire que par la voye des armes"; see Edouard de Barthélemy, ed., *Correspondance inédite de M. de Dinteville, lieutenant-général au gouvernement de Champagne, 1579–1586* (Arcis-sur-Aube, 1889), 91.

[46]Barthélemy, *Correspondance de Dinteville*, 90–91: "Ce n'estoit de leur faute et négligence, parce que suivant les lettres de S.M. et les miennes, ils s'estoient acquiteés de la garde de leur ville aussy soigneusement qu'on eust sçeu désirer, qui estoient tout le commandement qu'ils avoient receu. Au surplus ne leur estant apparu de la révocation du pouvoir de leur gouverneur, ils n'avoient sceu ni ozé se comporter en son endroict que comme ils avoient fait du passé. Je leur feis response que je ne pouvois encore rien juger de l'intention de Monseigneur de Guyse, mais que je les pouvois bien asseurer qu S.M. ne leur défauldroit aucunement de sa protection."

council concluded to ask Guise to limit the number of soldiers lodged in the city.[47]

Over the next few months, Guise further consolidated his hold over Châlons and Champagne. His forces occupied Epernay, and a garrison was stationed in Châlons under the same de Rosne who in 1576 had pressed Provins to join the League.[48] In June, Guise named de Rosne governor of Champagne in his absence, effectively replacing Dinteville. The same day, de Rosne ordered a list compiled of all the Protestants in Châlons. In addition, Guise exhorted the council to take a harder line against the Protestants, including the confiscation of their arms, the imposition of a curfew, and the billeting of soldiers in their houses.[49] The Treaty of Nemours, then, simply ratified Guise's occupation of Châlons.

Guise then set about establishing his military headquarters at Châlons. The first order of business was to secure the town's adherence to the articles of the League, recognizing the cardinal de Bourbon as Henry III's successor. On August 11, the council agreed to sign the Leaguer oath. Significantly, there is no record of the councillers' ever having done so. The page in the register where the oath would have belonged was left blank.[50] Thus, from the spring of 1585 until 1588, Châlons remained under the military occupation of Guise, de Rosne, and St. Mard.

Although the king had committed himself, through the Treaty of Nemours and the edict of July 18 that put the treaty into effect, to a new war of extermination against the Huguenots, he had no intention of seeing the war successfully prosecuted. To do so would have delivered the crown entirely to the League and perhaps have opened the way for Spanish influence in France. The resulting war was little more than a series of half-hearted and indecisive provincial campaigns.[51]

Meanwhile Guise was consolidating his hold on Champagne. The chief threat to the League's domination of the province came from the territories of the duc de Bouillon, based in Sedan, the "vray asile des obstinez hérétiques" and a "petite Genesve." Thus, in February 1586, Captain St.

[47]AD Marne E suppt. 4788, fols. 77–79.
[48]Poinsignon, *Histoire générale*, 2:280; Henry, *La réforme et la ligue*, 71.
[49]AD Marne E suppt. 4788, fols. 79, 112; 4789, fol. 13; Hérelle, *La Réforme*, 1:141–42; 2:137–38.
[50]AD Marne E suppt. 4788, fols. 83–84.
[51]Salmon, *Society in Crisis*, 239; Mariéjol, *La Réforme*, 254–55.

Paul, one of Guise's favorites, began the campaign by seizing the village of Douzy. In November, the Sedanais surprised Rocroy, killed the governor, and pillaged the town. Sedan was taken by Guise in December, and the conflict was ended by a truce signed in Reims in May 1587.[52]

This truce was occasioned by the fact that much bigger things were afoot. In the summer of 1587 an army of twenty-five thousand German mercenaries was in Lorraine, sacking, pillaging, and threatening to invade France in order to join with Navarre's forces in the south.[53] Henry III had sent his mignon Joyeuse against Navarre, hoping for a draw. Guise, meanwhile, had been named to command the royal army sent to stop the Germans. Henry secretly hoped that Guise would be defeated and that he could step in to dictate peace on his own terms,[54] but the king's scheming did not survive the fortunes of the battlefield. On October 27, 1587, Navarre crushed Joyeuse's army at Coutras, killing its commander. Guise meanwhile was dealing the Germans two severe blows at Vimory (October 26) and Auneau (November 24). Thus, the king's expectations were dashed. Rather than mediating, as he had planned, between two roughly equal but weakened factions, he was now faced with two immensely strengthened and mutually hostile forces. Guise was lionized in the pulpits of Paris as much as Henry III was vilified.

The national crisis was raised a notch in intensity by events in Paris in May 1588. Henry III, fearful of Guise's tremendous popularity in Paris, had forbidden the duke to come to the capital. However, the radical Leaguer organization in Paris, known as the Sixteen, invited Guise to the city, and he arrived on May 9, to the acclamation of the Sixteen and the Parisian crowd. Henry, in order to forestall a coup in Paris, had ordered six thousand Swiss mercenaries into the city in the early morning of May 12. The reaction was immediate and furious. Barricades went up in the streets and the soldiers were cornered and eventually spared only through Guise's intervention. Realizing that Paris was lost, the king slipped out of the Tuileries and fled the city. The Sixteen were now firmly in charge of Paris and sought to enlist the other Catholic towns of France in a grand Sainte Union and set up a series of Leaguer councils in the provinces.

[52]Henry, *La réforme et la ligue*, 84–87; Poinsignon, *Histoire générale*, 2:287–88.
[53]Mariéjol, *La Réforme*, 256, 260; Poinsignon, *Histoire générale*, 2:288–90.
[54]Salmon, *Society in Crisis*, 240–41.

Châlons, as Guise's military headquarters in Champagne, came under particular pressure to join Paris and the other Leaguer towns in swearing the oath of the Sainte Union. Châlons' security was, therefore, a matter of some importance. On May 15, Johannès, commander of the garrison in Châlons, exhorted the council to "faire bonne garde," and over the next several days brought more soldiers into the town.[55] The council resolved to ask the captain to order them out, and to send two deputies to Paris for Guise's instructions. Guise replied:

> It is very necessary that Captain Johannès have up to sixty men to be used for the necessary watch duty, and to go, when need be, before the troops approaching your city.... This small number cannot inconvenience you; to the contrary, they will help infinitely.[56]

The council, at this point, was trying to maintain a studied neutrality by emphasizing their obedience to both the king and Guise:

> The council concluded that this city be conserved under the obedience of the king and Monsieur de Guise, governor of the king ... and Sr. de Johannès ... be asked to content himself with the fidelity of the inhabitants for the service and obedience to the king and to M. de Guise under the authority of the king.[57]

The dilemma the councillors faced was forcefully brought home when, on June 4, they received a letter from the king, a letter which had found its way to Châlons by covert means:

> We never intended you to be surrounded by soldiers, who bring with them inconvenience and burden. For this reason, we find it very fitting that you conserve yourselves without receiving any garrisons.[58]

---

[55]AD Marne E Suppt. 4789, fols. 23–24. Johannès was an engineer who had arrived in Châlons with Guise in 1585, and who commanded the garrison in the absence of Guise and de Rosne. Presumably, this was the same person who, in 1584, attempted on Guise's behalf to assassinate Philippe du Plessis de Mornay, and whom Mme de Mornay called Guise's "assassin à gages"; see Mornay, Charlotte-Arbaleste de la Borde, Mme du Plessis de, *Mémoires* (Paris: Société de l'histoire de France, 1869), 1:149.)

[56]AD Marne E suppt. 4789, fol. 25: "il est trés nécessaire que le cappitaine Johannès ayt jusques à soixante hommes afin de s'en ayder aux courvées nécessaire, et mesmes pour envoier quant besoing sera au devant de trouppes qui pourroient aprocher vostredicte ville ... ce petit nombre ne vous peult en rien incommoder, au contraire servir infiniement."

[57]AD Marne E suppt. 4789, fol. 24.

[58]AD Marne E suppt. 4789, fols. 25–26.

Here was a seemingly insoluble problem: Guise's orders as governor were directly countermanded by the king. Yet, Guise obviously possessed the force to have his will obeyed. The council continued to try to maintain its loyalty to both. How long could such a situation continue?

Meanwhile, in Paris, where the Sixteen had taken control, the échevins sought to enlist the other cities of France in their cause. Thus, on June 7 the Châlonnais councillors received a letter from Paris that contained a solicitation of support in partisan language denouncing France's current "enemies":

> Since the misfortunes proceeding from the disunity of the French are known to everyone, and … as the root of them comes from the heretics, who by ruses and artifices wish to render the Catholic party so weak by its disunity that they may encompass our total ruin, and by the fog and obscurity of a miserable government, those who have abused the goodness of the king … wish … to grow fat on the substance of the people; we, who by divine grace, have up to now escaped the yoke of their tyranny … have sent a humble request to His Majesty, and also advised of the need to communicate to all other cities, notably your own … to request and pray you to immediately join your request to ours…. The king will be more faithfully served and the people more assured and otherwise relieved.

The Parisians then presented their request to the council:

> For this reason, we beg of you to continue the good beginning already established, and that this settlement which we request … be confirmed by our mutual oath and promise, under one God, one faith, one king, and one law … that by frequent conferences we may consider the expedient remedies for the restoration of a distressed state.[59]

---

[59]AD Marne E suppt. 4789, fols. 27–28: "Puisque les malheurs procédans de la désunion des Françoys sont congneus à ung chacun, et que les plus clairvoyans jugent que, comme la racine en est extraicte des hérétiques,… qui par ruses et artifices veulent rendre le party des catholiques si faible par leur désunion que avec le temps ilz puissent parvenir à nostre entière ruyne, et par le brouillart et obscurité d'ung si misérable gouvernement ceux qui ont abusé de la bonté du Roy se puissent, comme l'on voit, grandir de la substance de tout le peuple; nous, qui, de la grâce divine, avons eschappé jusques icy le dernier joug de leur tirannie,… avons envoyé nostre trèshumble requeste à Sa Majesté, avons aussi advisé estre besoing la communicquer à toutes les aultres villes, et notamment à la vostre … vous prians et requérans trèsinstamment de joindre vostre requeste à la nostre…. Le Roy en sera plus fidellement servy et le peuple mieulx asseuré et aultrement solagé."

The Châlonnais council responded with delaying tactics, requesting the text of the petition and oath before agreeing.[60]

The cardinal de Guise had secured the adherence of Troyes early in June.[61] From there he too pressed Châlons to join the *Sainte Union*, requesting the council to send two delegates to Troyes "firstly to rejoice in the day that God sent to the people of Troyes, and secondly to unite yourselves with them."[62] The council, on June 12, sent two of their number, Pierre du Moulinet and Pierre Daoust, to Troyes. On June 18 the two reported on their meeting with the cardinal to a joint assembly of the council and the "principal inhabitants." This assembly decided to play for time, asking the cardinal to wait for a further assembly of the three estates in Châlons to consider grievances to be treated at the Estates General to be convoked in Blois in September. On June 23, du Moulinet and Daoust returned once more from Troyes to inform the council of the cardinal's displeasure upon receiving their reply. The council concluded at this time to have the *capitaines cinquanteniers* consult with their men to see if they wished to adhere to the agreement in its present form. At the same time, the council concluded to inform the duc de Guise of their response to the cardinal, and to "assure him of the good will, zeal, and affection that the inhabitants have for the conservation of the Catholic, Apostolic, and Roman religion."[63] The duke replied:

> Your delays can only infinitely displease me, seeing that you are the last of the major cities of the kingdom to resolve yourselves to the service of God and your own conservation. I have made known to this courier my intention, which I pray you to satisfy immediately ... to send the necessary articles and instructions....
> Assuring myself that you will not fail to do so,
> Henry de Lorraine [64]

---

[60]AD Marne E suppt. 4789, fols. 27–28.   [61]Poinsignon, *Histoire générale*, 2:295.

[62]AD Marne E suppt. 4789, fol. 29: "Messieurs, je vous prie eslire deux d'entre vous pour venir de vostre part en ceste ville vous resjouyr, premièrement de l'heure que Dieu a envoyé à messieurs de Troyes, secondement afin de vous unir avec eux."

[63]AD Marne E suppt. 4789, fols. 30–32:"l'asseurer de la bonne volonté, zèle et affection que lesd. habitans ont à la conservation de la religion catholicque, apostolique, et romaine."

[64]AD Marne E suppt. 4789, fol. 33: "en quoy les longueurs dont vous usez ne me peuvent que desplaire infiniment, vous veoyant les derniers de toutes les principalles villes de ce royaume à vous résoudre à ce qui despend du service de Dieu et vostre conservation. J'ay faict entendre à ced. porteur mon intention, à laquelle je vous prie de satisfaire incontinent la présente reçceu et envoyer les articles et mémoires sur ce nécessaires, suivant l'instruction qui luy en a esté donné. Et m'asseurant que n'y ferez faulte,... Henry de Lorraine."

Clearly, the councillors were running out of room to maneuver. The decision could not be put off much longer. To consider the matter, a special assembly of inhabitants was convened on Sunday, July 3. At this meeting, held in the dominican monastery and attended by about four hundred men, Châlons appeared to have given in to the League. A closer examination of the conclusion, however, reveals further hedging and reservations:

> The *specialité* shall be approved at the pleasure and will of the king.... To the said delegates appointed to go to Paris be given power to negotiate, in the name of the inhabitants, the union and association ... with the prévôt des marchands and échevins of Paris and the deputies of the other Catholic cities of the kingdom.... All at the pleasure and will of the king ... the said delegates not having power to swear or oblige the city of Châlons to any onerous conditions without previous deliberation and resolution of the councillors or of a general assembly.[65]

On July 6, two councillors, Jean Aubelin and Claude François, were sent to Paris to negotiate.[66] Apparently these negotiations proceeded slowly but surely, for Aubelin and François returned from Paris at the end of the month with letters from the échevins of Paris and the duc de Guise. These letters both tend to the same effect: we have made a good beginning; it is now necessary to complete it.[67] Was Châlons now about to ally itself with the League and the Sixteen in defiance of the king? Clearly not, for the king himself had given in to the League.

Henry III, recognizing the superior power of the League, once again capitulated to it. On July 21 in Rouen, Henry signed an Edict of Union, thereby acceding to virtually all the League's demands: the Treaty of Nemours was reaffirmed, the cardinal de Bourbon was recognized as heir presumptive, the coup of the Sixteen was ratified, and all those who rejected the League were declared traitors. The king further agreed to publish in France the decrees of the Council of Trent and never again to

---

[65]AD Marne E suppt. 4789, fol. 34: "lad. spécialité sera passée soubz le bon plaisir et vouloir du Roy ... ausquelz procureurs a esté donné pouvoir et puissance pour et au nom de ladicte ville traicter de l'union et association d'icelle avec Messieurs les Prévosts des marchands et eschevins de Paris et députez des aultres villes catholicques de ce royaulme.... le tout soubz le bon plaisir et voulloir sad. Majesté, sans que lesd. procureurs puissent assermenter ou obliger lad. ville de Chaalons à quelques conditions onéreuses que ce soit, que préalablement il n'en ayt esté délibéré et résoult par les gens du Conseil de ladicte ville ou par assemblée générale."

[66]AD Marne E suppt. 4789, fol. 34.   [67]AD Marne E suppt. 4789, fol. 34.

conclude a truce or treaty with the Huguenots. Guise was given supreme military command as lieutenant-général of the kingdom, and Henry's favorite, Epernon (a particular object of hatred to the League), was disgraced.[68] When put in this context, Châlons' apparent willingness to submit to Paris and the League becomes somewhat less unequivocal, for were they not doing what the king had already done? And even so, they hesitated to give themselves over fully.

As he had done in the past, Henry was playing for time, hoping for a favorable outcome of the impending meeting of the Estates General at Blois. The Estates, which opened in October, were thoroughly dominated by the League. The relative unanimity of the deputies made it harder for the king to play them off against each other, as he had done in 1576. Nevertheless, Henry continued to resist their demands for a further strengthening of the League. In fact, in his opening address, the king declared his intention to outlaw again all political associations.[69] The most serious crisis yet to confront France was the direct result of Henry's inability to sway the Estates and his subsequent decision to sever the Gordian knot.

---

[68]Salmon, *Society in Crisis,* 243; Mariéjol, *La Réforme,* 277–78.
[69]Salmon, *Society in Crisis,* 244.

Chapter 7

The Community Liberated, 1588–1594

N DECEMBER 23, 1588, the duc de Guise was summoned to the king's chambers, where he was murdered by the royal guards. Simultaneously, Guise's brother the cardinal and other prominent Leaguers, including the cardinal de Bourbon, were taken prisoner. The cardinal de Guise was killed in his cell the next day. Henry clearly thought that he could destroy the League by cutting off its head; events throughout France were to prove him wrong. Although the assassinations cowed the Estates, news of the Guises' death provoked a swift and furious reaction. In Paris, the Sixteen replaced its members imprisoned at Blois and took an oath to "employ the last penny in their purse and the last drop of their blood" to avenge the dead princes.[1] The Sorbonne declared that Henry, by his tyranny, had abdicated the throne, and that his subjects were thereby absolved from further obedience. The Parlement was purged of royalist judges, Aumale was declared governor of Paris, and Mayenne lieutenant-général of the kingdom in place of his late brother.

Similar events occurred in the towns. Rouen, despite the precautions of the royalist governor Carrouges, adhered to the newly formed Conseil général de la Sainte-Union in February. Almost all of Provence subscribed, as did Toulouse and Lyon. And in Champagne, after a brief period of neutrality, Reims followed Troyes in declaring for the League, leaving only Châlons, Ste. Menehould, and Langres loyal to Henry III.[2]

---

[1]J. H. M. Salmon, *Society in Crisis: France in the Sixteenth Century* (London: St. Martins, 1975), 246 ; Jean Mariéjol, *La Réforme et la Ligue* (Paris: Hachette, 1904), 293.

[2]Philip Benedict, *Rouen during the Wars of Religion* (Cambridge: Cambridge University Press, 1981), 178–80; Mariéjol, *La Réforme*, 296; Maurice Poinsignon, *Histoire générale de la Champagne et de Brie*, 3 vols. (Paris, 1885, 1898; rpt. Paris: Guenégaud, 1974), 2:303–7.

The king related the events at Blois to the Châlonnais council in a letter received on December 28:

> There is no need to tell you the occasion given us by the late duc de Guise to feel the effects of the trouble he has sown in our kingdom, which we wished to forget and tried by every means possible to restore him to the path from which he had diverged. To the contrary, he had every day a new scheme against our person, which ... we thought it necessary to prevent and to guarantee our life by the loss of his.... And in order to avoid the trouble and dissension that could occur in your city, we wish you to expel the sieur de Rosne.[3]

The council's action was swift and decisive. Already on December 27, the council had intercepted letters carried by a certain Oudineau, apparently a representative of the Sixteen, which contained orders to conserve Châlons for the League.[4] De Rosne was now forcibly expelled, and his captains, Louis and Thomas D'Urbin, were arrested and imprisoned"to interrogate them regarding the attempt on this city of Châlons" ("pour yceulx oyr et interroger sur l'entreprise faicte sur cested. ville de Chaalons"). Louis D'Urbin was subsequently released into the custody of two inhabitants after having sworn an oath "to serve the king against all, together with the inhabitants at Châlons, under the authority of His Majesty" ("de servir le Roy envers et contre tous, ensemble les habitans dud. Chaalons soubz l'auctorité de Sa Majesté").[5]

What is striking about this chain of events is its swiftness and the apparent unanimity with which it was carried out. Unlike other cities such as Reims, which tried to remain neutral, or like Troyes, which was fully devoted to the League, Châlons had delivered itself wholly to the king

---

[3]AD Marne E suppt. 4789, fol. 41: "il n'est point besoing que nous vous représentions les occasions que nous ont esté données par le feu duc de Guise de nous resentir des troubles qu'il a semez en nostre royaume, lesquelles nous avons voulu oublier, et essaier par tous moyens à nous possibles de les ramener audict chemyn dont il s'estoit desvoyé. Mais il n'y a eu gratiffication ny bien faict qui l'aye peu faire ranger à son debvoir. Au contraire il avoit tous les jours quelque nouveau desseing sur nostre propre personne, laquelle ... nous avons pensé estre nécessaire de le prévenir et garentir nostre vye par la perte de la sienne.... Et afin d'éviter aux troubles et divisions que l'on pourroit esmouvoir en vostre ville, nous voullons que vous mettiez hors d'icelle le Sr de Rosne."

[4]Pierre-Victor-Palma Cayet, *Chronologie Novenaire, contenant l'histoire de la guerre*, ed. Michaud & Poujolat (Paris, 1857), 91.

[5]Edouard de Barthélemy, *Histoire*, 2d ed. (Châlons-sur-Marne, 1883), 294; Georges Hérelle, ed. *Mémoire des choses plus notables advenues en la province de Champagne 1585–98* (Reims: Trav. Acad. Reims, 68, 1879), 41–43; AD Marne E suppt. 4789, fol. 41.

within several days of the events at Blois. In a sense, the death of Guise freed the council's hands. There was no longer a question of divided loyalties and conflicting orders. Their governor was dead and now the king alone commanded their loyalty.[6]

The consensus which underlay the council's actions is brought to our attention by an oath sworn on December 30 by the clergy and lay inhabitants of Châlons "to guard and maintain this city of Châlons under the obedience and authority of the king and for the preservation of our Catholic, Apostolic, and Roman religion, and to employ to this end their lives, bodies, and goods, whether in their own name or in the name of the clergy of Châlons."[7]

Having thus declared for the king, the immediate task was to guarantee the city's security and maintain communications with the other royalist towns of the province, notably Ste. Menehould and Langres. Thus, on January 1, 1589, the council received as Châlons' new royal governor Dinteville's man, Philippe de Thomassin. Even in the midst of this crisis, however, the council made sure to retain its own role in the defense of the town by having Thomassin swear an oath to "aid and assist the inhabitants of this city for their conservation in the obedience of the king and under the authority of His Majesty."[8] In April, apparently dissatisfied with the division of powers, the council obtained modifications of Thomassin's commission. It now emphasized that his position was a temporary one, to last only so long as the "present troubles" continued. Furthermore, Thomassin was to acquire the council's assent for all his actions, none of which were to infringe on the city's "rights and liberties." Thomassin was also to do all in his power to prevent oppression by the soldiers garrisoned in Châlons.[9] Thus, even in a state of dire emergency, the council manifested a clear devotion to its independence and integrity, and a reluctance to give up any of its powers.

---

[6]Hérelle, *Mémoire des choses plus notables*, 41–42.

[7]AD Marne E suppt. 4789, fol. 41:"de garder et maintenir ceste ville de Chaalons soubz l'obéissance et l'auctorité du Roy et pour la manutention de nostre religion catholique, apostolique, et romaine, et ad ce employer leurs vies, corps, et biens tant en leurs privez noms que ceux … du clergé dud. Chaalons."

[8]AD Marne E suppt. 4789, fol. 42 "de ayder et assister lesd. habitans d'icelle ville pour leur conservation en l'obéissance du Roy et soubz l'auctorité de Sa Majesté."

[9]AD Marne E suppt. 4789, fol. 51.

Châlons now found itself in the anomalous position of forming its own garrison of outside soldiers instead of trying to avoid a garrison at all costs. On January 2, the council decided to raise four companies of fifty men each to guard the city, and on the seventh, they agreed to Dinteville's request to raise an additional four hundred to protect the countryside. Here again, the council demonstrated its determination to share in the conduct of affairs, controlling the appointment of the captains and lieutenants of the four companies that were guarding the city.[10]

The military necessity which lay behind these garrisons was the proximity of the Leaguer commander Antoine de St. Paul. Following the murders at Blois, St. Paul (along with de Rosne) was charged by Mayenne with command of Champagne and Brie in the absence of the young duc de Guise, imprisoned at Blois.[11] In January, after seizing Vitry-le-François, St. Paul operated in the Argonne. After being repulsed from Verdun, he seized Montfaucon and occupied villages and châteaux in the region, attempting to disrupt communications between Châlons, Sedan, and Langres. Following a defeat in February at St. Juvin, north of Ste. Menehould, he moved westward, seizing Bisseuil and Neufchâtel-sur-Aisne.[12] Meanwhile, Reims had ended its brief period of neutrality and declared for the League, pressuring other cities to do the same, thus providing a base for St. Paul and his men. On February 24, St. Paul wrote from Vitry to Chaumont of his intention to leave for Châlons the next day to confront Dinteville's troops.[13]

In light of these threats, the council took concerted action. On January 11, they ordered that a hundred men be stationed in Juvigny, and on the thirteenth posted twenty men at the château of Sarry, thus controlling the crossings on the Marne both above and below Châlons.[14] Juvigny resisted, and on January 13 the council concluded to send the prévost des maréschaulx or his lieutenant to Juvigny along with a body of archers "to have the inhabitants of Juvigny understand the necessity of securing the said bourg for the service of the king and welfare not only of Juvigny, but

---

[10]AD Marne E suppt. 4789, fols. 43–44.

[11]Hérelle, *La Réforme*, 1:169 n.1; Poinsignon, *Histoire générale*, 2:311.

[12]Poinsignon, *Histoire générale*, 2:311–12; Edouard Henry, *La réforme et la ligue en Champagne et à Reims* (St. Nicolas, 1867), 127–28; Hérelle, *La Réforme*, 2:233–37.

[13]Hérelle, *La Réforme*, 2:235.   [14]AD Marne E suppt. 4789, fols. 46, 47.

also of Châlons, and all the surrounding country." If Juvigny still resists, "the soldiers will be permitted to enter the bourg by any means necessary, even by assault and force."[15] On January 16, the council asked Dinteville to mount royal artillery on the ramparts, and on the eighteenth ordered a survey and subsequent distribution of all the arms in the city.[16] The League's campaign in Champagne continued throughout the spring and summer of 1589. In March, Epernay surrendered to St. Paul, and St. Paul himself was present just outside the walls of Châlons.[17] Reims, meanwhile, was attempting to enlist other cities in the League; those which accepted included Verdun, Laon, Rethel, and Mezières.[18] Despite its previous intransigence, Châlons was not exempt from solicitation. The council was entreated from all sides to swear the articles of the League. It was bombarded by letters from various members of the Guise family, from the échevins of Paris, and from the Conseil-général de l'Union. These appeals fluctuated between promises of goodwill and cooperation, and threats of dire consequences if Châlons persevered in its stubborn course.[19] The response of the council is best displayed in the responses to two of these letters. To de Rosne the council wrote:

> There is no need … to bother giving us advice about what we must do to remain in obedience to the king and the fidelity we owe to him, since we are certain of his orders…. We have received several letters from His Majesty amply enlightening us as to his will…. We intend to satisfy and follow completely His Majesty's commandments; therefore we request you not to bother yourself with the propriety of our actions and not to send anyone to us again.[20]

[15]AD Marne E suppt. 4789, fol. 47: "faire comprendre aux habitans dudict Juvigny la necessité qui est de tenir led. bourg de Juvigny en seureté pour le service du roy et bien publicq tant dudict Juvigny que de lad. ville de Chaalons et de tout le pays d'environ."

[16]AD Marne E suppt. 4789, fols, 48, 51.   [17]Hérelle, *La Réforme*, 2:237.

[18]Poinsignon, *Histoire générale*, 2:312; Henry, *La réforme*, 128–30.

[19]Thus Mayenne appealed to the council to guard against "les maulvaises intentions de ceulx qui veullent et ne recherchent que la ruyne des bons catholiques" Hérelle, *La Réforme*, 1:168–69. Catherine de Clèves, Guise's widow, threatened to send someone "vous peunir de vos ingratitudes"; Henry, *La réforme*, 143.

[20]Hérelle, *La Réforme*, 1:171–72"Il n'est point besoing, s'il vous plaist, de vous plus mectre en peine de nous donner advis de ce qu'il fault que nous fassions pour nous maintenir en l'obéissance du Roy…. Nous avons reçeu plusieurs lettres de Sa Majesté, par les quelles elle nous esclaircit amplement de sa volunté; … pourquoy nous vous prions de ne vous plus mectre en peine du comportement de noz actions."

And to the échevins of Paris:

> The union of which you write is nothing else than what we have sworn to
> the obedience of His Majesty and following his edict, which is to live and
> die in the Catholic, Apostolic, and Roman religion.[21]

At the same time that the council was resisting these blandishments
and threats, Châlons was being showered with praise and honors by the
king. The king recognized Châlons as "la ville principale de Champagne"
and transferred to the city a section of the Parlement of Paris, the cour des
monnaies of Troyes, and the grenier à sel and siège présidial of Vitry-le-
François.[22] All the while, Henry praised the Châlonnais' fidelity and stead-
fastness:

> We have heard … of the good work continued by your good comport-
> ment, not only to conserve yourselves in our obedience, as God and
> reason command you, but also to serve as an example, to show the way
> and encourage the other cities of my province of Champagne.[23]

One should not think, however, that the council's actions went unop-
posed within Châlons. Indeed, the anonymous author of the *Mémoire des
choses plus notables* explicitly states that following the murders at Blois, the
council acted decisively precisely to forestall Leaguer agitation.[24] In particular, opposition was to be expected from Bishop Clausse. Since the Day of
Barricades in May 1588, Clausse had boycotted the council to display his
displeasure at Châlons' hesitancy in joining the League. Thus, following
news of the events at Blois, he was presented with a fait accompli. In February 1589, Dinteville and the council tricked Clausse into leaving the city
at the very time his brothers, in command of a number of soldiers, were
approaching the city. The council remonstrated to Dinteville: "Because of
his [Clausse's] defiance, the people may revolt, if order is not promptly
established; the power of the bishop is inconvenient and prejudicial to the

---

[21]Hérelle, *La Réforme*, 1:181–82: "L'union de la quelle nous escripvez n'est aultre que celle
qu'avons juré soubz l'obéissance de Sa Majesté, et suivant son édit, qui est de vivre et mourir en la relligion catholicque, apostolique, et romaine."

[22]Hérelle, *La Réforme*, 1:198–200.

[23]Hérelle, *La Réforme*, 1:176–77: "Nous avons entendu … le bon debvoir auquel vous continuer
par voz bons comportments, non seulement pour vous conserver en nostre obéissance, comme Dieu et
la raison le vous commandent, mais pour servir d'exemple, monstrer le chemin et encourager les
aultres villes de ma province de Champagne à faire le semblable."

[24]Hérelle, *Mémoire des choses plus notables*, 45.

service of the king; for the welfare and tranquillity of the city, it is expedient that he leave, at least to go before his brothers and dissuade them from entering Châlons."[25] When Clausse attempted to return to Châlons, he found the gates closed to him. In a letter discussed in council on February 15, Clausse complained that he had been tricked, and he requested a hearing in the council. The council refused his request, and another to the same effect six months later.[26]

Dinteville and the council also acted to forestall opposition among the inhabitants. In January, the council had declared that "prohibitions are to be proclaimed with the sound of the trumpet in the squares of the city to all persons against sowing defamatory libels and maintaining scandalous propositions leading to sedition or popular agitation."[27]

Meanwhile, relations between Châlons and Leaguer towns, specifically Reims and Paris, were deteriorating further. On February 19, the council arrested a Rémois merchant.[28] More critical were relations with Paris and a hostage war between the two cities. Early in February, the échevins of Paris wrote to Châlons to ask for the release of two merchants held there along with their merchandise. These merchants, Nicolas Gombart and Fiacre Rolland, had apparently been arrested in retaliation for the Parisian authorities' refusal to permit two Châlonnais students at the Sorbonne, Michel Braux (son of Councillor Pierre Braux) and Louis Lallemant, to leave Paris, and because the Parisians had detained boatloads of Lenten provisions bound for Châlons. Gombart and Rolland then wrote to Paris of their predicament, stating that the condition for their release was the release of the students and the cargo held in Paris.[29]

The Parisians wrote to the council that Châlons had not been singled out for discriminatory treatment. The students had not been detained because they were from Châlons; on the contrary, they were detained as a

---

[25]Henry, *La réforme*, 139: "dans sa défiance, le peuple pouvoit se mutiner, si promptment n'y estoit mis ordre; que la puissance dudit évesque estoit incommode et préjudiciable au service du Roy; que, pour le bien public et repos de la ville, il estoit expedient qu'il sortist, du moins pour aller au devant de ses frères et les divertir de vouloir entrer à Chaalons."

[26]AD Marne E suppt. 4789, fol. 61.

[27]AD Marne E Suppt. 4789, fol. 51:"Que deffense seroit publié au son de trompette par les carrefours de ceste ville à toutes personnes ... de semer aulcunes libelles déffamatoires ny tenir propos scandalleux ou tendans à sédition ou émotion populaire."

[28]AD Marne E suppt. 4789, fol. 62.

[29]AD Marne E suppt. 4789, fol. 63; Hérelle, *La Réforme*, 1:177–86.

protective measure and in order to prevent the panic which might ensue from a general exodus of students. As to the seized merchandise, Châlons had been misinformed: the only merchandise seized was in retaliation for the alleged theft of one thousand écus by someone from Châlons. This affair, therefore, had nothing to do with the League or the war. The letter concludes with a veiled threat: if this matter is not resolved amicably, Châlons stands to lose more than Paris.[30] The Châlonnais reply is curt: "We have obtained from Monseigneur de Dinteville word that if you free the children of our city and permit the free transport of the seized merchandise he will discharge those whom he arrested with their merchandise.... Having nothing else to negotiate [i.e. Châlons' adherence to the League], there is no need to delegate anyone."[31]

Eventually, the cities worked out a complicated swap: Gombart, Rolland, and their goods for the Châlonnais students and goods held in Paris. This seems to have fallen through, however, for on March 20, we find the council at Châlons deciding to sell the wares of Gombart and Rolland in compensation for the goods seized in Paris and "for the deliverance of students and other persons detained in the city of Paris."[32]

The military situation in Champagne remained relatively stable throughout the spring and summer of 1589. That is, the Leaguer commander St. Paul and the royalist Dinteville occupied themselves with seizing the towns and châteaux held by the other without great change in the military balance. For Châlons, the most important question was whether or not the king would, or could, send additional military help. In response to numerous letters, the king wrote in March of his intention to send Louis de Gonzague, duc de Nevers, to Champagne, "when necessary." In addition, he was sending immediately Robert de Joyeuse, comte de Grandpré, to join Dinteville's forces. The need for Nevers seems to have arisen rather quickly, for a week later the king wrote that he was sending Nevers immediately.[33] Nevers then wrote to the council that he did indeed intend to

---

[30]Hérelle, *La Réforme*, 1:178–79.

[31]Hérelle, *La Réforme*, 1:181"Messieurs, nous avons obtenu de Monseigneur de Dinteville,... que licenciantz par vous les enffans de nostre ville et permettant le transport libre de marchandises arrestées, qu'il renvoyra ceux qui sont icy arrestez.... N'ayant aultre chose à traicter avec vous, il n'est nécessaire de déléguer aucuns de nous avecq procuration."

[32]AD Marne E suppt. 4789, fol. 67: "pour la déliverance des escolliers et autres personnes dud. Chaalons qui sont detenuez en lad. ville de Paris."

[33]Hérelle, *La Réforme*, 1:189, 191–92; AD Marne E suppt. 4789, fols. 68–69.

come, but could not until he could be assured that there was sufficient money.[34] In May, Nevers wrote again that he had been about to leave for Châlons from Noyers, "but this evening, the king ordered me to return to Nevers.... Therefore I greatly regret not being able to demonstrate to you the great desire I have to aid you."[35]

Châlonnais pleas for help became all the more urgent when Mayenne arrived in Reims early in July. The council wrote numerous letters to Dinteville requesting his presence.[36] Dinteville replied to all of them in the same fashion: The king had ordered him to escort Swiss mercenaries on their way to join the royal army; when he finally saw the king, he would do all he could to aid Châlons. In the meantime, "retain everything in such order that you render sure testimony of your perfect fidelity."[37]

Such was the situation in Champagne and Châlons on August 2, 1589, when Henry III was assassinated by Jacques Clément at St. Cloud. News of the regicide was greeted exuberantly in Paris and in other League towns.[38] News of the king's death came to Châlons on August 6 in a letter from Dinteville. He informed the councillors that the king had been stabbed, but "the doctors and surgeons unanimously agree that there is no danger, so that in a few days His Majesty will recuperate completely." The news of Henry's death was attached as a postscript:

> Since my letter, the tragedy of the king's death has occurred; the king [Henry IV] has today professed that he will change nothing in our religion and will expose all, including his life, to maintain his subjects in peace. The princes, royal officers, and captains, along with the colonels of the Swiss, have sworn fidelity to him. I wanted to advise you of this, and pray you to maintain your city in the repose that I wish for you.[39]

[34]Hérelle, *La Réforme,* 1:193–94.

[35]Hérelle, *La Réforme,* 1:200–201:"Mais cest apres disné, le Roy m'a commandé de m'en retorner à Nevers,... au moyen de quoy je porte infiny regret de n'avoir peu faire paroistre la bonne affection que j'avoys de seconder vostre bonne intention et l'amitié que m'avez monstrée."

[36]Hérelle, *La Réforme,* 1:202–10.

[37]Hérelle, *La Réforme,* 1: 206: "Cependant, je m'asseure que vous contiendrez toutes choses en si bon estat que vous rendrez certain tesmoignage de vostre parfaicte fidélité."

[38]Salmon, *Society in Crisis,* 157–58.

[39]Hérelle, *La Réforme,* 1:211–13: "Messieurs, depuis ma lettre close, il nous est arrivé le malheur de la mort de Sa Majesté; le Roy qui est aujourd'hui a pris les protestations de n'inover aucune chose en nostre religion, et d'aporter tout, jusques à la vye, pour maintenir ses subjectz en repos. Les princes, officiers de la couronne, seigneurs et cappitaines, avec les colonnelz des Suisses, luy ont juré fidélité. C'est de quoy je vous ay bien donner advis, et vous pryer maintenir vostre ville au repos que je vous désire."

Here was a situation totally unprecedented in French history: the legitimate heir to the throne was a heretic. Leaguers who had reviled Henry III were now redoubled in their opposition to the crown. Catholics who had supported Henry III, or at least not opposed him, were now faced with an awful choice. Could one swear allegiance to a heretic king? Or should one recognize the Leaguer king, Charles X, the elderly cardinal de Bourbon, proclaimed king by Mayenne and currently a prisoner of Henry IV?

The new king certainly appreciated the predicament into which his accession had thrown royalist Catholics, and acted immediately to alleviate their misgivings. As Dinteville had reported to the Châlonnais council, the new king swore to uphold the Catholic faith. Moreover, he declared his intention to receive instruction in the Catholic religion, and eventually to convert. Henry also wrote to the cities of France to the same effect. To Châlons he wrote:

> We are assured that, as you have always expressed your fidelity to and affection for the welfare and greatness of this crown, especially in the submission of your town to the authority and obedience, from which it had been distracted for some time previously, you will continue and persevere in the same devotion.... We hope to be in our province of Champagne soon, along with our army, to reestablish the repose which we desire for all our good and loyal subjects....[40]

Despite these assurances, however, many Catholics defected or withdrew into neutrality, including the potential savior of Châlons, the duc de Nevers, who retired to sort out his thoughts. Most towns which had previously not done so now went over to the League. Of the major Catholic towns of France, only Tours, Bordeaux, Langres, Compiègne, Clermont, and Châlons recognized Henry IV as king.[41]

Ironically, Henry IV's letter to Châlons, received on August 8, came after the Châlonnais declaration of loyalty. Immediately upon being informed of the king's death by Dinteville on August 6, the council swore

---

[40]"Nous nous asseurons que, comme vous avez tousjours rendu tesmoignage de vostre fidélité et affection au bien et grandeur de ceste couronne, spéciallement en la réduction de vostre ville soubz l'auctorité et obéissance, dont elle avoit été distraicte quelque temps auparavant, vous continuerez et persévérerez en la mesme dévotion.... Nous espérons estre bien tost en nostre province de Champaigne avec l'armée qui est de présent près de nous, pour y restablir le repos que nous désirons à tous noz bons et loyaulx subjectz..."; see Hérelle, *La Réforme*, 1:214; AD Marne E suppt. 4789, fol. 101.

[41]Mariéjol, *La Réforme*, 305.

unanimously "to conserve themselves in obedience and devotion to the king, legitimate successor to the Crown of France, provided they are maintained in the Catholic, Apostolic, and Roman religion, and without permitting in their town the exercise of any other religion."[42]

Given what we know of the predispositions of the councillors, and taking into consideration their actions over the previous year and a half, this allegiance can hardly be surprising. Nevertheless, it is significant enough to deserve brief reflection. It is obvious that the councillors swore this oath despite the new king's religion. No one can deny that they would have preferred a Catholic king. The proviso that they be allowed to maintain the Catholic religion, while of course important to the councillors, seems to have been a reiteration of their wishes, a formula. Had they not already received from Dinteville, a Catholic, the king's undertaking to preserve their religion? Even so, they preferred a legitimate king. This course of action was the only option available to them; it was the last step in a logical progression. They had remained loyal to Henry III after the Day of Barricades and the murders at Blois, events that had led many others into the fold of the League. They had rebuffed all efforts to enlist them in the Catholic League from 1576 onwards, even when the duc de Guise was in virtual military occupation of the city. Once they had started down this road, there was really no choice but to acknowledge Henry IV as king. Why indeed should they now submit to the blandishments of the Leaguers St. Paul, de Rosne, and Bishop Clausse? Loyalty had served their interests well. They had thrown off the domination of the Guises, they had been recognized by Henry III as the principal city of Champagne, they had become the seat of a Parlement and had been otherwise showered with favors by a grateful king. When one adds to all this the new king's promise to respect the Catholic religion and eventually to convert, the choice does not seem to have been difficult, and the speed with which the councillors swore loyalty only confirms this conclusion.

The council then wrote to their new king in the following terms:

[42]AD Marne E suppt. 4789, fols. 96–97: "A esté conclu que s'il a pleu à Dieu appeler ung seigneur Roy les habitans de ceste ville de Chaalons conserveront lad. ville en l'obéissance et devotion du légitime successeur Roy de la couronne de France et en continuant la première résolution desd. habitans de vivre et mourir en l'obéissance dud. seigneur Roy en conservant ... lesd. habitans en la religion catholique, apostolique, et romaine ... et sans qu'il soit faict aulcun exercice d'aultre religion audict Chaalons."

Your Majesty ... has declared to us ... his intention ... to conserve the Catholic, Apostolic, and Roman religion, with no innovations.... And on this assurance, even before the reception of your letters ... we had no difficulty, on the first news of this tragic accident, in resolving in our council, on the seventh day of this month, to keep and conserve this city under the obedience of the legitimate successor to the crown, while conserving ourselves in the ... Roman religion, protesting not to adhere to or favor any of those who caused the death of our lord king.... As to the state of this city and the countryside, we do not cease to represent to you the necessity and oppression of it.... We only advise Your Majesty of the necessity to send adequate forces here quickly, under the command of a Catholic chief and lord, to deliver the country from the incursions of the enemy.[43]

Indeed, now more than ever, Châlons needed royal reinforcements. The city was faced with pressure from without and subversion from within. Following the death of Henry III, the League had once again renewed its efforts to enlist Châlons. On August 5, a Franciscan monk carrying letters from the council of Troyes was arrested and imprisoned.[44] On August 9, the council received a letter from the council of Reims, asking what they intended to do following the king's death and imploring them to recognize Charles X. The council concluded not to respond.[45] The same day, St. Paul wrote from Reims that, as good Catholics, Châlons need not put up with the Huguenots; in an effort at reconciliation, St. Paul had ordered his soldiers to observe a truce of two weeks, during which time the council could decide to join the League.[46] The duc de Lorraine also wrote several letters in the first weeks of August soliciting Châlons' adherence to the League: "There being nothing of consequence separating you and us ... join your

---

[43]Hérelle, *La Réforme*, 1:219–21: "Vostredicte Majesté, Sire, nous a bien voulu déclarer par les mesmes lettres son intention et bonne volonté de conserver la religion catholicque, apostolique et romaine, sans qu'il y soit rien innové.... Et sur ceste asseurance, dès auparavant la réception de vosdictes lettres, n'avons fait difficulté aucune, aux premières nouvelles de ce triste accident, de prendre résolution en nostre conseil, dès le VIIe de ce mois, de garder et conserver ceste ville en l'obéissance du légitime successeur à la couronne, en nous conservant en ladicte religion ... romaine, avec protestation de n'adhérer ny favoriser aucunement ceulx qui sont cause de la mort dudict seigneur Roy.... Quant à l'estat de ladicte ville et du pays, nous ne nous arresterons davantage à vous représenter la nécessité et oppression d'iceulx.... Seulement nous advertirons Vostre Majesté qu'il est besoing d'envoyer de bref et en toute diligence de bonnes forces par deçà, soubz la conduicte d'un chef et seigneur catholicque, pour délivrer le pays des incursions des ennemis."

[44]AD Marne E suppt. 4789, fol. 96.   [45]AD Marne E suppt. 4789, fol. 103.

[46]Hérelle, *La Réforme*, 1:222.

counsels and means with ours to be employed in defense of this cause (our religion) and the welfare and repose of this state."[47] The duke and several of his relatives (notably the chevalier d'Aumale and Catherine de Clèves, Guise's widow) also wrote to Castel, hoping to gain Châlons through the defection of its captain.[48] The council's reaction to all these entreaties was the same: the council sent the pleas on to the king and Dinteville.[49]

At the same time, there was obvious dissent within the city. On August 9, a disturbance at the Porte de Marne was reported to the council.[50] The details of this disturbance are not recorded, but it is difficult to imagine that it could have been about anything other than the council's recognition of Henry IV. At the same meeting, Pierre Deu, an apothecary, presented a request on behalf of a number of other inhabitants. Again, the content of the request is not recorded, but it could not have been anything other than a request to join the League and recognize Charles X. Deu, upon his refusal to reveal the names of his copetitioners, was thrown into prison. Despite a number of requests from Deu and his wife, he was not set free.[51]

The council responded to these threats with unprecedented security measures. On August 7, they ordered a survey of all refugees in Châlons.[52] On August 8, Protestant refugees from Sedan and other foreign Huguenots were expelled. Native Huguenots were allowed to remain, provided they swore loyalty to the city, and held no assemblies nor exercised the new religion. At the same time, the council forbade *all* assemblies and prohibited *any* refugees from assembling in groups greater than three or four. The guards at the gates were ordered not to admit any soldiers or noblemen without Thomassin's and the council's express permission. And on August 10, the carrying of arms within the city was forbidden. Clearly, the council was just as anxious, perhaps more so, about the League as they were about the Huguenots.[53]

---

[47]Hérelle, *La Réforme*, 1:224: "N'ayant plus de subject qui vous puisse divertir et séparer de nous … vous joindrez vos conseilz et moiens avec les nostres pour emploier à la deffense de ceste cause (la religion) et au bien et repos de cest estat."

[48]Hérelle, *La Réforme*, 1:222.

[49]AD Marne E suppt. 4789, fol. 106.   [50]AD Marne E suppt. 4789, fol. 103.

[51]AD Marne E suppt. 4789, fols. 103, 104, 106.   [52]AD Marne E suppt. 4789, fol. 99.

[53]AD Marne E suppt. 4789, fols. 99–100, 104.

The Châlonnais council had good reason to worry that their hastily improvised solution in the wake of Henry III's death and Henry IV's accession might not stand up to unforeseen problems. In France as a whole the period between the assassination of Henry III in August 1589 and Henry IV's entry into Paris in 1594 are fraught with conditions bordering on anarchy. These years saw the final triumph of the Sixteen over royalist opposition in Paris (including the execution of *premier président* Brisson of the Parlement), the meeting of the Leaguer Estates General with its debates over the future of the monarchy, the military maneuvering between Henry and Mayenne (including the Battle of Ivry and the siege of Paris), and the king's conversion. During this period the fabric of French society also seemed to be unraveling, with the radical political theory of the Sixteen, inflammatory pamphlets such as the *Dialogue d'entre le Maheustre et le Manant* and the *Satire Menipée*, and widespread peasant unrest.

For Châlons, these outside developments were no less important than for France as a whole. Yet the Châlonnais responses were a logical progression from their actions taken in 1588 and 1589. In August 1589, Châlons had chosen loyalty to Henry IV, and the city was to maintain that loyalty until the final pacification of the province in 1594. This is not to say that nothing happened; on the contrary, Châlons, as the major royalist city of Champagne, became an important strategic focal point and was threatened from within and from without on several occasions.

As in previous years, there seems to have been a certain amount of dissent within the city. Now, however, Châlons was playing host to part of the Parlement of Paris; quite naturally, the city council receded into the background, allowing the magistrates of the Parlement to handle troublemakers. On June 7, the council resolved to ask the Parlement what to do regarding "defamatory libels" being spread in the city. The Parlement was, after all, the last court of appeal, and the councillors seemed content to hand over internal dissent matters to the magistrates while the council still directed the military security of the city. This tendency would only have been reinforced by the fact that among the avocats and procureurs competent to plead before the court there were a number of city councillors or their relatives.[54]

---

[54]AD Marne E suppt. 4789, fol. 88; Edouard de Barthélemy, "Le Parlement de Châlons-sur-Marne, 1589–94," *Revue de la Champagne et de Brie* (1884): 9.

In October 1589 there was a conspiracy led by Georges and Jacques de Berlize and Jehan Legros to open the city to St. Paul. Dinteville, at that time operating around Ste. Menehould, hurried back to Châlons to put down this plot. Jacques de Berlize and Legros were sentenced by the Parlement to be hanged, drawn, and quartered.[55] In April of 1591, a certain Claude Roussel, "serviteur de hostellerie de l'Ours," was condemned by an *arrêt* of the Parlement to be hanged "for … having made several intrigues to deliver the said city into the hands of the enemies of the king and of the said city."[56] The city was also troubled with preachers, especially Franciscans, who took the side of the League. In June 1591, Simon Gromard, a Franciscan, was reprimanded by the Parlement for "not having preached what he ought, and that he ought to preach the obedience due the king and against the rebels who have risen up against the State and who trouble the kingdom." In February 1592, Gromard was again reprimanded and again he promised to mend his ways. Similarly, another Franciscan, Claude Gourlier, was convicted in August 1591 of "having uttered many seditious, scandalous, and harmful statements against the memory of the late king, as well as against the honor of the present king." Gourlier was sentenced to public recantation and corporal punishment, and was then banished from France for life.[57]

The endemic provincial skirmishing by the League and its commanders, St. Paul and de Rosne, and the royalists under Dinteville and Thomassin continued. Châlons played an important part, both as a supplier of materiel and as an outpost of royalist forces. On several occasions the garrison posted in Châlons, in conjunction with the civic militia, took part in the localized campaigns, which consisted mostly of taking or retaking villages and châteaux held by the enemy.

Early in October 1589, St. Paul encountered a royalist force under Robert de Joyeuse, comte de Grandpré, at St. Amand, on the right bank of

---

[55]Barthélemy, *Histoire*, 2d ed., 307–8; Hérelle, *Mémoire des choses plus notables*, 96. The Parlement's sentence against Jacques de Berlize and Legros is included in Hérelle, *Mémoire des choses plus notables*, appendix 5, pp. 182–86.

[56]"pour avoir … faict plusieurs pratiques et menées pour livrer ladicte ville de Chaalons ès mains des ennemis du Roy et de ladicte ville"; see Poinsignon, *Histoire générale*, 2:349; Hérelle, *Mémoire des choses plus notables*, appendix 8, pp. 193–94.

[57]Hérelle, *Mémoire des choses plus notables*, appendix 11, pp. 204–9:"pour avoir blasphémé et renié Dieu et proféré plusieurs propos séditieux, scandaleux et injurieux, tant contre la mémoire du feu Roy que l'honneur du Roy à present regnant."

the Marne between Châlons and Vitry-le-François. The Leaguers soundly defeated the royalists, killing Grandpré and capturing his brother Tourteron, and forcing the survivors to retreat across the Marne to Pringy. Over the next three days (October 9–11), St. Paul attacked Pringy and actually took part of the village before the royalists were rescued by reinforcements from Châlons under the command of Thomassin, forcing St. Paul to retire to Vitry.[58]

The fighting continued for the next several years. In May 1590, the Châlonnais mounted an attack on Vitry where the royalist Tourteron (now comte de Grandpré) was being held prisoner. On the night of May 7 the royalists penetrated the citadel through a blockhouse and liberated Tourteron, killing the Leaguer governor de Mutigny in the process. St. Paul, laying siege to Vassy with four thousand men, quickly returned to Vitry, retaking the city on May 12.[59] Similar events took place throughout 1590, with the Châlonnais taking Conflans, Avize, Aulnay-aux-Planches, and Aulnay-l'Aistre.[60]

Apart from this localized skirmishing, Champagne was the scene of several large campaigns. A route through the province was critical if the king was to receive much-needed reinforcements from Germany, and to deny the same to his enemies. In the late summer of 1589, Henry IV ordered the maréchal d'Aumont to Champagne to counter the Leaguer forces in the province.[61] In August and September, d'Aumont, after establishing his camp near Châlons, took Château-Thierry, fortified Epernay, and made a feint toward Reims. In September, however, d'Aumont was recalled from Champagne by the king, who following his victory over Mayenne at Arques in Normandy, hoped to deal the League's army a crushing blow. Thus, Châlons was left on its own to uphold the royalist cause in Champagne.[62]

Following the royal victory over Mayenne at Ivry in March 1590, the way to Paris lay open to the king. From May to September, Henry besieged

---

[58]Poinsignon, *Histoire générale*, 2: 228–30; Hérelle, *La Réforme*, 2:287–90; Henry, *La réforme*, 161–63.

[59]Hérelle, *Mémoire des choses plus notables*, 104–6; Henry, *La réforme*, 169–70.

[60]Poinsignon, *Histoire générale*, 2:338; Henry, *La réforme*, 170; Barthélemy, *Histoire*, 2d ed., 311; Hérelle, *La Réforme*, 1:248–49; 2:316–20; AD Marne E suppt. 4789, fols. 136, 152, 154.

[61]Poinsignon, *Histoire générale*, 2:325.

[62]Poinsignon, *Histoire générale*, 2:327–28; Hérelle, *La Réforme*, 2:282–84.

Paris, and was forced to lift the siege only by the duke of Parma's invasion from the Netherlands. Parma's army then retreated through Brie and northern Champagne, retaking Provins for the League and threatening Châlons in the process.[63]

For Châlons, the next significant development was the entry into the conflict of Duke Charles III, ruler of the independent duchy of Lorraine. Prior to 1589, Lorraine, despite his position as the head of the senior branch of the Guise family, had clung to a position of cautious neutrality. Following Henry III's death, however, he declared himself the ally and protector of the League. Apart from the religious issues, Lorraine wished to put his son, the marquis du Pont, on the throne of France and to acquire for himself Metz, Toul, and Verdun.[64] It was not until the end of 1590, however, that his forces invaded France.

Lorraine's entry into the conflict was balanced by the reentry of the duc de Nevers on the royalist side. Henry III had appointed Nevers governor of Champagne following Guise's death. Nevers. who resigned the post on the accession of Henry IV, now ended his neutrality, declared his unconditional willingness to follow Henry IV, and accepted the governorship of Champagne on behalf of his young son, for whom he was to act until the boy was old enough to assume the post himself. The duke entered the province in late 1590, and over the next several years he attempted to pacify Champagne for the king.[65]

The League was weakened by the failure of its Estates General in Paris and fatally wounded by the king's conversion in 1593. One by one, the towns of Champagne came over to the king. Meaux submitted at the end of 1593, followed by Troyes, Bar-sur-Aube, Chaumont, and Vitry-le-François. By 1594 only Reims held firm for the League, primarily because of the military presence of St. Paul. Following St. Paul's death in April 1594 the city turned itself over to the king. With the submission of Reims, the Wars of Religion in Champagne were effectively at an end.

[63]Poinsignon, *Histoire générale*, 2:340; Hérelle, *La Réforme*, 1:263; 2:324.

[64]Salmon, *Society in Crisis*, 259, 268; Mariéjol, *La Réforme*, 333–35; Poinsignon, *Histoire générale*, 2:341–45.

[65]Poinsignon, *Histoire générale*, 2:345–46.

Chapter 8

Châlons, Ideal of the Bonne Ville

O A GREAT EXTENT, the questions addressed by this study are brought into clear focus by the dramatic events of 1588 and 1589 in Châlons-sur-Marne. In refusing to join the Catholic League, expelling the baron de Rosne, and proclaiming their loyalty to Henry of Navarre as the legitimate king of France, the councillors of Châlons had embarked on a very risky course, a course which is all the more intriguing because from a purely political or military point of view they did precisely the opposite of what would seem prudent. Throughout this study we have examined the actions of the council in terms of structure and policy. What choices were available to the councillors? What options were possible, given the structures of power both within Châlons and outside? Why did they choose the options they did? What factors led them in the path they chose?

The conduct and decisions of the city council were remarkably consistent throughout more than thirty years of civil war. The council's actions may be compared to a prism; by refracting the events and circumstances of the civil wars through this prism, we see revealed not only thirty years of Châlons' history, but also certain aspects of urban experience in a France torn apart by political and religious civil war.

In reading the *livres des conclusions* of the city council, it is impossible to avoid the impression that the councillors were overwhelmingly concerned with purely local matters. The momentous events taking place throughout France in these years have scarcely any echo in Châlons' records. The great battles, sieges, and treaties of the Wars of Religion pass virtually unnoticed in the minutes of the council. No doubt the councillors were aware of these events, but the way the councillors conducted city business was not affected until those events impinged upon Châlons

162

directly, whether it was the passage of an army through the city, the presence of a garrison there, or the city's role when Champagne was a theater of war. The great exception to this preoccupation with local affairs came after 1588 and 1589, when Châlons was thrust by the force of circumstances into a position of national political prominence. From then until the pacification of Champagne in 1594, every national development did affect Châlons directly, since its fortunes were now bound up with those of the royalists and Henry IV. This stubborn parochialism is in accord with the bonne ville as described by Bernard Chevalier. In Châlons, these attitudes of the bonne ville lasted throughout the wars.

The "treason of the bourgeois" and the impact of religious division did not spell the end of the bonne ville of Châlons sur Marne. Indeed, this seems to have been the case elsewhere as well. Much has been made of the idea that the Catholic League permitted the towns of France to recover the autonomy that the centralizing monarchy had taken from them. Robert Descimon, in particular, has argued that the Sixteen in Paris were motivated by a desire to preserve the urban communal values of the Middle Ages. He finds a number of congruencies between these values and the ideology of the Sixteen.[1] His antagonist, at least concerning this ideology, Elie Barnavi, has found a similar tendency for other French cities: "almost everywhere, indeed, the municipalities used the League to set themselves up as more or less autonomous entities."[2]

Yet in Châlons we find the same impulses working in the opposite direction. For Châlons, it was the League that threatened civic autonomy. Châlons had experienced the domination and occupation of the Guises and found such control not much to its liking. Châlons' adherence to the Sainte Union would have brought with it subservience to Paris and the Sixteen. In short, Châlons' civic autonomy and civic agenda were better

---

[1] Robert Descimon, *Qui étaient les Seize? Mythes et réalites de la Ligue parisienne (1585–1594)* (Paris: Fédération des sociétés historiques et archéologiques de Paris et de l'Ile de France, 1983), 281, 295–96.

[2] Elie Barnavi, "Centralisme ou fédéralisme? Les relations entre Paris et les villes à l'époque de la Ligue (1585–1594)," *Revue Historique* 259 (1978): 335–44, here 336. Marseille in particular used the League to assert its urban independence; see Wolfgang Kaiser, *Marseille au temps des troubles, 1559–1596: Morphologies sociales et luttes des factions,* trans. Florence Chaix (Paris: Editions de l'Ecole des Hautes Etudes en Sciences Sociales, 1992), 304.

served by loyalty than by rebellion. It may well be that this was short-sighted; having remained loyal, Châlons came to be more dependent on the royal fiscal system for its revenues. How Châlons' autonomy fared under Henry IV after the Wars of Religion is beyond the scope of this study. What is clear is that the ideals of the bonne ville and Châlons' own historical and political circumstances combined to produce loyalty instead of rebellion. Conversely, many other towns felt that their agendas were better served by the League and Guise than by the crown. Or perhaps they simply did not have the same range of options available to them as the councillors of Châlons. In any case, local elites were not merely the pawns of powerful outsiders. They had interests of their own, and given the proper circumstances and configurations of power, they were not diffident about pursuing them.

One item on the agenda of the Châlonnais council was longstanding rivalry with other cities of Champagne: Troyes, Reims, and especially the new city of Vitry-le-François.[3] While it is true that these cities were capable of cooperation and consultation when matters of mutual interest were at stake, the dominant tone of intercity relations is one of rivalry.[4] This rivalry had many facets: social, economic, political, and eventually during the wars, military. The collapse of the central government gave hostile cities increased scope in which to pursue their rivalry. It was the new city of Vitry-le-François which was the particular focus of Châlonnais hostility. The two cities schemed to steal each other's marks of honor and

---

[3]For a more complete treatment of this subject, see Mark Konnert, "*Bonne Ville* or 'Treason of the Bourgeois?' Civic Rivalry and the Boundaries of Civic Identity in the French Wars of Religion: Châlons-sur-Marne and the Towns of Champagne," *Renaissance and Reformation/Renaissance et Réforme* 21, no. 1 (1997).

[4]Regarding this cooperation, in 1559 the council of Châlons wrote to the councils of Troyes and Reims concerning a royal loan of 50,000 livres from the cities of Champagne; see AD Marne E suppt. 4785, fol. 2. In 1576, Châlons, Troyes, and Vitry submitted joint remonstrances at court regarding the amount of the taille; see AD Marne E suppt. 4787, fol. 83. Even in the middle of civil war in the 1590s, royalist Châlons and Leaguer Reims signed a truce that permitted local workers to reap the harvest in peace; see Maurice Poinsignon, *Histoire générale de la Champagne et de Brie*, 3 vols. (Paris, 1885, 1898; rpt. Paris: Guénégaud, 1974), 2:385–91; Edouard Henry, *La réforme et la ligue en Champagne et à Reims* (St. Nicolas, 1867), 249–77; Edouard de Barthélemy, *Histoire*, 2d ed. (Châlons-sur-Marne, 1883), 314–19; Georges Hérelle, ed., *La Réforme et la Ligue en Champagne*, vol. 1, *Lettres*; vol. 2, *Pièces diverses* (Paris, 1888-92), 1:305–21, 325–53.

importance, and eventually, in 1590, entered into armed hostilities, with the Châlonnais attempting to persuade the king to destroy the rival city.[5]

Châlons was rewarded for its loyalty to the crown by the transfer of several bodies and jurisdictions from League towns to Châlons. The king transferred to Châlons not only a section of the Parlement of Paris, but also the cour des monnaies of the Troyes, and the grenier à sel and siège présidial of Vitry-le-François.

While no one would suggest that Châlons remained loyal to Henry III simply because Reims, Troyes, and especially Vitry were League towns, one cannot deny that it must have been a factor. The political divisions of the time allowed the Châlonnais council to finally obtain these longstanding goals at the expense of its neighbors and rivals. This was also a factor in the decision to recognize Henry IV; not recognizing him as king would have meant the loss of all they had acquired.

As discussed in chapter 2, the crises of the Wars of Religion seem to have revived interest in civic affairs among the city councillors. What we see here is a strengthening of the bonne ville's autonomy and self-aware-ness, not its attenuation, as the city council was forced to come to terms with the forces and events that threatened the city and its inhabitants. Indeed, the period of the Wars of Religion may in this respect be compared to the Hundred Years' War, which gave birth to the bonne ville.[6] Indeed, the crises of the Wars of Religion seem to have combined to produce a final and spectacular, if short-lived, blossoming of the ideal of the bonne ville. In Châlons, this ideal was expressed in opposition to the Catholic League; in other cities, no doubt, it was expressed in adherence to the League. What is important is that it was a decision, at least in Châlons (and

---

[5]Thus, in 1577 the Châlonnais council schemed to have suppressed the élection and grenier à sel of Vitry, raising a war chest of eighteen thousand livres from the leading inhabitants for the suppres-sion of the former. The Châlonnais council repeatedly attempted to have Vitry's *siège présidial* trans-ferred to Châlons. In 1582, as Vitry's fortifications neared completion, the Châlonnais council petitioned the king to have them destroyed, and when this failed, they raised a further twelve thousand livres to gain the transfer to Châlons of Vitry's *siège particulier* of the *bailliage* of Vermandois and its *siège présidial*, again, unsuccessfully; see AD Marne E suppt. 4785, fols. 18, 22–23, 236; 4787, fols. 138, 139; 4788, fols. 37, 39–40. For the Châlonnais petition to demolish Vitry, see Hérelle, *La Réforme*, 1:243. On Vitry-le-François, see René Crozet, "Une ville neuve au XVIe siècle: Vitry-le-François," *La vie urbaine* 5 (1923): 291–309; idem, "Le protestantisme et la Ligue à Vitry-le-François et en Per-thois." *Revue historique* 156 (1927): 1–40.

[6]Bernard Chevalier, *Les bonnes villes de France du XIVe au XVIe siècle* (Paris: Aubier Mon-taigne, 1982), 94–100.

presumably in other cities) that was made by civic elites on the basis of their perception of their own and their towns' interests. The autonomy and identity of the bonne ville could be equally well expressed in either royalist or Leaguer affiliation.

According to Chevalier, unity of religion was one of the strongest bonds that tied the bonne ville together, and it was the "'saison des Saint-Barthelemy' which closed this phase in the history of cities."[7] Yet, in Châlons the existence of a religious minority does not seem to have been so divisive.

The city council exhibited a rather paradoxical attitude towards the Huguenots. On the one hand, the council on numerous occasions requested the authorities to prohibit Protestant worship in Châlons. Even after the Edict of Nantes settled the religious question for nearly a century, the city council still petitioned the king to prohibit Protestant worship within city walls.[8] On the other hand, the council was generally tolerant of individual Huguenots. In several instances the council acted to protect Huguenot property and lives: the council resisted Bussy's wish to expel all Huguenots from Châlons in 1562 and 1563; it warned the Huguenots of the impending searches for grain in 1567; and, in the midst of the most horrifying example of religious passion run wild, the St. Bartholomew's Day Massacre, the council promised to protect the Huguenots' lives.

How are we to interpret this paradox? The answer becomes evident when events in Châlons are given their proper perspective and put into a national context. First, the actions taken by the council against Protestants were essentially nonviolent, whether it be expulsion from the city council, exclusion from the watch, or subjection to discriminatory taxation. These measures were unpleasant, but not violent or life-threatening. There were no massacres or religious riots of any consequence in Châlons such as have been observed in other French cities.[9] Châlonnais religious persecution was extremely mild by contemporary standards.

---

[7]Chevalier, *Les bonnes villes*, 288; see also 302–8.

[8]See Barthélemy, *Histoire*, 2d ed., 323–27.

[9]On Paris, see Barbara Diefendorf, "Prologue to a Massacre: Popular Unrest in Paris, 1557–1572," *American Historical Review* 90 (1985): 1067–91. For Lyon, see Natalie Z. Davis, "Strikes and Salvation and Lyon," and "The Rites of Violence," in *Society and Culture*. The whole issue of the nature of religious violence has been undergoing substantial revision, most particularly due to the publication of Denis Crouzet's massive work, *Les guerriers de Dieu*, 2 vols (Seyssel: Champ Vallon, 1990). Crouzet argues that the violence of the Wars of Religion can be explained only by religious motives, and that

Second, the impetus for such persecution generally came, directly or indirectly, from outside Châlons. Protestant councillors are expelled from the council in anticipation of the arrival of the elder duc de Guise, fresh from his "triumph" of Vassy and tumultuous reception in Paris. At the end of the first war of religion, the council resisted reinstatement of the Protestants largely at the insistence of Guise's brother, the duc d'Aumale. The council moved reluctantly toward compiling a list of Huguenots to be expelled from the city, and did so only when forced to by Bussy, the garrison commander and royal governor of Châlons. The council seized the property of the Protestant refugees only as a last resort, when paying the soldiers became a matter of the greatest urgency. Virtually every example of harassment or persecution of Protestants in Châlons can be traced to outside agents and pressures.

In short, in the minds of the councillors, religious division was less important than the integrity of their city and the bonds that they shared as Châlonnais. Clearly, they would have preferred a totally Catholic city. Given the circumstances, however, they realized that this would be possible only at the price of expelling, perhaps of exterminating, their fellow inhabitants. This was a price they were not willing to pay.[10] Moreover, in the course of the wars Châlonnais Catholics and Huguenots exhibited a measure of confidence in each other: the Catholics realized that the

---

Catholics and Huguenots had their own distinctive modes of violence, based upon their differing responses to a deep-seated crisis of eschatological expectations. Catholic violence in particular was characterized by a kind of divine frenzy, by people losing themselves in divine violence, hoping to purify the world in expectation of the Second Coming. Crouzet's work has initiated a huge debate, but he is, I believe, mistaken on several important issues; specifically, in his quest for a monocausal explanation of the violence of the Wars of Religion, in his assertion that since the violence cannot be explained completely by social, economic, or political motives, then religion must be the real and only motive. Nor do people generally lose themselves in violent behavior; this goes against all the findings of social psychology and sociology. See Mack Holt, "Putting Religion Back into the Wars of Religion," *French Historical Studies* 18, no. 2 (1993): 524–51, and Mark Greengrass, "The Psychology of Religious Violence," *French History* 5, no. 4 (1992): 467–74.

[10]Wolfgang Kaiser, *Marseille au temps des troubles*, 219–20, 273, notes a similar sort of tolerance in Marseille, based on the desire not to interfere with business. Indeed, it was dissatisfaction with this de facto tolerance which prompted the most the radical phase of the League in Marseille, the dictatorship of Charles de Casaulx. Such dissatisfaction was presumably not present in Châlons, or at least those who felt it were unable or unwilling to act on it. For a similar albeit less dramatic instance where city fathers put unity and order ahead of religious uniformity, see Muriel C. McClendon, "'Against God's Word': Government, Religion and the Crisis of Authority in Early Reformation Norwich," *Sixteenth Century Journal* 25 (1994): 353–69.

Huguenots were not about to betray the city by opening the gates to a Protestant army; the Huguenots understood that while they might be subjected to certain types of discrimination, their property and lives were as secure as the circumstances of the times allowed.

Tolerance, like bigotry, is self-reinforcing. Cities which experienced massacres generally had a history of contention and violence between Protestants and Catholics—a vicious cycle set in, with each incident of religious intolerance reinforcing the strife.[11] But Châlonnais Catholics and Huguenots had acquired a measure of confidence in each other, and as they overcame each incident and each crisis together, the bond of confidence was only reinforced.

However tolerant the councillors might have been of native Huguenots, this tolerance did not extend to foreigners. Non-Châlonnais Huguenots were expelled on several occasions throughout the wars. The councillors' attitude towards foreign Protestants was the same as its attitude towards foreign sick and foreign vagabonds. The council recognized an obligation to its own, whether they be sick, poor, or Protestant. Foreigners were afforded no such toleration—not because they were sick, poor, or Protestant, but simply because they were foreign. Foreigners had no claim on the council's benevolence. Nor could the councillors express the same measure of confidence towards foreigners that they did towards their own native Huguenots. What lay behind this attitude on the part of the councillors? A definitive psychological explanation is probably impossible. Nevertheless, there are certain factors which, taken together, go a long way towards an explanation.

Châlons-sur-Marne was a city with a well-defined sense of community despite the fact that the city's very existence was only customary. This sense of community was born out of the inhabitants' struggles against the bishops for a voice in the government of their city. It was born out of the calamities of the Hundred Years' War, when the inhabitants were forced to cohere as a community to guarantee the survival of their city. It was born out of a geographical position which exposed them to an extensive cross-

---

[11]Philip Benedict, "The Saint Bartholomew's Massacres in the Provinces," *Historical Journal* 21(1978): 220–21.

fertilization of ideas and ideologies, contributing to a sense of tolerance for the unusual and the different.[12] The city's geographical position also exposed it to less benevolent forces. Lacking natural defenses and situated near the frontier of France, on the major invasion routes, the inhabitants very early pieced together an effective structure for their own defense. This defensive apparatus predated the upheavals brought by religious schism; those who might have wished to transform it into an instrument of repression against their fellow inhabitants would have found it very difficult to do so.

This sense of community was also facilitated by the city's size. Châlons in the sixteenth century had about ten thousand inhabitants or about twenty-five hundred households, or *feux*. It is likely—especially in the confined area of an early modern city—that the heads of the households knew each other, at least by sight or reputation. Clearly, there were cities of Châlons' size, and even smaller, which did experience the confessional violence that Châlons avoided. Religious violence does not automatically take place where the preconditions and occasions for it exist. What Natalie Davis has called the "conditions for guilt-free massacre" must also be present.[13] This is, of course, more likely in the anonymity of a large city than in a place such as Châlons, where there was no faceless mob of heretics or idolaters to be massacred; instead, there were neighbors, friends, childhood playmates, and relatives. The "heretic" or "idolater" is likely to be one's classmate, brother-in-law, or neighbor. Instead of asking why a place like Châlons avoided religious violence, we ought to turn the question on its head and ask what extraordinary pressures and experiences led neighbors in similar communities to slaughter one another.

---

[12]Roger Zuber, "Les Champenois réfugiés à Strasbourg et l'Eglise Réformée de Châlons," *Mémoires de la Société d'agriculture, commerce, science, et des arts du département de la Marne* (1964): 45–46. For examples of different civic cultures and identities, specifically ones closely linked with the Catholic Church and the defense of Catholic orthodoxy, see Barbara Diefendorf *Beneath the Cross: Catholics and Huguenots in Sixteenth-Century Paris* (New York: Oxford University Press, 1991), 48, on Paris; Mack Holt, "Wine, Community and Reformation in Sixteenth-Century Burgundy," *Past and Present* 138 (1993), 58–93, on Dijon; and Kaiser, *Marseille au temps des troubles,* 170, 190–91, on Marseille.

[13]Davis, *Society and Culture*, 181: "The crucial fact that the killers must forget is that their victims are human beings. These harmful people in the community—the evil priest or the hateful heretic—have already been transformed for the crowd into 'vermin' or 'devils.'" See also Denis Crouzet, *Les guerriers de Dieu,* 1:254–71.

Another part of the explanation for Châlons' toleration lies in the professional and occupational character of the city. Then as now, Châlons was primarily an administrative rather than industrial center. There were no large-scale industries such as weaving, as there were at places like Troyes and Amiens, and thus no large urban working class, which often produced the most radical Huguenots, who inspired the fear and hatred of the local elite. On the other hand, Châlons lay in the *ressort* of the Parlement of Paris and had no sovereign court of its own. As J. H. M. Salmon has written, the magistrates of the sovereign courts "remained generally hostile to reform," and "consistently resisted the crown's endeavour to tolerate religious dissent."[14] Châlons therefore lacked the two most potentially antagonistic and volatile ingredients for social and religious violence— ingredients which combined to produce religious violence in Paris, Rouen, and Toulouse.

When presented with the choice of remaining loyal to their king and the traditions of hereditary succession, or joining the rebel Catholic League—an organization predicated on the persecution and elimination of the Huguenots, whom the council had tolerated for almost thirty years—the councillors' choice was obvious.

⌐

SOME OF THE ANSWERS to the questions that concern us here lay in Châlons' own peculiar circumstances and historical experience. Châlons was certainly an ordinary city—it was neither especially large nor especially important on a national scale. Yet, beneath this seemingly ordinary surface, extraordinary things were taking place. This should remind us that other communities were shaped by their own experiences and their governments' perceptions of their own and their city's interests. Who knows what exceptional events are hidden in the histories of other ordinary cities? Answers to the more important question transcend Châlons itself. If we are correct in postulating that devotion to the ideals of the bonne ville—the same ideals which for Descimon brought forth the Sixteen in Paris—could also lead to the contrary result, the question, then,

---

[14]J.H.M. Salmon, *Society in Crisis: France in the Sixteenth Century* (London: St. Martins, 1975), 133.

should be why it cost the whole of France thirty-five years of civil war to arrive at the solutions which Châlons had adopted from the beginning. The Edict of Nantes is essentially no more than the extension to all of France of the type of tolerance displayed in Châlons: recognition that while the Huguenots may have been heretics, they were also French, and that the price demanded for religious uniformity was simply too high to be paid.

Bibliography

ARCHIVES

The relevant archival material is housed in the Archives Départementales de la Marne in Châlons. Formerly catalogued separately as the Archives Communales de Châlons, the records of the city have now been incorporated into the departmental archives. Throughout, I have used the cataloguing system of the Archives Départementales. For reference and comparison, here are the relevant *fonds* according to both the Archives Communales (AC) and Archives Départementales (AD) systems:

	AC Châlons	AD Marne
Fêtes et cérémonies publiques	AA 13	E suppt. 4764
Livres des conclusions	BB 11–16	E suppt. 4785–4790
Registre des réfugiés	BB 47	E suppt. 4823
Financial affairs	CC 12–96	E suppt. 4843–4927
Military affairs	EE 1–36	E suppt. 5239–5274

MANUSCRIPTS

Annales du diocèse de Chaalons en Champagne, mises en ordre par M.P.G., ancien curé du diocèse. Bibliothèque Municipale de Châlons-sur-Marne, Fonds Garinet, 2535.

Fradet. *Mémoires concernant les évêques et la ville de Chaalons.* 2 vols. Bibliothèque Municipale de Châlons-sur-Marne, Fonds Garinet, 1875.

Histoire des évêques de Châlons jusqu'en 1624. Bibliothèque Municipale de Châlons-sur-Marne, Fonds Garinet, 9803.

Histoire du diocèse de Châlons-sur-Marne, par D. François, religieux bénédictin de la congregation de Saint-Vanne. Bibliothèque Municipale de Châlons-sur-Marne, Fonds Garinet, 1851.

Recueil historique de la ville et des évêques de Châlons, en Champagne. Bibliothèque Municipale de Châlons-sur-Marne, Fonds Garinet, 9803.

Histoire de la Ligue. Bibliothèque Nationale, Manuscrits Français, 23295–96.

OTHER SOURCES

These sources are arranged alphabetically by author. Original works precede works edited, compiled, or translated by the same person. Each author's works are arranged chronologically by date of publication. Compiled, edited, or translated works are grouped, in that order, following the authored works.

Ascoli, Peter. "French Provincial Cities and the Catholic League." *Occasional Papers of the American Society for Reformation Research* 1 (1977).

Babeau, Albert. *La ville sous l'ancien régime.* 2 vols. Paris, 1884.

Barbat, Louis. *Histoire de la ville de Châlons-sur-Marne et de ses monuments depuis son origine jusqu'en 1855.* Châlons, 1865.

—————. *Tablettes historiques de Châlons-sur-Marne.* Châlons, 1879.

Barnavi, Elie. "Centralisme ou fédéralisme? Les relations entre Paris et les villes à l'époque de la Ligue (1585–1594)." *Revue Historique* 259 (1978): 335–44.

—————. *Le parti de Dieu: Etude sociale et politique des chefs de la Ligue parisienne, 1585–1594.* Brussels: Editions Nauwelaerts, 1980.

—————. "Réponse à Robert Descimon." *Annales: Économies, Sociétés, Civilisations* 37 (1982): 112–221.

Barthélemy, Edouard de. *Essai historique sur la Réforme et la Ligue à Châlons-sur-Marne.* Châlons, 1851.

—————. *Correspondance inédite des rois de France avec le conseil de ville de Châlons-sur-Marne.* Châlons, 1855.

—————. *Diocèse ancien de Châlons-sur-Marne, histoire et monuments.* 2 vols. Paris, 1861.

—————. "Catherine de Médicis, le duc de Guise, et le traité de Nemours." *Revue des questions historiques* 27 (1880): 465–95

—————. *Histoire de la ville de Châlons-sur-Marne et de ses institutions, des origines à 1848.* Châlons, 1st ed., 1854, 2d ed., 1883.

—————. "Le Parlement de Châlons-sur-Marne, 1589–94." *Revue de Champagne et de Brie* (1883): 5–41.

—————, ed. *Correspondance inédite de M. de Dinteville, lieutenant-général au gouvernement de Champagne, 1579–1586.* Arcis-sur-Aube, 1889.

Beik, William. *Absolutism and Society in Seventeenth Century France: State Power and Provincial Aristocracy in Languedoc.* Cambridge: Cambridge University Press, 1985.

Benedict, Philip. "The Saint Bartholomew's Massacres in the Provinces." *The Historical Journal* 21 (1978): 205–25.

—————. *Rouen during the Wars of Religion.* Cambridge: Cambridge UniversityPress, 1981.

—————, ed. *Cities and Social Change in Early Modern France.* London: Unwin Hyman, 1989.

Bèze, Théodore de. *Histoire ecclésiastique des églises réformées au royaume de France.* 2 vols. Ed. G. Baum and E. Cunitz. Paris, 1883.

Brady, Thomas A. *Ruling Class, Regime and Reformation at Strasbourg 1520–1555.* Studies in Medieval and Reformation Thought, 22. General editor, H. A. Oberman. Leiden: E.J. Brill, 1978.

Brunet, Roger. *Atlas et géographie de Champagne, Pays de Meuse, et Basse Bourgogne.* Paris: Flammarion, 1981.

Buirette de Verrires, Claude Rémi. *Annales Historiques de la ville et comté-prairie de Châlons-sur-Marne.* Châlons, 1788.

Carorguy, Jacques. *Mémoires.* Ed. E. Bruwaert. Paris, 1880.

Cayet, Pierre-Victor-Palma. *Chronologie Novenaire, contenant l'histoire de la guerre.* Edited by Michaud and Poujolat. Paris, 1857.

Châlons-sur-Marne, 2000 ans: Mélanges d'histoire, de géographie, d'art, et de traditions. Châlons-sur-Marne: Association Bimillénaire, 1980.

Chevalier, Bernard. *Les bonnes villes de France du XIVe au XVIe siècle.* Paris: Aubier Montaigne, 1982.

Clause, Georges, and Jean-Pierre Ravaux. *Histoire de Châlons-sur-Marne.* Le Coteau-Roanne: Horvath, 1983.

Collins, James B. *The Fiscal Limits of Absolutism: Direct Taxation in Early Seventeenth-Century France.* Berkeley and Los Angeles: University of California Press, 1988.

Couvret, Anne-Marie. "Les Châlonnais du XVIe siècle, propriétaires ruraux." *Mémoires de la société d'agriculture, commerce, sciences, et arts du département de la Marne* 78 (1963): 61–81.

Crouzet, Denis. *Les guerriers de Dieu.* 2 vols. Seyssel: Champ Vallon, 1990.

Crozet, Réné. "Une ville neuve du XVIe siècle: Vitry-le-François." *La vie urbaine* 5 (1923): 291–309.

———. "Le protestantisme et la Ligue à Vitry-le-François et en Perthois." *Revue Historique* 156 (1927): 1–40.

———. *Histoire de Champagne.* Paris: Boivin, 1933.

Crubellier, Maurice, and Charles Juilliard. *Histoire de Champagne.* Paris: Presses Universitaires, 1969.

Davies, Joan. "Persecution and Protestantism: Toulouse, 1562–1575." *Historical Journal* 22 (1979): 31–53.

Davila, Enrico Caterina. *The History of the Civil Wars of France.* Trans. E.Farnsworth. London, 1758.

Davis, Natalie Z. *Society and Culture in Early Modern France.* Stanford: Stanford University Press, 1975.

Descimon, Robert. "La Ligue à Paris (1585–1594): Une révision." *Annales: Économies, Sociétés, Civilisations* 37 (1982): 72–111.

———. "La Ligue: Des divergences fondamentales." *Annales: Économies, Sociétés, Civilisations* 37 (1982): 122–28.

———. *Qui étaient les Seize? Mythes et réalités de la Ligue parisienne (1585–1594).* Paris: Fédération des sociétés historiques et archéologiques de Paris et de l'Ile de France, 1983.

Desportes, Pierre, ed. *Histoire de Reims.* Toulouse: Privat, 1983.

Diefendorf, Barbara. *Paris City Councillors in the Sixteenth Century: The Politics of Patrimony.* Princeton: Princeton University Press, 1983.

———. "Recent Literature on the Religious Conflicts in Sixteenth-Century France." *Religious Studies Review* 10 (1984): 362–67.

———. "Prologue to a Massacre: Popular Urban Unrest in Paris, 1557–1572." *American Historical Review* 90 (1985): 1067–1091.

———, "The Background to the League: Civic Values in Paris at the Beginning of the Wars of Religion." Address delivered to the Society for French Historical Studies, Quebec, 1986.

————. "The Catholic League: Social Crisis or Apocalypse Now?" *French Historical Studies* 15 (1987): 332–44.

————. *Beneath the Cross: Catholics and Huguenots in Sixteenth-Century Paris.* New York: Oxford University Press, 1991.

Dolan, Claire. "L'image du protestant et le conseil municipal d'Aix au XVIe s." *Renaissance and Reformation/Renaissance et Réforme* 4 (1980): 152–64.

————. *Entre tours et clochers: Gens d'église à Aix-en-Provence au XVIe siècle.* Sherbrooke, Québec, and Aix-en-Provence: Presses de l'Université de Sherbrooke and Edisud, 1981.

Doucet, Roger. *Les institutions de la France au XVIe siècle.* 2 vols. Paris: Picard, 1948.

Drouot, Henri. *Mayenne et la Bourgogne: Étude sur la Ligue.* 2 vols. Paris: Picard, 1937.

————"Les conseils provinciaux de la Sainte-Union (1589–1595): Notes et questions." *Annales du Midi* 65 (1953): 415–33.

Duby, Georges, ed. *Histoire de la France urbaine.* 3 vols. Paris: Seuil, 1980.

Farr, James R. "The Rise of a Middle Class: Artisans in Dijon, 1550–1650." Ph.D. diss., Northwestern University, 1983.

————. "Popular Religious Solidarity in Sixteenth-Century Dijon." *French Historical Studies* 14 (1985): 192–214.

————. *Hands of Honor: Artisans and Their World in Dijon, 1550–1650.* Ithaca: Cornell University Press, 1988.

François, M., ed. *Lettres de Henri III, roi de France.* Paris, 1884.

Galpern, A.N. *The Religions of the People in Sixteenth-Century Champagne.* Harvard Historical Studies, no. 92 (1976). Cambridge, Mass: Harvard University Press, 1976.

Garrisson-Estèbe, Janine. *Tocsin pour un massacre. La saison des Saint Barthélemy.* Paris: Le Centurion/Sciences Humaines, 1968.

Greengrass, Mark. "The Psychology of Religious Violence." *French History* 5, no. 4 (1992): 467–74.

————. "The *Sainte Union* in the Provinces: The Case of Toulouse." *Sixteenth Century Journal* 14 (1983): 469–96.

Grignon, Louis. *Topographie historique de la ville de Châlons-sur-Marne.* Châlons, 1889.

Grosjean, Ernest. *Implantation de la Réforme en France (1561–98) vue et vécue depuis Châlons-sur-Marne.* Châlons, 1980.

Guggenheim, Anne. "The Calvinist Notables of Nîmes during the Era of the Religious Wars." *Sixteenth Century Journal* 3 (1972): 80–96.

Guilbert, Sylvette. "Les fortifications de Châlons-sur-Marne à la fin du Moyen Age." *Actes du 95e congrès national des sociétés savantes, Reims, 1970.* Section d'archéologie et d'histoire de l'art. Paris (1974): 195–203.

————. "A Châlons-sur-Marne au XVe siècle: Un conseil municipal face aux épidémies." *Annales: Économies, Sociétés, Civilisations* 23 (1968).

Harding, Robert. *Anatomy of a Power Elite: The Provincial Governors of Early Modern France.* New Haven: Yale University Press, 1978.

————. "The Mobilization of Confraternities against the Reformation in France." *Sixteenth Century Journal,* 11 (1980): 85–107.

————. "Revolution and Reform in the Holy League: Angers, Rennes, and Nantes." *Journal of Modern History,* 53 (1981): 379–416.

Haton, Claude. *Mémoires contenant le récit des événements accomplis de 1553 à 1583 principalement dans la Champagne et la Brie.* 2 vols. Ed. F. Bourquelot. Documents inédits sur l'histoire de France. Paris, 1857.

Harding, Robert. "The Mobilization of Confraternities against the Reformation in France." *Sixteenth Century Journal* 11 (1980): 85–107.

————. "Revolution and Reform in the Holy League: Angers, Rennes, and Nantes." *Journal of Modern History* 53 (1981): 379-416.

Hauchecorne, François. "Orléans au temps de la Ligue." *Bulletin trimestriel le de la Société archéologique et historique de l'Orléannais,* n. ser. 5, vol. 5, no. 39 (1970): 267–78.

————. "Orléans ligueur en 1591." *Actes du 93e congrès de la Société des savants, Tours, 1968/Bulletin philologique et historique du comité des travaux historiques et scientifiques* 2 (1971): 2, 845–59.

Heller, Henry. *The Conquest of Poverty: The Calvinist Revolt in Sixteenth-Century France.* Studies in Medieval and Reformation Thought, 35. Ed. Heiko A. Oberman. Leiden: J. Brill, 1986.

————. *Iron and Blood: Civil Wars in Sixteenth-Century France.* Montreal and Kingston: McGill-Queen's University Press, 1991.

Henry, Edouard. *La réforme et la ligue en Champagne et à Reims.* St. Nicolas, 1867.

Hérelle, Georges, ed. *Mémoire des choses plus notables advenues en la province de Champagne 1585-98.* Trav. Acad. Reims, 68 (1879).

————, ed. *Documents inédits sur le protestantisme à Vitry-le-François.* 3 vols. Paris, 1906.

————, ed. *La Réforme et la Ligue en Champagne.* Vol. 1, *Lettres;* vol. 2, *Pièces diverses.* Paris, 1888-92.

Hickey, Daniel. *The Coming of French Absolutism: The Struggle for Tax Reform in the Province of Dauphiné, 1540–1640.* Toronto: University of Toronto Press, 1986.

Hoffman, Philip. *Church and Community in the Diocese of Lyon.* New Haven: Yale University Press, 1984.

Holt, Mack P. "Wine, Community and Reformation in Sixteenth-Century Burgundy," *Past and Present* 138 (1993): 58–93.

————. "Putting Religion Back into the Wars of Religion." *French Historical Studies* 18, no. 2 (1993): 524–51,

Huppert, George. *Les Bourgeois Gentilshommes: An Essay on the Definition of Elites in Renaissance France.* Chicago: University of Chicago Press, 1977.

————. *Public Schools in Renaissance France.* Urbana: University of Illinois Press, 1984.

Kaiser, Wolfgang. *Marseille au temps des troubles, 1559–1596: Morphologie sociale et luttes des factions.* Trans. Florence Chaix. Paris: Editions de l'Ecole des Hautes Etudes en Sciences Sociales, 1992.

Kingdon, Robert M. *Geneva and the Coming of the Wars of Religion in France, 1555–1563.* Geneva: E. Droz, 1956.

————. *Geneva and the Consolidation of the French Protestant Movement, 1564–1572.* Geneva: E. Droz, 1967.

Konnert, Mark W. "A Tolerant City Council? Châlons-sur-Marne during the Wars of Religion," *Proceedings of the Annual Meeting of the Western Society for French History* 16 (1989): 40–47.

———. "Urban Values versus Religious Passion: Châlons-sur-Marne during the Wars of Religion," *Sixteenth Century Journal* 20 (1989): 387–405.

———. "*Bonne Ville* or 'Treason of the Bourgeoisie'? Civic Rivalry and the Boundaries of Civic Identity in the French Wars of Religion: Châlons-sur-Marne and the Towns of Champagne." *Renaissance and Reformation/Renaissance et Réforme* 21, no. 1 (1997).

Laronze, Charles. *Essai sur le régime municipal en Bretagne pendant les guerres de religion.* Paris, 1890; rpt. Geneva: Megariotis, 1981.

Lamet, Maryélise S. "French Protestants in a Position of Strength: The Early Years of the Reformation in Caen, 1558–1568." *Sixteenth Century Journal* 9 (1978): 35–56.

Laurent, Jean. *Atlas de la région Champagne-Ardennes.* Aulnay sous Bois, 1962.

"Lettre de Pierre Fornelet à Neuchâtel du 6 octobre, 1561." *Bulletin de la Société de l'histoire du protestantisme français* 12 (1863): 361–66.

"Lettre de Pierre Fornelet à Calvin du 6 octobre, 1561." *Bulletin de la Société de l'histoire du protestantisme français* 14 (1866): 364–67.

Maillet, Germaine. "Plans de Châlons du Moyen Age au XVIIIe siècle." *Bulletin du comité du folklore champenois* 104 (1971).

Mariéjol, Jean. *La Réforme et la Ligue.* Vol. 6, Histoire de France. Edited by E. Lavisse. Paris: Hachette, 1904.

McClendon, Muriel C. "'Against God's Word': Government, Religion and the Crisis of Authority in Early Reformation Norwich." *Sixteenth Century Journal* 25 (1994): 353–69.

Mentzer, Raymond A. "Heresy Suspects in Languedoc prior to 1560: Observations on their Social and Occupational Status." *Bibliothèque d'Humanisme et Renaissance* 39 (1977): 561–68.

Mieck, Ilja. "Die Bartolomäusnacht als Forschungsproblem: Kritische Bestandaufnahme und neue Aspekte," *Historische Zeitschrifte* 226 (1973): 73–110.

Mornay, Charlotte-Arbaleste de la Borde, Mme du Plessis de. *Mémoires.* Paris, 1869.

Mousnier, Roland. *The Institutions of France under the Absolute Monarchy 1589–1789: Society and the State.* Trans. B. Pearce. Chicago: University of Chicago Press, 1979.

Nicholls, David. "Social Change and Early Protestantism in France: Normandy, 1520–1562." *European Studies Review* 10 (1980): 279–308.

———. "The Social History of the French Reformation: Ideology, Confession and Culture." *Social History* 9 (1984): 25–43.

Pelicier, Philippe. *Inventaire sommaire des Archives Communales antérieures à 1790; Ville de Châlons-sur-Marne.* Châlons, 1903.

Perret, André. *Les hôpitaux de Châlons-sur-Marne jusqu'au XVIIe siècle.* Thèse manuscrite de l'Ecole des Chartres.

Poinsignon, Maurice. *Histoire générale de la Champagne et de Brie.* 3 vols. Paris, 1885, 1898; rpt. Paris: Guenégaud, 1974.

Read, Charles, ed. "La Saint-Barthélemy à Orléans racontée par Joh.-Wilh. de Botzheim, étudiant allemand témoin oculaire." *Bulletin de la Société de l'Histoire du Protestantisme Français,* 21 (1872): 345–92.

Reuss, Rodolphe. "Un nouveau récit de la Saint-Barthélemy par un bourgeois de Strasbourg." *Bulletin de la Société de l'Histoire du Protestantisme Français* 22 (1873): 374–81.

Roberts, Penny. "Religious Conflict and the Urban Setting: Troyes during the French Wars of Religion." *French History* 6 (1992): 259–78.

Rosenberg, David. "Social Experience and Religious Choice: A Case Study; The Protestant Weavers and Woolcombers of Amiens in the Sixteenth Century." Ph.D. diss., Yale University, 1978.

Rublack, Hans-Cristoph. "Political and Social Norms in Urban Communities in the Holy Roman Empire." In *Religion, Politics, and Social Protest.* Ed. K. von Greyerz. London: George Allen and Unwin, 1984.

Salmon, J. H. M. "The Paris Sixteen, 1584–94: The Social Analysis of a Revolutionary Movement." *Journal of Modern History* 44 (1972): 540–76.

———. *Society in Crisis: France in the Sixteenth Century.* London: St. Martins, 1975.

Sutherland, Nicola. *The Massacre of St. Bartholomew and the European Conflict.* London: n.p., 1973.

Thompson, James W. *The Wars of Religion in France 1559–1576.* Chicago: University of Chicago Press, 1909.

Van Doren, L. Scott. "War, Taxes, and Social Protest: The Challenge to Authority in Sixteenth-Century Dauphiné." Ph.D. diss., Harvard University, 1970.

Viard, Georges. "Propaganda politique et compagnes d'opinion à Langres au temps de la Ligue." *Cahiers Haut-Marnais* 138 (1979), 121–33.

Wolfe, Martin. *The Fiscal System of Renaissance France.* New Haven: Yale University Press, 1972.

Wolff, Philippe. *Histoire de Toulouse.* Toulouse: Privat, 1961.

Zeller, Gaston. *Les institutions de la France au XVIe siècle.* Paris: Presses Universitaires, 1948.

Zuber, Roger. "Les Champenois réfugiés à Strasbourg et l'Eglise Réformée de Châlons." *Mémoires de la Société d'agriculture, commerce, science, et des arts du département de la Marne* (1964): 31–55.

Index

*A*bbeys
of Benedictines, 30
St. Memmie, 30, 31
St. Pierre-aux-Monts, 30, 31
St. Sulpice, 30, 31
Toussaints de l'Ile, 31, 32, 83, 107
Aetius (Rom. general), 28
d'Alençon/Anjou, duc, 116, 122
Alfeston, Michel, 73
Alpin (saint), 28
Ambloff (colonel), 119
Amboise tumult/conspiracy, 91, 93
d'Andelot (commander), 105
d'Anjou/Alençon, duc, 116, 122, 134
d'Apremont, Antoine, 111
arms, and military security, 63, 64-65, 132-33,
138, 157
Aubelin, Jean, 143
Aubelin family, 42
d'Aultry (seigneur), 110
d'Aumale (Claude de Lorraine), 58, 84, 96, 102,
104, 110, 134, 145
d'Aumont (maréchal), 46

*B*abeau, Albert, 4, 15
de Bar, Jacques, 106, 109
de Bar family, 42
Barbezieulx (Charles de La Rochefoucald), 59,
92, 106, 125, 129, 131
Barnavi, Elie, 12, 166
Beik, W. H., 17
Belin, Pierre, 114
Benedict, Philip, 6, 7, 14, 113, 114
Benedictine abbey, 30
Berliz, Georges, 159
Berliz, Jacques de, 159
Berlize, Marc de, 77
Beschefer, Jacques, 111
Beschefer family, 42
Billet, Claude, 111
Birague (captain), 57
Blois Estates General, 124
bonne ville
Châlons as ideal, 162-71
defined/described, 6-7
Bourbon, Charles X (cardinal) de, 145, 154
Bourgeois/Burgensis, Jérôme de (bishop), 44,
94, 95n9

Braulx, Pierre, 43, 93
Braulx family, 42
Braux, Michel, 151
Braux, Pierre, 151
Bricquenay village, 101
Broyes-lez-Sézanne, and Catholic League, 133
Bussy (Antoine de Clermont), 58, 66, 67, 103,
132
anti-Huguenot measures, 98-101, 102

*C*alvin, John, 91, 93
Carolingians, and Châlons, 30
Carrouges (royalist governor), 145
Casimir, John, 108, 116
Castel (Thierry de l'Hôpital), 52, 55-56, 94, 96,
102, 109, 111-12 130
Catalauni (Catuvellani) tribe, 28
Catherine de Médicis, 80, 91, 102, 135
Catholic League
Leaguer Estates General, 158
outlawed, 124
in Paris, 139
rise of, vii-viii, 122-23
and the Sixteen, 75, 145, 158
war preparations, 108
Cauchon, T., 43
Celtic names, in Champagne, 28
Châlons-sur-Marne. *See also* city council.
and Catholic League, 122-24
ceded to Guises, 122-44
challenged (1560-76), 91-121
chronology (1588-94), 145-61
civic identity, 34-35
subdued (1576-1588), 122-44
early history, 30-39
finances, 72-90, 74
fiscal administration, 72-90
fishing rights, 44, 45
as focus of study, viii-ix, 15-21
fortifications, 51-52, 53, 54
geographical importance, 25-29, 169
governors of, 58
hostage negotiations, 151-52
Huguenots, 99-104
and security, 62, 132-33, 138, 157
ideal bonne ville, 162-71
institutional developments, 37-38
intercity rivalry, 164-65

Châlons-sur-Marne (*continued*)
  legal existence lacking, 17, 49
  no St. Bartholomew's Day massacre, 113
  at outbreak of Wars, 91-99
  parishes of, 31
  and Parlement of Paris, 158
  power structures, 25-39
  religious toleration, 97, 171-73
  royalist, 36, 147, 150, 155-56
  security measures, 59-71, 147-50, 157
  self-governing, 33-34
  in sixteenth century (*map*), 39
  St. Martin's Day Assembly (Nov. 11), 41, 43, 73, 94
  subdued (1576-1588), 122-44
  and Wars of Religion, 30-39
Chambre des Comptes, in Paris, 77
Champagne
  and Catholic League, 124-25
  end of Wars of Religion, 161
  geographical importance, 25-27
  Leaguer/Guisard region, viii
  military campaigns in, 160
  Roman period, 28
Champagne, Guillaume de (seigneur de Vary-mont), 43, 56, 84, 93, 130
Champagne, Hugues de (sieur de St. Mard), 55, 56, 57, 137
Chapelle des Sybilles, council meetings in, 40
Charles V, 64, 71
Charles VII, 38
Charles IX, 80, 91, 103
Charles the Bald, 30
Chastillon, Pierre, 73
Chastillon family, 42
Cheppes, fortification at, 28
Chevalier, Bernard, 7, 8, 15, 51, 54, 62, 163, 166
Church of St. Pierre, 30
city council. *See also* Châlons-sur-Marne.
  and civic finances, 72-90, 74
  composition of, 42
  establishment of, 37
  expenses of, 80
  and Huguenots/Protestants, 104, 166-69
  meeting frequency/attendance, 47-49, 168
  oaths of allegiance, vii, 43-44, 140, 146-47, 154-55
  portrait of, 40-50
  revenues, 74
  St. Martin's Day Assembly, 41, 43, 73, 94
  toleration, 97
Clausse, Cosme (bishop), viii, 44-45, 49, 57, 119, 135
  and Catholic League, 131
  and petition to worship, 125-26

Clausse, Cosme (Bishop) (*continued*)
  tricked by council, 150-51
Clausse, Nicolas (bishop), 44
Clément, Jacques, 153
Clément family, 42
Clermont, Antoine de (sieur de Bussy), 58, 66, 67, 103, 132
  anti-Huguenot measures, 98-101, 102
Clèves, Louis de (abbot), 45, 125-26
Cognac, 111
Coligny (admiral), 106, 107
Collins, James, 17
Company of the Crossbow, 64
Condé, Prince de, 91, 105, 106-7, 116, 123
Cuissotte family, 42

*D*aoust family, 42
Davis, Natalie Zemon, 9, 169
Descimon, Robert, 6, 12, 13, 15, 163
Desportes, Pierre, 5
Deu, Pierre, 157
Deux-Ponts (duke of Zweibrucken), 110
Diefendorf, Barbara, 8, 12, 18, 71
Dinteville, Joachim de, 59, 60, 136, 137, 149, 151, 153, 159
  royalist, vii, 78, 131, 132
Dolan, Claire, 6, 20
Dommengin, Jean, 43
Doucet, Roger, 4
Drouot, Henri, 12
Duby, Georges, 6
Du Pont (marquis Lorraine), 161

*E*dicts
  of Amboise, 101, 104
  of Beaulieu, 116, 122, 123, 125
  of Poitiers, 124
  of Romorantin, 91, 93
  of St. Germain, 91, 111
Elbeuf (cousin of Guises), 134
Erchenré (bishop), 30
Estates General, at Blois (1576), 124
d'Estrées (captain), 101

*F*arr, James, 9
feudal system, 32
Fornelet, Pierre, 93-94, 97, 103, 104, 111
fortifications, expenditures for, 54
Franciscans, and Catholic League, 159
Francis II, death of, 91
François, Charles, 81, 95, 103
François, Claude, 143
François, Pierre, 73, 78
François family, 42

*G*alpern, A. N., 26, 92
Godet, G., 42, 46
Godet family, 42

Gombart, Nicolas, 151
Gonzague, Charles de (duc de Rethelois), 58
Gonzague, Louis de (duc de Nevers), 58, 60, 93, 94, 96, 129, 152-53, 154
Gorlier family, 42
Gourlier, Claude, 159
Grandpré (Robert de Joyeuse), 152, 159-60
Gromard, Simon, 159
Guise family, and Catholic League, 122
Guise (François de Lorraine), 58
Guise (Henri de Lorraine), 58, 107, 109
    and Catholic League, 122-23, 125-44
    correspondence with Châlons, 117-20
    murdered, vii, 2, 60, 145
    and petitions on worship, 125-27
    and Wars of Religion, 91
Guise (Louis de Lorraine), 142
    murdered, vii, 122, 145

Harding, Robert, 69
Harouys, Jean, 114
Haton, Claude, 129, 133
Hauser, Henri, 10
Heller, Henry, 11-12
Hennequin, Nicholas, 42
Hennequin family, 42
Henry II, 80
Henry III, 86
    assassinated, vii, 153
    and Catholic League, 122, 124, 130, 143
    flees Paris, 139
    murder of Guises, vii, 1, 60, 122, 145
Henry IV (Henry of Navarre), viii, 60-61, 116, 139
    and Catholic League, 122
    and Châlons, 150
    heir to throne, 134
Hickey, Daniel, 17
historiography, of Châlons, 19-21
Hoffman, Philip, 9
l'Hôpital, Jean de, 55
l'Hôpital, Thierry de (sieur de Castel), 52, 55-56, 94, 96, 102, 109, 111-12
    and Catholic League, 130
Hôpital St. Jacques, 83, 107
Hôpital St. Lazaire, 45-46
Hôtel Dieu, 83, 107
Hôtel du Saint Esprit, 40
hôtel épiscopal, 40
Huguenots, 84
    armed conflicts, 105, 106
    arms, and military security, 132-33, 138, 157
    boycott of Estates General, 124
    Bussey's measures against, 98-101
    and Catholic League, 122, 133
    in Châlons, 93-94, 125-27, 166-69

Huguenots (*continued*)
    and Edict of Beaulieu, 124
    and Edict of St. Germain, 111
    exiled, 97, 103, 109, 111
    expelled, 95, 96, 110, 157
    and Massacre of Vassy, 92
    and Peace of Bergerac, 124
    and Peace of Monsieur/Beaulileu, 123
    and petitions on worship, 125-27
    protected, 83
    as security threat, 67, 132-33, 138, 157
    synod at Blacy, 111
d'Humières, M., 123

Johannés (captain), 57
John the Fearless, of Burgundy, 37
Joyeuse, Robert de (comte de Grandpré), 152, 159-60
Joyeuse, Tourteron, 160

Kaiser, Wolfgang, 14

La Charité, 111
La Ferté-sous-Jouarre synod, 105
Lallemant, Louis, 151
La Marck, Henri-Robert de (duc de Bouillon), 104, 138
Langault, Jacques, 93
Langres, 147
La Rochefoucald, Charles de (sieur de Barbezieulx), 59, 106, 125, 131
    and Catholic League, 129
    and Châlons, 92
La Rochelle, 111, 115
Laronze, Charles, 9-10
Le Goff, Jacques, 7
Legros, Jehan, 159
Lenoncourt, M. de, 57
Le Roy Ladurie, Emmanuel, 9
Lignage, Claude, 77
Lignones tribe, 28
Lorraine, Charles (duc de Mayenne), 58, 122, 134, 145, 153
Lorraine, Charles III (duke), 122, 156, 161
Lorraine, Claude de (duc d'Aumale), 58, 84, 96, 102, 104, 110, 134, 145
Lorraine, François (duc de Guise), 58
Lorraine, Henri de (duc de Guise), 58, 60, 107, 109
    and Catholic League, 122-23, 125-44
    correspondence with Châlons, 117-20
    murdered, vii, 2, 60, 145
    and petitions on worship, 125-27
    and Wars of Religion, 91
Lorraine, Louis de (cardinal de Guise), vii, 122, 142, 145
Lorraine, (marquis du Pont), 161

Louis of Nassau, 108
Louis (saint), 33
Louis XI, and bonne villes, 7
Loup (bishop), 30
Lyon, Adolphe de (seigneur d'Espaulx), 59, 83, 94, 105, 107, 111-12

*M*argaine, Pierre, 111
Maupeou, Pierre, 77
Maurroy, Henry, 93
Mayenne (Charles de Lorraine), 58, 122, 134, 145, 153
Memmie (St.), 28
Mercoeur (cousin of Guises), 134
Merovingians, and Châlons, 29, 30
Michelet, Jules, 25
military security, 59–71, 132-33, 138, 140, 157
Montauban, 111
Moulinet, Pierre du, 42-43
Mousnier, Roland, 3
Mutigny (governor) de, 160

*N*eufbourg, 32
Neuville de Vigne-l'Evêque, 32
Nevelet, Pierre, 115
Nevers (Louis de Gonzague), 58, 60, 93, 94, 96, 129, 152-53, 154
Nicaise (saint), 28
Notre-Dame-l'Epine regiment, 66, 107, 139

*O*udineau, M., 146

*P*aris, 71, 92, 139
Parlement of Paris, and Châlons, 158
Parma, duke of, 161
peace treaties
    Beaulieu/Monsieur, 116, 122
    Bergerac, 124
    Joinville, 134
    Longjumeau, 108
    Monsieur/Beaulieu, 116, 122, 123,
    Nemours (Châlons ceded), viii, 122-44
Péronne, 123
Philip II of Spain, 134
Philip the Fair, 33, 35
Pigalle, Fleurant de, 199
plague, 45, 65
Poissy conference, 91
Porcien (Antoine de Croy), 97, 101, 102
power structures, episcopal, 31
Privat press, 5
Protestants. *See Huguenots.*

*R*eims, 115
Remi tribe, 28
Renty, Robert de, 111
Rethelois (Charles de Conzague), 58
Roger I, 31nn, 32

Rolland, Fiacre, 151
Romans, in Champagne, 28
Rosne, baron de, vii, 58, 59, 60, 70, 85, 149
    and Catholic League, 129
    expelled, 146
Roussel, Claude, 159
Roussel, Jacques, 106

*S*almon, J. H. M., 12
Schneider, Robert, 6
Schomberg (commander), 119
Sixteen, the, 75, 139, 141, 145, 158
St. Bartholomew's Day Massacre, 112, 13
St. Lazaire college, 45-46
St. Mard (Hugues de Champagne), 55, 56, 57, 130-31, 137
St. Martin's Day (Nov. 11), assembly, 41, 43, 73, 94
St. Memmie Abbey, 30, 31
St. Paul, Antoine de, 59, 70, 85, 138-39, 148, 156, 159
St. Pierre-aux-Monts Abbey, 30, 31
St. Sulpice Abbey, 30, 31
Ste. Menehould, 147

*T*avalle, M. de (commander), 133
Thomassin, Phillippe de, 58, 60, 147
Toussaints de l'Ile Abbey, 31, 32, 45, 83, 107
Tousson, Antone (abbot), 45
treaties. *See* peace treaties.
Troyes, and Catholic League, 129
Tumult of Ambiose, 91

*U*nivers de la France et de pays francophones, 5
D'Urbin, Louis, 146
D'Urbin, Thomas, 146

*V*agrancy, 65
Varymont (Guillaume de Champagne), 43, 56, 84, 93, 130
Vassy, massacre of Huguenots, 91
Vermandois, and city council, 41
Vikings, and Châlons, 30
Vitry, resistance to octroi, 77\

*W*ars of Religion, impact on Châlons, 72-90, 161
William of Orange, 109, 110
Wolfe, Martin, 81\
Wolff, Philippe, 5
wool industry, in Châlons, 35

*Y*tam family, 42

*Z*eller, Gaston, 4, 5
Zweibrucken, duke of (Deux-Ponts, 110